GUIDING THE AMERICAN UNIVERSITY

American higher education is under unprecedented pressure, beginning with the public funding and student debt crises and extending to inadequate performance in student retention and growing global competition. Respected educator and scholar Peter N. Stearns breaks down the underlying problems, exploring the most contentious issues for university leaders and administrators today. *Guiding the American University* covers the major facets of university operation—administration, faculty and students—and discusses what should be changed and what should be preserved. Covering major topics for debate and real problems facing American higher education today—including the tenure system, online learning, administrative bloat and campus culture—this book is a critical resource for aspiring and current higher education administrators. Research based and stemming from a range of case studies, this book's insightful and fresh recommendations serve as an important contribution to the conversation on the future of American higher education.

Peter N. Stearns is University Professor and Provost Emeritus at George Mason University.

GUIDING THE AMERICAN UNIVERSITY

Contemporary Challenges and Choices

Peter N. Stearns

NEW YORK AND LONDON

First published 2016
by Routledge
711 Third Avenue, New York, NY 10017

and by Routledge
2 Park Square, Milton Park, Abingdon, Oxon, OX14 4RN

Routledge is an imprint of the Taylor & Francis Group, an informa business

© 2016 Taylor & Francis

The right of Peter N. Stearns to be identified as author of this work has been asserted by him in accordance with sections 77 and 78 of the Copyright, Designs and Patents Act 1988.

All rights reserved. No part of this book may be reprinted or reproduced or utilised in any form or by any electronic, mechanical, or other means, now known or hereafter invented, including photocopying and recording, or in any information storage or retrieval system, without permission in writing from the publishers.

Trademark notice: Product or corporate names may be trademarks or registered trademarks, and are used only for identification and explanation without intent to infringe.

Library of Congress Cataloging-in-Publication Data
Stearns, Peter N.
 Guiding the American university : contemporary challenges and choices / Peter N. Stearns.
  pages cm
 Includes bibliographical references and index.
 1. Universities and colleges—United States—Administration. I. Title.
 LB2341.S764 2016
 378.1'01—dc23
 2015017181

ISBN: 978-1-138-88926-2 (hbk)
ISBN: 978-1-138-88927-9 (pbk)
ISBN: 978-1-315-71301-4 (ebk)

Typeset in Bembo
by Apex CoVantage, LLC

Printed and bound in the United States of America by Publishers Graphics, LLC on sustainably sourced paper.

CONTENTS

Preface		*vi*
Acknowledgments		*viii*
1	Introduction: Crisis and Opportunity	1
2	Universities on Trial	11
3	Essential Strengths: From Defense to Offense?	40
4	Shared Governance	57
5	Academic Administration: "Dark Side" or Positive Force; or Both?	75
6	The Faculty	111
7	Students and Their Services	148
8	Beyond the Campus: Regional and Global Roles	176
9	Adding It Up: "The University of the 21st Century"	192
Index		*197*

PREFACE

Americans need a better conversation about higher education than we have been offered in recent years. Voices attacking universities and urging massive change have, frankly, been too loud. Yet at the same time, within the academy, reactions have often been too quickly defensive, as if any reference to a topic like faculty teaching loads must prompt us to circle our wagons and claim that nothing is amiss. Current prospects, namely that higher education is likely to be dragged more directly into partisan political battles (already active in several states), enhance the need for a constructive middle way.

Given the recent volume of publications about American colleges and universities, the wary reader legitimately asks: why yet another entry? What's distinctive about this effort? This book offers two related strengths, while also benefiting from several of the current studies. First, it does seek to strike a balance between the need for innovation, for recognition of undeniable deficiencies, and the preservation of vital strengths. Second, it applies the conversation to many of the real and practical issues that universities face—it reflects insider grasp. For example, instead of invoking the need for greater efficiency in a general way, or assuming that technology or some other *deus ex machina* is about to solve all our problems, it deals with the actual domains where efficiencies might be achieved—and the downsides of wielding an axe too crudely.

The result takes us into some areas that are commonly referred to more than really analyzed—or simply kept in the cupboard, away from critical view. We will be discussing the tenure system and some badly needed reforms. We will admit the need to deal with teaching loads. We will talk, with some regret, about constraints on research, as well as the vital need to maintain the research-education interaction. We will offer more detailed data about administrative bloat, and we will introduce a fairly comprehensive assessment of that strange American animal, student services. We will be talking about priorities and goals that higher education must embrace but also some otherwise desirable targets that may lie beyond our grasp.

The goal is realism about how contemporary universities work, and should work in the near future, from someone who's been actively engaged in academia for some time, but someone also with a willingness to invite a fresh look at many of the key issues involved in light of the very real, and often very new, policy dilemmas that now confront the higher education field.

Aspirations are not neglected: the book covers exciting if sometimes complex agendas in teaching, in global and regional outreach, and in maintaining the commitment to significant new knowledge. However, aspirations that are not grounded in current realities are vulnerable. New teaching and student success standards? Great, but what about the expansion of adjuncts? The research mission? Unquestionably, but how do the costs involved square with the crisis over tuition?

This is a crucial moment in the contemporary history of higher education in the United States. After World War II, American universities moved successfully from largely supporting the preservation of a privileged class, either regionally or nationally, to more massive outreach. The system soared to unprecedented prominence in the process, which long shielded it from extensive critique. This pattern of expansion has in many ways continued—witness the 45% increase in the student body over the past decade plus—but many of the assumptions of the postwar decades are now called into question by changes ranging from a new kind of student mix to social decisions about what governments will support to a new level of public skepticism—all in a (largely unacknowledged) climate of growing international competition in higher education. Hence the need for a new look but based on the understanding of real university practice.

I side neither with the systematic disparagers nor with the systematic defenders of the American university. I want to challenge the disparagers by noting the complexity of the contemporary university but also its very real strengths—strengths that we must preserve unless we simply agree to offer a lower-quality product. I want to challenge the defenders not only by mentioning hot button issues like tenure or research evaluation but by urging very real changes in the status quo and in aspects of academic culture.

The basic goal, of course, is not the challenge but the belief that a current evaluation from a distinctive vantage point can help structure the kinds of constructive conversations that should guide us going forward. Whether for those inside the academy or for members of the large external audience of policymakers, alumni, and even prospective students, the need for a focus on real decision points and for a balance between appreciation and self-criticism is pressing.

ACKNOWLEDGMENTS

All sorts of people have contributed to this book, directly and indirectly—the list is too long to detail fully. I've had the privilege of working closely with several university presidents who taught me a lot, even when I occasionally disagreed. Interactions with other provosts at a variety of conferences have been invaluable and indeed continue to be. Hollie Chessman has been an unusually capable researcher and editor, and I am particularly in her debt. A host of colleagues at George Mason have given me all sorts of guidance. I am particularly grateful for the direct involvement of Jan Arminio, Karen Gentemann, Rose Pascarell, Jack Censer, Kim Eby, Vikas Chandoke, Renate Guilford, Michelle Marks and Kris Smith, though of course they are not responsible for the resulting discussions. Donna Sundre, at James Madison University, provided helpful information, and Deborah Stearns, from Montgomery College, offered suggestions. Cody Vander Clute assisted with manuscript preparation. My wife, Donna Kidd, has taught me a great deal about budget and planning processes, as well as putting up with my writer's excitement and occasional frustration for many months.

1

INTRODUCTION

Crisis and Opportunity

Universities in the United States are caught between a host of strengths, measurable and otherwise, and a growing range of attacks from within as well as outside the academy. We sorely need new opportunities to navigate among these tensions and, over time, to reduce the tensions themselves.

For the plus side: American higher education produces more top-ranked schools—regardless of the whims of any particular global ranking system—than any other nation, by a huge margin. As quick cases in point: American institutions comprise 62% of the top 100 on the 2014 Shanghai Jiao Tong list and 38% of the top 50 in the Q4 scale. Population size has something to do with this disproportion, but there is far more involved.

For the expanding minus column: American higher education faces an arguably unprecedented array of attacks and critiques, generating gleeful calls for systematic disruption or dire forecasts about going the way of the printed newspaper or, even worse, Border's bookstore. In a half century of academic experience, I have never seen anything like it.

The disparities clearly affect governing boards. Five years ago, the board at my university was vigorously focused on making us a "world-class" university. The term was a bit grandiose, but the goal clearly was to improve quality and visibility. Its successor group, beginning just four years back, dropped "world-class" entirely and developed a laser focus on real or imagined inefficiencies plus budget and tuition constraints. The same story could be told at many institutions over the past half-decade. Admittedly, changes in state politics and above all the ramifications of economic recession factor into the variability, but there's more to the inconsistency than this. It is hard to decide what universities should concentrate on in the mix of strengths and vulnerabilities. The result is a distracting impulse to zig and then zag.

This is a book about running American universities today and tomorrow amid these striking polarities. The book joins the discussion of basic priorities to an assessment of core issues in actual academic administration, urging more candid exchanges about the choices that must be made going forward.

Combining Management Realities with the New Terrain

We begin with the claim that the present level of incoherence in the higher education context is undesirable and—in most respects—unnecessary. It has several harmful consequences. It leads to unconstructive divides within the university and between external power sources and the academy. Priorities are obscured: lots of faculty don't have a clear sense of where their institution is going and what, other than the struggle to survive, should engage them. Ill-considered experiments are given too much credence, at least until they collapse: a case in point was the notion that free online courses (the fabled MOOCs) represented the wave of the future for universities—with little initial thought to the obvious point that the courses could not be generated or sustained without a substantial revenue source. What was interesting here was not the offering—it was fine for institutions that could afford to offer free wares as a form of advertising or as a means of learning more about online education—but the fact that an inherently flawed business plan—a plan without financial compensation—seemed so promising reflects serious academic disarray. Otherwise sensible academic leaders and observers spent more than a year grasping at straws. Finally, amid all the confusion, many universities arguably do not put their best feet forward, conceding too much ground to groups that have their own agendas—beginning with politicians who want at all costs to avoid a careful conversation about budget priorities. Higher education leadership can and should be doing better.[1]

It's time—and I know this is a brash claim—for some renewed common sense. We'll proceed step by step.

First, let's accumulate all the significant current attacks on American higher education briefly but honestly. The purpose here, aside from trying to generate a constructive agenda, includes a recognition of the mutual incompatibility of many of the attacks, which is a problem in its own right. The main point is to suggest how we can select two or three primary deficiencies from among the crowd and argue that these should guide the next stages of change and remediation.

Second, and equally important, let's also identify existing strengths that can and should be preserved. As noted, American universities for all their woes are in some respects riding high, not only in international rankings but also in terms of many aspects of what in business might be called customer satisfaction.

And third, let's frame this conversation, and apply the results, to the way American colleges and universities actually operate. How, for example, should the tenure system be considered, or reconsidered, in light of the current context? What about the hallowed notion of shared governance between faculty and administration (with some external authority tossed in as well)? Do we need radical reconsideration of what student life operations are doing; if so, on what basis? We need to address not just general views of the university—the problems, the strong points—but their application to real issues, to the actual kinds of decisions administrators and faculties, and those who aspire to join them, make or should make.

The Need for Balance: Change and Cherish

This is a book about balance. Good universities have long had to worry about balance—between teaching and research, for example, where new issues link to older models and concerns—and about professional and liberal training goals, another tension that, despite current hyperbole, should feed into our basic approach. More recently, universities have worried about global versus regional interests, but the big balancing act now is between preservation and innovation, both essential but both by themselves inadequate in dealing with what universities need to do in the near future.

Balance wars against both disrupters and traditionalists, though hopefully it can also bring some of them together. The disruption movement is fascinating, and again quite new in my experience—save perhaps for some of the extreme, and short-lived, anti-intellectualism of the 1960s protest. Lots of bright, well-meaning people sincerely believe that almost every aspect of the American university must be rethought and transformed. Some of them are fully sincere. Some, probably, operate, whether consciously or not, under generational banners: let's find any way possible to penetrate a power structure dominated by baby boomers (with a few preboomer hangers-on). Some are out to make a buck. It's really interesting to realize how many academic audiences—particularly administrative audiences—pay big money to hear themselves attacked at leadership or planning conferences. It's rather like the liberal segment of the French aristocracy in 1789.

Traditionalism is currently far less fashionable and has fewer spokespeople, but surely it exists. Michael Crow and William Dabars' recent study, urging a new model for American universities, notes regretfully that "few institutions of modern society so rigidly adhere to tradition as academe," with only religion and the courts as rivals. And surely, as the disrupters claim, though with exaggeration, many universities do change slowly. Many faculty are quite eager to continue doing, for the next two decades, what they did the previous two.[2]

The balanced approach urges, however, that both extremes are off base. We need change, in some cases serious change. This book will focus directly not only on several policy areas but on some deep-seated aspects of academic culture that need to be altered. I personally think that innovation is the best way to describe the shifts that are required because it is a less combative term than disruption. Whatever the vocabulary, we do have some sacred cows that must be desacralized. At the same time we need to be able, against the current fashion, to point out what should not be fully altered—what existing strengths go into quality education—while also recognizing several adjustments that have already begun to emerge and that should be more respectfully recognized. Even a glance at the differences in the courses and undergraduate majors offered in a quality public university today, compared to its counterpart half a century ago, at least should raise questions about some of the more systematic accusations about unaltered traditionalism.

It is indeed true, as the critics say, that universities cannot continue on their present path and that academic life must become more complicated than it was a few decades ago. But—against this claim alone—it is also true that significant change has already been occurring AND that a range of basic practices must be very carefully and explicitly enhanced.

Balance isn't sexy. It does capture, however, how most constructive change occurs: few frontal attacks ever succeed entirely. Balance—real change but also real preservation—more accurately conveys what is possible in reviewing the interests of the key players in higher education and how they can work together toward future success. As we explore the core features of the contemporary university, the plea for balanced priorities is no evasion. It's the only way to combine existing achievement with the kinds of adjustments that simply have to be faced.

One of the problems with the current atmosphere around higher education is that a plea for balance risks seeming purely defensive, hopelessly retrograde. In some versions, advocacy of disruption makes any objection look feeble and evasive. Add to this some other obvious points that disrupters also make. For example, this book is written by someone who has been in academic administration and therefore has a stake in elements of the existing system. It is written by someone well past youth; a key disrupter argument is that change must come from those who are young, who have more than a decade or so left in the system and who therefore can espouse fundamental change with more conviction. Obviously, I think those arguments are wrong, but that might merely confirm my irrelevance. I also think they are wrong because they downplay some real changes that are already underway, by faculty and administrative leaders and because they bypass the elements of preservation that are also essential. Not everything is broken. Not every new idea is worth investment.

The goal is evolution, admittedly accelerated evolution, rather than revolution. Evolution is inherently more achievable and normally has fewer unpredictable or undesirable side effects than its more disruptive cousin. In this case, evolution has a chance to appeal to those many faculty and students (more on the student claim later) who find lots of merit in existing academic practices. More people can be drawn into discussions of change if, first, they have a clear sense of priorities among current problems and, second, they can see connections to established systems. For—and again this will be more fully defended in Chapter 2—it is not for the most part fundamental goals that are in question but how best to reach these goals. This is not a plea for a stand-pat approach, however modest the rhetoric of balance may seem. Movement is essential but not frenzy. Evolutionary change will get us to where we should be.

The Nature of University Management

The evolutionary approach is enhanced by the nature of academic organization—which, I admit, some disrupters see as a key problem. Academic administration is, and should be, an exercise in persuasion and discussion. It is not a *diktat*. One of the tensions between the academic world and some of its governing boards is a real difference in management style. There are, and again there should be, relatively few opportunities for academic administrators to tell faculty and staff: do this. Not a few administrators, even some with academic experience, get into trouble because of an exaggerated sense of hierarchy. Of course, there is a power structure in the university, but it operates amid consultation, wide contributions and abundant persuasion.

This point, too, can be confused. It does not mean that administrative leaders do not have goals and priorities or a sense of where the university should be heading. If they do not, the institution can be in serious trouble. But the goals themselves should be formed, and recurrently tested, by presentations to and discussions with other internal constituencies. They should be open to modification on that basis, and they should certainly be receptive to valid initiatives proposed by other sectors. Good administration is an exercise in interactivity. This entails a lot of meetings, I admit, but it can also generate real and intelligent engagement as to where the institution should be heading.

The interactive style does not mean that fairly rapid change is impossible, another target of disrupters and external critics. We must also talk about important cases where major new decisions were made and implemented reasonably quickly and about how entrepreneurial flexibility is a vital academic attribute. Persuasion and interaction do not prevent significant redirections, but they help assure that the redirections will be appreciated and amplified by those involved.

Despairing advocates of academic change sometimes refer to the difficulty of turning a battleship on a dime. I claim that the image is misleading on two counts. First, we don't really want a full turn—whether the "we" here is faculty and administrations, or students and their families, or American society more generally. Second, the academic enterprise can set some new patterns pretty quickly, and there's real evidence of this in recent university experience.

But the ship will run better, and will adjust course more smoothly, if participants have more opportunity to discuss the priorities of current challenges and their intersection with established strengths. It will run better as well if this discussion refers to the real issues with which academic decision makers deal, from installing new academic programs or ending old ones to deciding the best size for various categories of faculty to assessing actual student progress. The goal is the kind of realistic presentation—the explicit discussion of how things work amid the cluster of current problems—that will inform some existing administrators and also the many people in training programs for higher education (many of whom already have relevant staff positions). I hope the result will also interest those faculty—like participants in faculty senates—whose contributions will be improved if they have access to fuller knowledge of what contemporary academic administration is all about. I don't despair of even serving some of the outside observers, from accreditation officials to members of governing boards, who again will function more effectively if they have a more grounded sense of current operations and current debates.

The focus is on academic systems and decisions themselves, but the discussion must also reference some wider factors in the higher education context. American universities operate in a really odd organizational structure in which federal decisions influence basic activities strongly, and may impinge even more in the future, but in which there is no real federal authority and relatively few opportunities for systematic policy discussion about higher education overall. This haphazard system may have real advantages—most academics believe, whether correctly or not, that more federal involvement would be detrimental—but it has real drawbacks, for the feds' intrusions are not leavened by any overall responsibility. (Correspondingly, one of our future challenges in international higher education competition may involve our patchwork policy structure; or perhaps this will be a saving grace, as against the more rational but arguably more bureaucratic systems elsewhere.) Or take the unquestionably legitimate plea that our universities improve their performance on student retention and graduation rates—a key subject of the following chapter. I fully agree, but to discuss this obligation without some attention to P–12 operations would be folly. Part of our challenge—not most of it, as I will argue in closing this chapter—involves factors that impinge on us but operate beyond our full control.[3]

Blending Data and Experience

As it approaches current problems and future prospects, the book combines general information about higher education and university administration in the United States and (to a degree) their comparative context, with various case studies. It also builds directly on what I think I have learned from my own experience, or what I wish I had learned (I've also benefited from some postadministration months, which have admittedly allowed more time for reflection). The following chapters discuss educational goals and innovations where several recent studies have at least partially pointed the way, but they combine this with (I hope) a concrete sense of what universities, administrations and personnel are all about. It's the mix of basic responses with practical operations that is distinctive and, I believe, distinctively useful: where we should be heading combines practical considerations of how we might get there.

This is, of course, where the experience part comes in, so I'll provide a very brief word about that angle. Like many academic administrators, for better or worse, I had no formal leadership training. I had a few vainglorious organizational positions in high school and college, but I first went from frying pan to fire as a history department chair, initially at Rutgers then later, after a long return to faculty purity, at Carnegie Mellon. I still view the department chair position as particularly demanding, a clearly middle-management role located awkwardly between actual students and faculty on one hand and deans and decanal staffs on the other—a clear learning experience. I moved to a deanship at Carnegie Mellon for several years and then applied for and won the provost position at George Mason University, where I served for 14½ years before recently stepping down to return to full-time faculty. This, of course, was my fullest exposure to the kinds of issues with which this book deals. It also allowed me to interact with all sorts of people at Mason but also with some valued colleagues from other institutions, from whom I learned much of what I now seek to convey. It was a terrific experience, with some perfectly awful days; it was unquestionably the most interesting job I ever had.

A word as well about George Mason. This is not a book about Mason, and again examples from various institutions will illustrate key points, but what I learned at Mason looms large at least indirectly. Mason is a relatively young (43 years as an independent institution) public university in Northern Virginia. It takes pride, some of which is legitimate, in being agile and entrepreneurial—hence, among other things, consistent rankings in the top five of US News' up-and-coming universities. (This is a double-edged honor, admittedly: at some point, one must be able to declare that one has up and arrived.) Mason now has 34,000 students, a roughly 50% growth over the past decade plus, making us the largest public institution in the state; it has tripled the number of PhD programs in the same span; it has quadrupled its externally funded research; it has introduced more new academic programs that all the other public Virginia universities combined during most of the past decade (an achievement that has not always pleased our State Council). We're not a flagship and suffer some of the reputational and fiscal disadvantages of lower status. We have an unusually diverse student body, not only ethnically but also in terms of socioeconomic status, though our progress on faculty diversity has been far less impressive. We've gone global big-time, including currently running a promising branch campus in Incheon, South Korea. We have had, in quick summary, a number of experiences that have kept us relatively lively despite the many difficulties of the past decade. We have also made some mistakes and suffered some deficiencies that can also contribute to an understanding of what American universities are facing as they move forward.

Mason serves, in sum, as an example of an institution that has managed to maintain real momentum despite recent challenges, though facing even more challenges to come. It is also not at the top of the academic pecking order, which helps link its experience to the situation of many other schools.

Mason is not Everyplace, of course. Indeed, our higher administration (myself until recently included) spends a great deal of time trying to persuade itself and others about how distinctive we are—a proclivity characteristic of many institutions and one I want to discuss later, warts and all. But Mason's experience, along with broader data and additional examples, does capture much of the dilemma and promise of American higher education. The focus is disproportionately on public institutions (which currently educate 67% of all undergraduate students enrolled in college in the United States, with about two-thirds of the remainder in the privates, one-third in for-profits), but other types of universities figure in as part of the competitive environment. Many problems and experiences are widely shared, and at the same time the diversity of American institutions forms part of the academy's tool kit going forward. Again, without belaboring any single case, the goal is to use familiarity with real academic operation and decision making as a key element in exploring the higher educational future.

> **Varieties of Higher Education**
>
> Except for discussion of research mission, in chapter 3, this book will not usually differentiate among institutional types in the United States, partly to avoid distracting detail, partly because of the self-serving belief that much of the discussion will be widely useful across international lines. But a brief guide may help. Currently—and the list does change, most recently with several colleges closing—there are approximately 287 doctoral and fairly to quite high research universities in the United States; the highest level, with 108, is about 65% public, but the publics loom larger in the category overall. In the fairly to quite substantial Masters degrees group, the United States has 1,124 institutions, mainly public, with about 900 bachelor's colleges of various types. Approximately 1,100 public colleges offer mainly associates degrees, along with 94 privates and about 650 for-profits, with 211 other institutions in the category overall. Quite obviously, the best-known American institutions are atypical, and in some cases truly misleading guides to the educational issues and opportunities facing the United States. Nonflagship publics, including the array of schools in the Masters categories, arguably deserve more attention than they normally receive.[4]

The book proceeds largely in terms of academic structure, though always emphasizing interrelationships and shared concerns. After two focused chapters on the challenges that critics say we are facing and those we do face, and on the qualities we should preserve, the book deals, in sequence, with the complexity and opportunity of shared governance; with issues of academic administration; with faculty issues; with student and student life topics; and then more briefly with obligations of outreach and global connection. Always, the emphasis is on the implications of a balanced approach, combining change and enhancement, for all the key sectors of the American university. Always, as the conclusion emphasizes, the focus is on where we should be heading for the future and what combination of innovation and preservation we can and should be promising.

Here I will add a final personal note. I have been an academic administrator of one sort or another for a long time and hope that some distillations of my experiences and deficiencies will be useful to others. I was trained as an academic—a historian—and never gave that up. I continued to teach a course a term and to do some research and writing, even as provost. Though provost, and regarded (usually but not always humorously) by the Faculty Senate as having gone over to the Dark Side, I always regarded myself as faculty, too. (Faculty who have never been adulterated may of course take issue with this claim, particularly as they read some of the recommendations in Chapter 6.) And I have returned to faculty life with relative ease, even to the point of wondering already what our central administration is really up to. My point is that faculty values inform my sense of American higher education at least as much as administrative privilege does, and here, too, I would like to believe that the combination is constructive.

* * *

These are tough days for American higher education, though not without some points of relief and reward. They will get tougher still in the foreseeable future, perhaps particularly for faculty, which is one of my real concerns in what follows. Those of us involved—administrators, faculty, staff, students—must be aware of our external environment. We should not give up on working with key components of that environment—with politicians and P–12 officials as well as, obviously, with governing boards and state or accreditation agencies—to seek improvements going forward. A core challenge, indeed, involves striking an assertive balance between accepting current realities—budget realities first and foremost—and insisting that recent deteriorations should be addressed by those in charge.

But most of our future is up to us, however persuasive we may prove to be with other actors. We can hope to improve the decisions made without our full involvement, but there will always be limits. Self-reliance raises the stakes in deciding what our key problems are when identifying our core strengths. Vital goals—whether they be research achievements, or the liberal component of an undergraduate curriculum, or a knowledge of real student needs, or even the invitation to address growing global opportunity and competition—simply will not get much attention if we do not insist on essentials in our own house. And there's a further element: a real responsibility for appropriate standards. One of the depressing features of much current public discussion of higher education is the absence of much clear attention to quality. Innovation and disruption, yes; efficiency and low cost, hallelujah; ever more degrees, without question. But none of this will add value if basic quality is not attached—whether the standards are novel or not. Right now at least, it's the academy itself that must insist on this. The responsibility is an inescapable part of our future, and we must continue to discuss how to fulfill it. Here, above all, no one will save us except ourselves.

Further Reading

Several books contribute to a basic sense of what American higher education is all about.

Henry Rosovsky, *The University: An Owner's Manual* (Princeton: Princeton University Press, 1991), is still valuable reading on how systems work from a former provost, though obviously written before the current malaise.

Philip G. Altbach, Patricia J. Gumport, and Robert O. Berdahl, eds., *American Higher Education in the Twenty-First Century: Social, Political and Economic Challenges*, 3rd ed. (Baltimore: Johnson Hopkins University Press, 2011), proves remarkably prescient about a host of issues.

Also on basic functions, John V. Lombardi, *How Universities Work* (Baltimore: Johns Hopkins University Press, 2013), and Derek Curtis Bok, *Higher Education in America* (Princeton: Princeton University Press, 2013) are valuable contributions.

Goldie Blumenstyk, *American Higher Education in Crisis? What Everyone Needs to Know* (Oxford: Oxford University, Press, 2015) offers a good summary, though with a prospective student audience particularly in mind.

Daniel M. Fogel, ed., *Precipice or Crossroads: Where America's Great Public Universities Stand and Where They Are Going Midway through Their Second Century* (Albany: State University of New York Press, 2012) offers a more scholarly assessment.

Arthur M. Cohen, *The Shaping of American Higher Education: Emergence and the Growth of the Contemporary System*, 2nd ed. (San Francisco: Jossey-Bass, 2010) provides fuller historical perspective.

See also the recent entry based extensively on the experiences and aspirations of Arizona State but with wider historical reference: Michael M. Crow and William B. Dabars, *Designing the New American University* (Baltimore: Johns Hopkins University Press, 2015).

Notes

1 A. Bozkurt and others, "Trends in Distance Education Research," *International Review of Research in Open and Distributed Learning* 16 (2015): 330–63; Li Yuan and others, "Beyond MOOCs: Sustainable Online Learning in Institutions," *Cetis* Publications (Jan. 31, 2014). See also the experiment launched by Arizona State in 2015 using a MOOC-like approach for potential first-year students but with later possibility for credit.

2 Michael Crow and William Dabars, *Designing the New American University* (Baltimore: 2015) emphasizes innovations but with attention to preservation as well; for straight out disruption, Kevin Carey, *The End of College* (New York, 2015).

3 George Clark, "A Diverse Educational System: structure, standards and challenges," *American Studies Journal* 45 (1998); Arthur Cohen, *The Shaping of American Higher Education*, 2nd ed. (San Francisco, 2010).

4 Carnegie Foundation for the Advancement of Teaching, *The Carnegie Classification of Institutions of Higher Education,* Jan. 3, 2010; see also the Foundation's website, particularly the communications since Jan. 1, 2015, under new auspices: http://carnegieclassification.iu.edu

2

UNIVERSITIES ON TRIAL

The accusations are multiple, in combination almost overwhelming. "At the colleges and universities attended by most American students, costs are spiraling out of control and quality is declining just as increasing international competition demands that higher education be more productive and less expensive" (Jeff Selingo). Even worse, higher education institutions themselves are probably incapable of generating the remedies to this downward trajectory. As a prominent innovation advocate, Clay Christensen, puts it (worth noting that he is an academic himself): "The history of innovation tells us those new models are not going to come from within higher ed. They will come from new entrants." And from a leader in the New America Foundation: "Colleges can't forever continue raising prices, shortchanging their teaching responsibilities." In the same vein, from another observer: "Universities in the United States extract a lot of money without delivering value." The towers of academia must be collapsing.[1]

And indeed, if it is true that we are raising costs heedlessly even as our product deteriorates, quite probably someone else should take over. Or at the very least, as many disrupters advocate, we should throw open the ivied gates to external entrepreneurs. Though it is worth noting, even at this early stage of the argument, that the most popular alternative in recent years, the for-profits, have done an absolutely miserable job in the main, enhancing problems in areas like student debt in ways that tar the rest of us. There are, to be sure, more responsible entities, but an initial word of caution is not out of place.

But back to the defendant's table. Some huge problems have emerged in American higher education, and some core deficiencies cry out for attention. Indeed, we will argue that the potential list of concerns may be a bit longer than some of our fiercest critics suggest, but the overall accusation—offering less for more—is overly simple at best and actually misleading as a guide to those of us in academe or to those who seek to supplant us. It's important to recognize the attacks and the climate in which some wild statements emerge, but it's equally important to push back against the extremes and to focus more precisely on what, in fact, requires redress.

This chapter will contend that there are two issues of overwhelming importance—which unfortunately point in partially opposing directions—with a number of other concerns that either distract or can be acknowledged but clearly should be relegated to a lower priority. Budget comes first, educational outcomes are second on the list of inescapable issues, and then we can talk about how the priorities that result relate to other aspects of the university agenda.

The Budget

Most of us know the basic story here, but it has some fine points that demand attention—including the vital fact the fundamental problems are not just of recent vintage. Academic finances have been under pressure for over a decade. Some types of expenditures have risen, but the real revolution involves the dramatic reduction of state support for the operating funds of the public universities, combined with the stagnation of average family incomes. The initial response to this revolution, heightened tuitions, worked for a while but then generated its own backlash. A durable solution has yet to be found.

Like most important topics, this one offers some complexities. Public funding for higher education had been rising, on the whole, in the decades before 2000, though amid oscillations. If 2015 levels are compared with those of 35 years ago, they are still ahead. But even here there's a joker in the pack: in the meantime, enrollments have risen massively, which means that, on a per student basis, the situation has deteriorated even when, in the long view, public commitment seems high—and it's on a per student basis that education occurs. States have encouraged, even prodded this kind of enrollment growth (though some public institutions, perhaps wisely, have stood aside), but they have not maintained the funding part of the bargain and in recent years have cut on an absolute basis as well.

Revolution is not too dramatic a term for what's been happening. Since the first years of the new century, huge cuts in state allocations for higher education (with one exception: fracking-rich North Dakota) have converted attendance at the most widely attended universities and colleges from a public good to a private good. When I became provost at George Mason in 2000, 68% of our annual operating budget was provided by the Commonwealth of Virginia. The figure now stands at 23% and dropping. Other institutions in other states can tell an even more dramatic story, with state support in some cases falling below 10%. Community colleges suffer with the rest of us: the Lone Star system in Texas, for example, once saw the state providing 70% of its operating budget, but this has plummeted to 23%.

It is vital to emphasize that this huge change has not merely been a response to the admittedly dire recession that began in 2008, though reactions here have made things worse. State funding first declined in the economic downturn of 2001–2002. At the time, most administrators assumed that this was an annoying but transitory phenomenon. Such had been the pattern, for example, in the 1990s: a dramatic cut early in the decade, recession induced, was followed by so much new state largesse that many schools actually cut their (already low) tuition rates. So, around 2002, state universities howled a bit but mainly waited.

But the anticipated return to prosperity simply never occurred. There was a slight rebound by the middle of the decade, but nothing to write home about. Those of us in academic administration began to realize that states had changed: limits on revenue in the fierce antitaxation climate, plus other demands including unfunded federal mandates, most obviously in the health sector, had fundamentally altered the rules of the game. Then came 2008 with an understandable new budget downturn that occurred, however, in the midst of the existing slide. Here is the core dilemma for the public universities: the need to craft a new, long-term financial model that assumes a minority shareholder role for the state.[2]

The whole process of budget transformation, further, has been accompanied by no small amount of obfuscation. Indeed, it is interesting to speculate about how much of the current crisis atmosphere for higher education is the result purely and simply of new budget vulnerabilities combined, of course, with the self-serving public rhetoric that tries to pin the blame on the universities themselves—seeking or claiming additional weaknesses beyond the fiscal realm.

Political Challenge and University Response

We've never had a real discussion about the shift from public to private funding for state systems. Obviously, the omission reflects the lack of comprehensive federal involvement (which may be a good thing in other respects); there is no clear national stage for this kind of policy debate. Each state pecked away on its own, and while the result was revolutionary, the process was haphazard.

Of course, the state politicians had every reason to want to avoid the issue. They were not happy with their role, in many cases. The pressures they were confronting—stagnant and then falling revenues, new obligations to Medicare, antipathy toward taxes—were real and painful, but they were also delighted to hide behind the widespread beliefs that somehow universities were spending money on frivolous things or that, because they were not businesses, they must be inherently inefficient. ("If I can cut this in my company, surely you can hack 15% off of your operations.") As word spread about mounting student debt—a potential political hot button—it was particularly convenient to attach blame to higher ed. (This despite the fact that there is a clear correlation, among the publics, between reductions in state funding and rising student debt: every $100 in state cuts means $66 more debt among those students who have to borrow at all.)

In this context, universities themselves faced clear dilemmas and face them still. There was a lot of pressure simply to accept the gradual budget slide, even before 2008; then for a time, economic realities seemed even more incontrovertible. Too much complaining might antagonize our masters. We were frequently told to stop whining, and we certainly did not want to jeopardize any small scraps that might be sent our way. By now, many existing legislators honestly don't remember that things were once dramatically different: they accept a 10–20% state contribution as new-normal generosity.

For whatever combination of reasons, we higher ed officials did not manage to mount the kind of discussion that should have occurred within either state or national contexts. We had some options at first about raising tuition, and then we were semiparalyzed by the widespread conviction that we ourselves were primarily responsible for driving up student loan burdens. There was a need, whatever our views, to figure out how to manage the budgets we did get; we could not focus primarily on lament. So we began to assume that the sea change was permanent, planning our futures with no hope of significant new public infusion.

Is this the best course going forward? I know that many faculty are deeply concerned that top administrators have given up too readily, without advancing fully adequate alternatives.

And they may be right; we—higher ed administration—may have retreated too quickly. We're not necessarily serving the national interest well by letting the issue drop from sight. Other societies are upping university investment (if sometimes inadequately), not dropping it, and this is a competitive issue that will bite us in the future. (Germany, for example, has just returned to a no-tuition policy on the strength of 80% state support for university operating budgets.) Global posture aside, social justice concerns might reasonably prompt a new kind of funding discussion. Many observers, including some in the Obama administration, are clearly hoping that universities will find some way to partially compensate for growing social inequality by providing new levels of opportunity through education. This is a challenge we should want to take up but not without some come-to-Jesus budget talks. Even more broadly, we are as a society increasingly privileging funding for the older sector of the population over what is being directed to the young; the university situation is part of this broader shift, which is arguably not in the long-run national interest.

I know it is grandiose to invoke national priorities, but the fact is that in this case the shoe fits. We should not abandon the issue of public commitment to higher education, and we should indeed work to find ways to

> become more collectively effective in organizing a conversation. Currently, some university systems are seeking to provoke some discussion by another round of fairly dramatic tuition increases—California currently heads the list here, hoping that this will provoke greater responsibility by the state governments involved, but the tactic is rather crude and carries clear political risks. It does not excuse us from a more straightforward approach to the discussion we need so vitally.
>
> We will still face real budget challenges, even should renewed public effort bear some fruit. Some combination of cost-cutting efficiencies and identification of alternative revenue sources will be required even in the most enlightened settings. Administrations and faculties must assume a new level of budget responsibility as part of the larger pattern of taking greater charge of our own destiny.
>
> In this case, however, we should combine this burden with renewed energy in the corridors of political power.

As public funding began to drop, universities for the most part—initially, with some encouragement from embarrassed state officials—sought the logical alternative: higher tuition. In some cases, this recourse was combined with enrollment growth, and the combination could indeed bring in some much-needed compensatory funds. Without question, tuitions rose far more rapidly than inflation. To enhance the problem, this occurred at a time when—thanks to growing income inequality as well as periodic economic downturns—median household income was actually declining. The result was mounting student debt and, in short order, an anguished chorus from a host of real or self-appointed education experts. From 19% of the median annual family budgets, costs at four-year colleges mounted to 25% or even higher, while community colleges rose to near 20%; here was a very real human challenge.[3]

Not surprisingly, a fierce backlash resulted, which often further reduced clarity. Two common approaches emerged. The first simply noted that "they" were raising tuition quite rapidly, which was true enough: the "they" being universities themselves, without any particular explanation attached. Thus, a 2014 *Wall Street Journal* article simply claimed that tuitions had increased 1000% since the 1970s, without bothering to note that the biggest overall factor was the reduction in public support. The second approach probed more deeply, if selectively, to find examples of how universities were using their ill-gotten gains on truly frivolous expenditures (here the examples came mainly from the privates, but the brush tarred all institutions). The recreational climbing wall became the dominant image, though more recently the apparent plans of some football-rich southern schools to build lakes and water parks have stimulated concern—as well they might.

As large, complex and varied places, universities surely have made mistakes in their spending plans. We'll discuss in a later chapter the challenges of students-as-consumers, where some problems may rest. Research costs constitute another issue, where the publics need at the least to improve their justifications. Private universities and certainly the for-profits may have been less than responsible in some cases, though in fairness any tuition trend analysis that does not allow for discounting practices—the amounts of money devoted to scholarships, effectively reducing overall costs for many undergraduates— is misleading as well.

But there is no question that, in the public sector, the supreme cause of tuition increases has been the decline in public funding. Knowing that does not fix the problem, but at least it identifies a rational starting point. The familiar phrase—college costs have been rising rapidly—is true from the standpoint of students and their families. But in fact, per student costs have not risen much: it's the source of payment that has been dramatically transformed.[4]

National trends are indisputable and should be far more widely understood. In 1990, states contributed $8,500 in operating costs per student in public institutions; by 2013, this had dropped to $6,100. During the same period, tuitions rose from an average of $2,645 to $5,475—or about $400 more than had been required to fill the gap.

George Mason, as a single institution, mirrored the wider pattern: Over the first 13 years of the new century, Mason's tuition rose 6% above the levels needed to cover inflation plus the multimillion dollar drop in state funding. Six percent, to be sure, is six percent. It went to cover the costs of a growing research operation, which arguably provided clear benefit to students and alumni alike; plus a greater IT investment, recently including the need to address cybersecurity concerns; plus wider overall security costs amid new threats to campus safety; plus some costs resulting from the increasingly detailed regulatory requirements including demands from our accreditation body. It is possible, to be sure, that even this modest increase should have been more tightly controlled, but it was not frivolous: we have no climbing walls (which would not be directly covered by tuition in any event), and our only pond is for drainage purposes (though it is quite pretty). Mason, like public universities generally, has simply reacted to the state's long-term decision to recast its priorities. Any other diagnosis is frankly irresponsible and distracts from the real job of figuring out what to do next.

For—and again this can be readily conceded; it's simple fact—our first recourses, however understandable, have clearly become unsustainable.

1. Those of us who helped shape public university policy did increase tuition, though not gleefully, and fairly soon realized that we were also increasing student debt. We can't continue at this pace, and indeed for the most part have stopped already, or at least cut back. One can argue a bit on the margins of the debt crisis: it is a greater issue for the privates and for-profits than for publics. Some debt is surely a good investment, given the clear career profitability of higher education degrees overall; indeed, in a few cases, students may actually have become too timid

about some debt, working too much to the detriment of their educational experience. But no question: we can't continue the trends of past six to eight years. Already, rates of tuition increase (and student borrowing) are slowing, though we have not yet reached the end of that path.

2. We also face increasing challenges concerning the second recourse, expanding enrollments with a special eye to out-of-state and international clientele. Domestically, demography is against us for a while: typical student populations are not growing; indeed community colleges, as potential transfer sources, are actually shrinking overall. Competition for out-of-staters will become ever fiercer. Some schools, faced with huge enrollment shortfalls, have already cut their out-of-state tuitions to near in-state levels, which is another case of a panic response that masks the ongoing fiscal challenge; the students will not be paying enough to cover their costs. More generally, discounting from listed tuition prices expands steadily, for privates but also publics competing for the out-of-state crowd—another blow to revenues because of market realities. The online field is even more constricted, for competition systematically prevents charging out of state rates; it may still be possible to win a slight margin over in-state tuitions, but successful expansion will depend on serious cost cutting (particularly on the faculty labor side). International opportunities will remain greater for a while at least, but competition here, too, will accelerate. Bottom line: enrollments and tuitions will not, by themselves, bail us out.

> **The Student Numbers Game: Another Reality Check**
>
> Undergraduate enrollments have grown rapidly over the past two decades, as many universities—particularly, the nonflagship publics and the for-profits—sought to respond to popular demand and also increase revenues as a partial response to public disinvestment, thus the 45% jump in overall student numbers between 1997 and 2011. But relevant American demography is now stagnating: the 18–24 year old age group has actually shrunk by 4%, and it won't increase again for several years; by 2025, it will stand only 3% above 2011 levels—a mere 100,000 people. Current projections then have it declining once again. Enrollments may go up anyway—the feds predict a 13% jump between 2012 and 2022—but this will reflect higher percentages, not population growth. Easy access to additional tuition payers domestically is a thing of the past—compounding the declining access to public funds.[5]

3. But many institutions also began, even as they upped their charges and their headcounts, to introduce new "efficiencies" as well. This was a less visible, but very real, part of the response. Class sizes became larger. Composition classes that had been capped at 20, which is a defendable size for writing-intensive work,

moved up to 25. Minimal enrollments to continue a course moved from 12 to 15, at some cost to available specialty offerings. More sweepingly still, the faculty mix began to change, with a greater number of adjuncts and full-time teaching faculty, at the expense of the traditional research-and-teaching tenure track staple. Most systematically of all, in many places, faculty salaries stagnated despite ongoing if modest inflation: here was the clearest sacrifice, one that deserves more widespread notice. These reductions, in combination, explain how the increasing numbers of in-state students could be handled, with their tuitions welcome but ultimately inadequate to cover the actual costs of education.

4. By 2013, the whole situation generated a further problem: adverse credit ratings by Moody's and other agencies that increased the costs of borrowing, jeopardizing even those capital expansions that might bring in additional student bodies and dollars. Investment analysts confirmed the extent to which established business models had gone awry.

So where do things stand now, after well over a decade of budget frenzy?

The clear fiscal challenge remains. Conventional budget sources, including state contributions but now tuition levels and easy enrollment growth as well, newly constrained by public and political outcry and the student debt concerns, exacerbated by the lagging demography, are not keeping pace with basic costs. Library acquisitions and software contracts that have long outpaced inflation are now joined in many cases by rapidly rising health insurance and pension expenses, over which individual institutions have little or no control. Every year also sees irresistible new demands for heightened security commitments.

And there is no dramatic remedy. Basically, we have entered phase two of the new budget era, with public funding still down but the initial responses—except for the cost cutting—now curtailed as well. Strategies that worked in initial response to public funding reductions—tuition hikes, enrollment growth, reliance on higher out-of-state pricing—have either ended or encountered serious new limitations. The future depends on a different mix of approaches, none very glamorous, as well as open and honest communication among the various constituencies of the university as we move forward. Here's the increasingly familiar formula:

1. *New sources of revenue.* Obviously, do continue to develop or expand programs that fit within the university mission but that bring in revenues above costs. Here is the current field of dreams in higher ed, the hope that some combination of initiatives will produce a rush of funds independent of both state and student tuition, allowing a renewal of dynamism and a pledge to quality that may be impossible without this component. While relevant projects are not entirely within institutional control, this is the approach that indeed deserves particularly aggressive attention. Revenue-generating moves can of course include a larger number of out-of-state and particularly international students, despite the growing recruitment challenges (and necessary compensatory investment in admissions efforts). They can certainly include, where appropriate, more robust executive education

efforts and possibly some other premium-priced projects. A number of universities also have direct business opportunities, including commercial uses of available land, that must be entertained, though there are some potential distractions here from the core mission. It's possible, as well, that some online operations may fall within the new-revenue-generation category, though their dependence on low labor costs raises questions that belong more properly in our larger discussion of faculty issues. Overall, there is no question that a new entrepreneurial spirit is called for, and signs of new attention abound. What is not yet certain—except for a few early entrants into the new cash cow game, such as Oregon State and its very profitable embrace of new recruitment arrangements for international students—is how much durable profit is really available. When every institution is recruiting in China, just as that nation's relevant demography also recedes, can we really be sure that we've identified a major option for the future? But, of course, we must try, and it's appropriate to begin watching which universities really gain ground through new options.

2. *Push philanthropy.* A logical response to the tension between university constraints and growing income inequality would entail ever-greater contributions from the wealthy, but logic does not always apply. Philanthropy is hard work. It involves its own investments—some contend that a dollar is required for every five dollars raised. And it is certainly a competitive field, as the richest institutions continue to have the easiest time getting richer. This is already an area where public institutions are becoming more like the privates, and there is every reason to hope for even greater success in the future. Gifts won't bail us out entirely, but we can hope that alumni and friends will play a real role in addressing the ongoing budget dilemma.[6]

Making Philanthropy Pay

As we face our budget challenges candidly and work development campaigns even more fully into the mix, we need innovation in this category as well. Too often, "development" is invoked rather generally, with insufficient connection to real priorities. Greater discipline here is part of meeting budget needs but also central to the broader process of administrative self-scrutiny.

Quite simply, investments in development must be measured, more carefully and openly than has commonly been the case to date, against contributions to core mission. It's understandable that development staffs and materials must be expanded: the accepted 1:5 (one dollar invested for every five brought in) funding formula makes this clear. It's inevitable that some donors will want to give to the university for purposes that are acceptable but frankly tangential, and this is fine so long as there are no additional costs attached (too often the case in actual fact; beware the gift—for example, the endowed chair—that demands new operating funds to complete). We must measure our success, our return on investment, primarily by gifts that really do fit basic goals of education and research (and student support, always a priority category), and we should not mislead ourselves or others by citing larger totals that add less direct value. An accounting system of this sort, which distinguishes categories within the totals in order to clarify what gifts actually support the institutional mission, will help faculty and staff alike keep track of this aspect of university endeavor. The result will allow all concerned, inside and outside the institution, to appreciate whether the investment in development is really paying off or whether it needs to be more tightly focused on the real priorities. A relevant set of accounting categories might also guide some potential donors to understand more fully how their gifts can best help the cause. There is danger, otherwise, of a rather expensive operation that looks good on paper but somehow never seems to pay off.

3. *Don't give up on the state.* I agree that we will not see a return to the 60–70% funding for public universities that once prevailed, but some compromise improvements are not just theoretically possible. As state revenues recently improved, for example, an adept chancellor in Massachusetts was able to persuade his state to pick up half of the annual operating costs of the public university system in return for two years of tuition stability and a pledge of prudence thereafter. The state price tag was $100 million, with the university promising to "keep the overall cost of education affordable while"—revealing addition—"not compromising on quality."[7] A pattern of this sort would be huge if spread more widely. It would repair some prior damage; above all, it would help immensely in compensating for limiting future tuition increases to inflation levels and no more. Unfortunately, the case is also unusual: while a few states have used better fiscal times for modest increases in university funding—Iowa, for example, has increased state support to preempt tuition hikes for three straight years—the earlier reductions have not been significantly repaired. Further, even when some states seem to regain their footing, though without major repair work, growing health and pension costs are often passed on to universities with no compensatory funding—effectively reducing operating budgets yet again. There's no escaping the need to find better ways to talk with states about some new tradeoffs, for without some greater public commitment, the other budget remedies will be inadequate to stop the bleeding. Even worse: in several cases, amazingly, outright cuts actually continue, even as the national economy rights itself. States like Wisconsin, with rising tax revenues, still talk of targeting higher ed for further slashes, as tax reductions—not just avoiding increases—seem more attractive to some politicians than higher education maintenance, much less fiscal redress. The trends seem out of hand in some states, when in fact what we should be discussing is a compromise approach to recovery.

4. *The efficiency commitment.* Cost cutting of various sorts—or, should enrollment growth continue, new levels of stability—remain an inescapable part of the picture. There is no way to avoid ongoing discussions about faculty productivity, program effectiveness, and what is so charmingly termed administrative bloat. These will be central topics in our review of academic operations in chapters that follow.

5. *Adding it up.* Increasingly, the operating budget future for most higher education institutions in the United States must be built from new revenue sources; private contributions, hopefully constructively targeted; a possible, partial public reinvestment; and cost containment, with inflation-level tuition increases added in. The sum total, obviously, requires huge effort and a willingness to make hard decisions. There is no panacea, no alternative to a careful combination of piecemeal approaches.

Two points, however, are abundantly clear. First: the more challenging our budget future—and I see no ease on the horizon—the more important it is to assure *extensive* and open communication among administrators, faculty, staff and students. While I shudder at the term transparency—and have privately concluded that whoever invokes transparency is probably concealing something—we do need to develop or maintain frequent conversations on where things stand, recurrent opportunities to offer suggestions or question imminent decisions. At Mason, we've found that fairly frequent budget forums to update faculty and staff (and interested students) on budget issues have created a widely positive atmosphere even in tough times. Periodic updates to faculty and student senate groups pay off as well. It's clearly better to share bad news, and resultant options and adjustments, than to leave people guessing.

And second: a word of caution. Public attacks on real or imagined cost centers have made it increasingly easy for universities to feel defensive. In fact, and with full agreement that efficiencies need regular review, there is very little fat in most operating budgets. Accusations to the contrary are off the mark, if not deliberately irresponsible, and this means that too much budget constraint will cut into quality. On balance, in universities as in other areas, you get what you pay for. This thread, along with the new budget realities, must be maintained in the chapters that follow.

But the challenging bottom line remains: budgets have been disrupted, and innovations are essential in response.

Educational Quality

Accusations of deteriorating quality form the second big academic target in recent years. Here, too, some serious confusions and dubious claims adorn the crudest attacks. Not surprisingly, soaring tuitions have raised varied questions about accountability, and precision is not always a strong point. At the same time, a core concern must be granted, and this sets up the second spur to significant change.

This is our wheelhouse, and if we can't improve our collective performance, we should indeed turn the ship over to someone else.

Defining the problem in this category is harder than dealing with budgets, for we're talking about inherently looser data. Budgets, after all, hit you in the face, whether you're a parent contemplating tuition trends, a faculty member wondering about salaries that lag behind inflation, or an administrator trying to make ends meet. Learning results are inherently difficult to measure, and debate about results is inevitable and, up to a point, quite healthy.

This being so, let's make the central point clear at the outset: I do not think it is true that learning is deteriorating, though there is unquestionably a batch of issues that warrant serious attention. The real dilemma—upon which critics also seize—involves graduation rates, an area in which universities in the United States have long fallen short. The students who finish do learn and, as we will demonstrate more fully in the next chapter, do benefit as a result. Those who drop out may learn a bit, but they are also saddled with a variety of burdens, and they have far less to show for their efforts. We need to sort through the various accusations about outcomes but ultimately zero in on the real vulnerability. For while, as with budget, some of higher education's detractors are truly fanciful in their claims about meager learning results, it IS incontestable that American higher education overall has been shortchanging an unacceptably large number of students for quite a while and that (even more than with budgets) a focused commitment for the future is overdue.

Concerns about student learning, and therefore higher education's effectiveness, have certainly accelerated during the past 15 years, though they are not brand new. The Department of Education under George W. Bush cast doubt on achievement levels. The main report, *A Test of Leadership,* contended that "the quality of student learning at U.S. colleges and universities is inadequate, and in some cases, declining."[8] Employers added to the charge a decade ago (though they had complained in earlier years as well): "the current state of affairs is unacceptable." In their view, only about 16% of graduates excelled in writing skills and only 28% in critical thinking and problem solving. Obviously, how the deficiencies were being measured and defined left a huge area for debate—excelling is not the same thing as adequacy—but it certainly looked like there was a problem.

Of course, everybody knew that grade levels had been going up, most obviously at the elite universities where, without question, almost every student was above average—often massively above average. This was not necessarily a problem: what used to be accepted as tolerable—the famous "gentleman's C" of the 1950s—had simply been moved up a notch. However, the process did raise questions about deteriorating academic rigor: it was and is unlikely that student performances have improved as much as grades have.

The newest blast came in 2011, with the publication of Richard Arum and Josipa Roksa's book, *Academically Adrift*—a must read, still, for academic administrators and faculty, despite some important flaws. Relying centrally on a careful examination of over 2,000 results of the Collegiate Learning Assessment Test (ACT), *Adrift* concluded that upwards of 45% of all college students had not improved in writing, critical-thinking or problem-solving ability during their first two years of study; even after four years, 36% fell into this category. As the authors noted, "American higher education is characterized by limited or no learning for a large proportion of students." Many undergraduates were "drifting through college without a clear sense of purpose."[9]

These were, and remain, huge and deeply troubling claims. The authors themselves were actually appropriately cautious in their ultimate conclusions (with good reason, as we will note):

> the limited learning that exists on U.S. college campuses . . . qualifies today as a significant social problem and should be a subject of concern of policymakers, practitioners, parents and citizens alike. While the phenomenon can accurately be described as a social problem, the situation that exists on today's college campuses in no way qualifies as a crisis, and we have consciously avoided the use of rhetoric here that would point to a 'crisis in higher education.'

Even so, the charges were serious. In the hands of other observers, bent on painting as dark a picture as possible, they could quickly turn into a much more systematic indictment—particularly when coupled with an oversimple picture of rising college costs. For Jeff Selingo, the whole situation had a bad odor. He wondered if colleges weren't deliberately ignoring the accusations and seeking to distract the public from paying the necessary attention. Arum and Roksa, indeed, had, despite their circumspection, added that "you can't trust these institutions to police themselves." Back in the hands of the fiercer critics, the limited learning results reflected deep inadequacies not only in student culture (a major target in the study itself: far too much campus consumerism, too little study time) but also in universities' blithe insouciance as they favored research over teaching, failed to evaluate instruction with any seriousness, and threw part-time faculty into the classrooms with little interest in consequences. The lessons? We—the American public— must give up its faith that institutions of higher education are really assuring the quality of their produce. Campuses were suffering from a "systematic dumbing down." Jeff Selingo put it, extending the claims in *Adrift:* "The evidence, from grades to achievement tests to graduation rates, is pretty damning—students are skating through college, if they make it through at all."

This was not, of course, exactly what *Adrift* had concluded. It resolutely ignored the implicit finding that the majority of students did in fact improve their basic analytical skills, but it is obviously much easier to condemn a whole process than to tackle even rudimentary complexities in the larger public atmosphere in which universities were becoming unprecedented targets for attack. (Where is critical thinking when we need it?) And the charges were recurrently repeated in new ways. Arum and Roksa offered a follow-up study that noted problems recent college graduates were having in finding appropriate jobs. William Deresiewicz issued a book condemning the intellectual conformism of Ivy League students—described as *Excellent Sheep*—from a lockstep admissions process on through four years of classroom regurgitations. The case for inadequacy, and possibly deterioration, seems to mount steadily. American higher education quality has clearly become fair game.

As with budgets, the new critical climate makes it easy to seem defensive. But if we are seriously to address necessary remedies—again, as with budgets, a central theme in the chapters that follow—we need a more careful diagnosis than the most cavalier critics offer, more careful indeed than can be found in the pages of *Adrift*.

There are two problems with the measurements offered up in *Adrift*. First, as the authors essentially acknowledge, there is relatively little evidence that things have actually been getting worse, which is the critics' preferred claim. We have simply not been assessing students' analytical skills for a long enough period of time—aside from evaluation systems in individual classes, which of course have been longstanding—to offer careful judgments about historical trends. *Adrift* does cite one study that suggests that, in the 1980s, learning progress during the first two years was greater than what has been found more recently. The authors have some very interesting evidence about changes in study time, which we will address again in Chapter 7, but we really don't know for sure that students are learning less than they once did. This may be a cold comfort; it might suggest that we're just now finding out that our colleges have been inadequate for ages. The United States does arguably face enhanced global competition that may make previously permissible levels of underperformance unacceptable. Still, for the record as against the most facile blasts; we are not necessarily getting worse and might in fact be improving a bit.

More important is the dubious quality of *Adrift*'s core evidence, along with some ancillary claims. The Collegiate Learning Assessment test—the basis for the contention that a large minority of students were learning nothing—is an interesting but flawed exercise, which is why most colleges do not use it (NOT because we are trying to hide from the TRUTH). It asks students to do some really interesting writing assignments around a carefully prepared problem set in a 90-minute timeframe. The exercise is given to entering students and then repeated with comparable questions at the end of sophomore and then again at the end of senior year. The results are worth attention but—and this is the key point—not as a real basis for evaluating achievement. For the problem is that the tests are what the assessment trade calls low stakes. Entering first-years, eager to please, arguably take them pretty seriously; often, they form part of a battery of tests, some of which will directly impact placement. But sophomores and seniors (who have to be pressed, sometimes bribed outright with small payments, to take the tests at all) have no reason to worry about the results, which have no impact on their futures. So they may or may not see them as significant or put forth real effort. The verdict?

The mixed results of the follow-up tests feed a claim that must not be ignored but one that ultimately, essentially, remains unproven.

> **Learning More about Outcomes**
>
> The minority of schools that do use assessment testing outside of individual courses report results that, like the more general information we have about student progress, run counter to the claims in *Adrift*. James Madison University tests entering students and then repeats the process for completing sophomores in areas such as writing, scientific and quantitative reasoning, the humanities, and ethical reasoning. The tests have been carefully prepared by teams of faculty and assessment experts. The sophomore checkup reveals that the average student improves in each area by about half a standard deviation. The gains are not huge, but they are definite and consistent against the generalizations about massive stagnation reported in *Adrift*. Schools like JMU are justly pleased with their system and its clear validation of their general education programs.[10]
>
> Examples of this sort deserve more attention, not just to correct irresponsible attacks but to further the process of improving how we assess learning quality and make the higher education case to a newly skeptical public. Unless we cave in entirely, and only count degrees and first jobs as the measure of student success, regardless of more basic learning gains, assessment must be a growth area for the future.

Adrift adds in a few other elements that can also be contested. Particularly interesting is the recurrent lament about the number of college students who are not asked to write essays of more than 20 pages, either as first-years or as seniors. Actually, most writing experts would argue that the long paper is much less useful, for training or for evaluation, than a series of shorter efforts (particularly for first-years). So it's not clear that we're actually falling down on the job in this category, either.

All this said, I have no intention of throwing the baby out with the bath. After all, we have not only the Arum and Roksa efforts but also Derek Bok's careful and sobering analysis in his 2006 *Underachieving Colleges* to suggest that (whatever the historical trends) we are not doing as well as we might in our core product area.

Without backpedaling on the concerns about *Adrift*'s evidence base, here's what we probably know.

A recommitment to student learning is imperative. American colleges may have long been too cavalier about those of their students who were not being reached, but that is all the more reason for redress. Increasing international competition is a valid reason for new concern. Even more important—and highlighted in *Adrift*—is the growing number of first-generation or minority college students who may in some cases (not all) more readily get lost in the college experience than was true of student cohorts in the past. We don't have to accept blanket indictments. Many institutions and certainly many individual professors are already active. Here, too, *Adrift* offers really welcome evidence that learning results respond to careful attention. We need to generalize these efforts, expand our grasp of best practices, and make the goal explicit and public.

This means also that we must continue to work on our assessment procedures. A number of instruments already exist. We need to pay more attention to schools that do offer high-stakes testing of general analytical gains; without necessarily generalizing this approach, we should certainly be open to the results. Though impressionistic in its base in student questionnaires, the National Survey of Student Engagement can be helpful, for example, in assessing student study time and comparing data with other institutions in the survey. A few years ago, Mason used NSSE results, suggesting that more students felt underchallenged in the classroom than was desirable, to undertake serious conversations with and among faculty, with a much improved result in this category next time around. Here, too, examples can be generalized. Other assessment procedures, required by various accreditation agencies, actually produce even more systematic and credible data about student learning, substantially qualifying some of the claims in *Adrift*, and we must return to this point. The whole commitment to assessment and utilization of results needs ongoing attention and must be a central part of our discussion of higher education components in later chapters. We need to find additional ways to measure whether appropriate goals are having appropriate results but also to make the relevant public more aware of what we can already demonstrate.[11]

(Note to prospective students and their parents: if you want a good question to ask of the colleges you are considering, have them tell you about their learning assessment procedures and how they are used to improve instruction. A dry topic but very revealing. Lots more relevant than dorm amenities.)

Along with further commitment to student learning and its evaluation, we must also extend the growing interest in degree completion, where we have a far more extensive and measurable problem than with student learning overall. Currently, taking American higher education as a whole, 59% of entrants to four-year colleges complete a bachelor's degree in six years. High rates of incompletion play a key role in the American slippage in the overall percentage of college graduates: a nation that was first, twenty-five years ago, now stands in 12th or 13th place internationally. Doing better with and for the students who enter is by far the best way to address this growing challenge. Here, too, it's important to note that the dilemma is not new; lots of universities and colleges have long assumed that high dropout rates were simply part of the territory. The assumption was deeply flawed, in terms of the costs, in self-perception and in wasted resources, that the customary levels of failure imposed. It has now—given still-higher costs and the increasingly competitive global standards—become genuinely self-defeating, for institutions as well as individuals.[12]

There is a slight caveat here: a growing number of American students do not complete their degrees at the same school where they matriculated, and there is a problem capturing the results in the completion figures. Two groups are working on the issue: The National Student Clearinghouse and Student Achievement Measures (SAM), a project backed by several higher education associations. These are projects in progress, but a more realistic set of figures should emerge soon that will make the national higher education system look less bad. It will remain true, however, that too many students begin college, spend some serious money, and simply do not complete their work or win substantial results. Improving this record will remain the core measurement for greater student success.

International Standing

As the relative percentage of American college graduates in the overall population has slipped, thanks to inattention at home and gains abroad, completion rates for those who start the process also lag. Finding clearly comparable data across national lines is not easy, but there is no question that the United States is well behind in the retention game. A recent study of 18 countries, by the Organization for Economic Development and Cooperation, rates the United States 14th on the list in degree completion rates among entering students, virtually 50% behind Japan, Turkey and Australia, 12% behind Germany, and 10% under the group average—and this is without South Korea, one of the world's higher ed leaders, on the list at all. The United States still benefits from relatively robust college entry rates (well behind Finland and Korea, but about 8th internationally overall); despite tuition challenges and shifts in demography, we're not doing as badly in this category as some imagine, though there is room for improvement. Still, the poor retention figures significantly reduce the resulting impact, causing the lion's share of the comparative problem. Improving completion rates, in other words, is the best single step toward redressing the national position in college graduate percentages overall—as well as being a humane efficiency for all concerned.[13]

The priority of higher graduation rates operates in close relationship to the pledges over student learning and assessment. We must obviously be careful NOT to seek greater retention by lowering standards, which is frankly more than a minor risk in the current national mood. The mutual relationship is vital: higher education institutions of various sorts need to combine greater attention to learning outcomes—making sure that there is no slippage and hopefully some progress—with improvements in degree completion. This is the combination that best serves students and best measures the success of institutions themselves. We have long known that it is easier and cheaper to retain students than to recruit new ones. We need to more forcefully translate this understanding, and the parallel commitment to greater student success, into better performance.

The Key Priorities: Better Budget Results, Better Student Outcomes

Agreeing on these priority areas—with attention to budget stability virtually forced on us and enhancements in learning and graduation rates a public but also ethical imperative—offers a certain degree of harmony. It will certainly be easier to defend the new tuition levels if we can simultaneously point to better student performance. The fabled "return on investment" will be even clearer (though note: it's pretty clear already, despite our problems). Logically—if not necessarily politically—it should be easier to talk to our government masters about reconsidering the extent of public university budget reductions if we simultaneously link remediation to higher graduation rates. We will be improving efficiency and wasting less of our time and above all that of some students and their families on educational investments that yield incomplete results.

For students and their families, the compatibility of priorities may be even clearer. With greater budget stabilization and less reliance on tuition increases beyond inflation, student debt and financial pressures should also ease. This in turn will have direct impact on retention, for financial issues heavily contribute to at least a large minority of student dropouts.

Yet the goals are by no means entirely harmonious. Some of the key measures that must be considered in improving student learning and retention—obvious example: more courses offered by full-time faculty—war against budget limitations. Remediation or some polite equivalent is another area where learning needs struggle against cost constraints. Trying to assure greater student success sometimes sees universities forced to compensate for clear deficiencies in P–12 preparation for many students. How many students, for example, come into to college STEM fields having "taken" calculus in high school but prove unable in fact to function at a university level? These problems can be addressed through at least implicit remediation, smaller class size and more tutoring and advising, plus possibly some self-paced online programs that can help students through the rough spots; but every single one of those approaches does cost additional money for the institution, the student or both.

For administrators, faculty and staff, there is no alternative to a juggling act. Measuring major policy decisions by their impact on the basic business plan—the budget focus—but also by their potential encouragement to active learning and graduation commits universities to criteria that are rarely if ever entirely compatible. Yet there is no real option. Simply working on the budget—developing a new profit center, cutting costs, or even persuading a legislator—makes no sense if we can't also measure student payoff. Yet working on student results without the budget essentials will bring us down as well. If asked which priority really comes first, the student outcomes are inherently the more attractive but the only honest answer is: both.

The Plus Side of Priorities: Items Lower on the List

The tension of trying to balance the top priorities can be eased a bit by a recognition that a number of other commonly cited issues—some of them related to the Big Two, others rather separate—can be downgraded, in a few cases sidestepped altogether. Here is another discussion that will carry through the following chapters, but a brief sampling will support the prioritization process. Obviously, the list is subjective: some readers will want still other items identified as lower priority, while others will object strenuously that at least two of the following topics should be moved right to the top. At least we can promote a discussion that is not entirely random.

1. *Research growth.* This is the most painful one. Research *expansion* is simply not quite on the top priority list, even amid our real anxieties—for our institutions and for the national future—about the reductions in funded support that have occurred, particularly at the federal level, since the Great Recession. Indeed, the clear point is that, by themselves, universities cannot be asked to compensate for probably misguided decisions in this vital area. Research at a significant level remains essential, and indeed it can relate directly to student success; more on this in the next chapter. We also must be honest: even funded research requires institutional investment. Quite apart from faculty time removed from teaching, funded research normally costs about twenty cents in operating budget increase for every dollar brought it. Expenses often include substantial startup packages required to lure talented faculty, even at early ranks, and make them functional once they arrive but also includes fields such as lab safety where external overhead does not cover full need. The amortization of the investment required to construct and equip research facilities themselves can be a budget backbreaker. This is why the research sector has to be evaluated carefully in light of the top two goals. It can and should be maintained. Even roughly current levels of research will remain essential to institutional performance, to the social good, and to student advancement. Ultimately, we will have little to teach if new knowledge dries up. In the present circumstances, however, a commitment to expansion, as opposed to healthy maintenance, is a small notch down from the top, given the toll it takes on budget stability and tuition outlays.[14]

Especially for Any Faculty Readers

The research budget dilemma deserves just a bit of emphasis, for many experienced faculty blithely assume that universities have been using their research overhead to cover all sorts of other items; frivolously, some would add. It's hard to realize that even overheads of 50% or more don't do the trick, given the types of expenses noted above; they are far from serving as a profit center. The situation tends to get worse with greater federal

> constraints on what overhead can cover plus a welter of new regulations that require staff attention. This is where the approximately twenty-cent outlay for every external dollar comes in, as a recent American Association of Universities report reemphasizes—making universities themselves the second greatest source of research funding after the federal government. The point is not just setting the record straight. Understanding the extra costs of funded research supports our later discussion of the need for more careful evaluation and justification of the research we must maintain, and it helps clarify those disruptive (and, in my view, errant) proposals that would do away with research altogether.

There is, of course, an escape clause here. We must hope that the constraints will ease, allowing a return to sensible growth. This will involve, however, not only new federal funding largesse but also an improvement in some combination of state and philanthropic support to cover the expenses that even federal overheads to not reach—the twenty cents on the dollar. Research advocates—for hopes here die hard, quite understandably—urge more reliance as well on private research funding from the fabled American corporate sector. This is indeed desirable for national and regional growth futures, but a further warning here: experience to date suggests that businesses and foundations are far less willing than the feds to provide much overhead—they are looking if not for a free ride at university expense, at least for a cheap date, and this merely enhances the budget dilemma. Again, an escape hatch exists that might allow resumption of expansion, but it must be defined very carefully for all parties concerned.

2. *Athletics.* For many alumni and for a wider public, American universities have become synonymous with entertaining sports. My university happens not to have a football team (above the club level), yet when, for example, a new president came on the scene, football issues constituted far and away the number one topic of conversation. We simply have to dispute this prioritization. I know that few academic colleagues will disagree, however much we enjoy sports as spectators and also genuinely admire the qualities and achievements of many student athletes. But there is real danger, in the contemporary context, that public enthusiasm plus the big business lures of the top athletic programs will pull our attention away from the top goals. Simply trying to keep up with league realignments and television contracts, not to mention alumni insistence that this coach be fired, that one retained, constitutes a serious drain on administrative attention. Once more, eyes on the prize. College sports rarely (just a few big-time football schools excepted here) fail to cost money, with serious resultant burdens on student fees. Their role in retention, though not necessarily nonexistent, is surely secondary for most students. Here is another category to keep in proper perspective, though admittedly this is a challenge amid the current frenzy.

3. *Four-year graduation.* For some schools, trying to be sure that most students not only graduate but do so in four years will remain a desirable and achievable goal, important to parents as well. For most of us, too much pressure to speed things up can be counterproductive. In point of fact, only 19% of all entering American undergraduates finish in four years, and it would be folly to assume this can or even should change dramatically. Our students come in many flavors. Some have or get jobs as students that are directly related to career goals, and while we may worry about distractions from the educational process, the combination will make sense to them, even if the result is a six-year horizon. Others simply have to work, for other personal or family reasons. Many, as our student body increasingly expands its age range, have serious family obligations of their own. I admit that I used to think that universities should uniformly strive for the four-year goal because that's what my friends and I assumed and that's what attaches to the prestige institutions. We should make sure there are no artificial barriers and indeed create opportunities (for example, through careful summer options) that allow a few to accelerate even further—for this can, among other things, ease tuition burdens. Other patterns warrant attention as well. There are paths for some to a three-year degree and even more interesting opportunities for five-year bachelors/masters combinations, which can have powerful results. For most institutions, however, chasing an invariable four-year standard is a needless distraction, and we need to help the wider public to understand this as well. A variety of options and timetables, all assessed for quality outcomes and ultimate degree completion, responds to what students need overall. Our top priorities are demanding enough, and they meet responsible requirements.

4. *Rapid expansion of enrollments.* This is an interesting one; some rethinking seems unavoidable, but the issue needs to be explored even more carefully than was the case for research. As noted, until recently, many institutions (including my own) found it essential to expand enrollments as part of the strategy of meeting budget cuts, along with higher tuitions, and was at the same time possible because of population growth. When universities could recruit fee-paying, out-of-state students but accompany this by measurable though more modest in-state growth, the proposition clearly paid off. It was acceptable to most political authorities, and a responsible expression of the obligations of public institutions. This may still hold true in some instances, but slowing demographics, increased competition for students, and the new constraints on in-state as well as out-of-state tuitions may change the ballgame; hence, the altered priority.

Politicians will still press for more. This is part of the Obama strategy to put the nation back on top in percentage of college graduates. In my own state of Virginia, a previous governor talked boldly about the need for 100,000 new degrees over ten years. It was a great appeal, recognizing the importance of higher education for additional individuals and for society; but he offered no funding to cover the gap between diminished state support plus tuitions and the actual cost of education. So though a few universities talked about responding, the proposition ultimately made little sense. Larger enrollments may indeed be quite desirable in terms of personal and societal economic futures, but we as institutions must now be more cautious. We must measure expansion prospects by the two top priorities. On the budget side: if growth does not at least break even, I think we have to be leery. If growth stretches available resources, we also risk jeopardizing investments in student success and higher graduation rates. Improved retention will, by itself, move the numbers up noticeably, and this should be accepted as part of the basic priority scheme. Growth beyond this must be tested carefully; its inclusion, however attractive, should not be automatic.

Public institutions must accept a clear social mission, which is why the enrollment growth issue needs such careful treatment. Where many elite privates, and candidly some public flagships, make their tasks easier by limiting admissions, seeking to be as exclusive as possible, the public commitment must be different, particularly as wider patterns of social inequality continue to deteriorate. The responsible public university should at least maintain current admissions levels, should accept students from a wide range of socioeconomic backgrounds, and—Priority #2—should steadily improve the completion rates. It should welcome evaluation in these terms. The result will be student diversity of various sorts, at least modest growth (through better retention), and improved institutional and individual success. Adding more rapid expansion to the list of essentials must drop down a notch.

5. *Bringing back adult noncompleters.* Here is another attractive goal, unquestionably worth attention, but again requiring careful vetting in relation to the top priorities. There may be as many as 30 million American adults who have had some college but for whatever combination of reasons failed to complete an undergraduate degree. The number is staggering, potentially a major invitation to extend more active recruitment, particularly given the sluggish demography of the conventional age group. This issue is not just numbers, however; there are lots of individuals whose lives might be better, particularly in terms of job credentials, by completing a degree. In a changing economy, having a larger percentage of adults with college degrees is in the national interest as well. So there are many reasons to attend to the subject; in fact, the age of the average undergraduate is already going up, a sign that returnees are already reentering at a higher pace. Caution is needed as well. There are lots of enthusiastic proponents of a massive degree completion campaign, some with attractive foundation grants to offer, but the business plan (once an inspirational donation expires) is challenging: this population may actually be somewhat more expensive to educate than the average, given reentry and retooling issues. Regular in-state tuition may fall even shorter of real costs than is usually the case. There's a retention issue as well: right now, returnees persist to graduation at only a 41% rate, well short of the average. If we are to serve these people responsibly, we probably need more advising and mentoring—again a cost category. Here, too, there may be some escape hatches: the push to give credit for competencies acquired in adulthood could help on the cost side and improve

motivation, but obviously this approach must be accompanied by careful assessments of academic quality. Some states might even be willing, in this case, actually to cover costs above in-state tuition—though this has not yet materialized. There are a host of valid reasons for colleges, particularly in the public sector, to pay attention to this category, but many reasons as well not to be pulled off track by overambitious claims. As with overall enrollment growth, let's be interested but realistically wary. The target is important, but its pursuit must depend on a business plan that is at worst cost-neutral—and this is not easily attained.

6. *The rankings.* This is an easy one, in principle. It's impossible not to worry about rankings a little bit, and there are, unfortunately, some reasons that our worry may increase in the near future. There's also no question that, except for a few daring (misguided?) institutions, this is a category that should be well down the priority list.[15]

Study the granddaddy ranking, *US News* (as I'm sure many readers have). There's no question of its influence, not only in the United States; Chinese mothers, thinking about where to send their kids abroad, are well versed. Yet the ranking measures very few things that we should both be interested in and capable of doing anything about. It does give credit for retention and (four-year) graduation rates. Its interest in reputation might or might not be relevant. Beyond these factors, the premium goes to selectivity—how many students you manage to attract but exclude as opposed to how many you manage to include and advance—and above all to funding. The rich, as a result, are always at the top of the heap, and the magazine simply shuffles them around a bit to justify selling a new copy every year. Public institutions, and particularly those devoted to serving a wide spectrum of qualified students, can't really compete.

On balance, there's not much point trying. A recent study from a highly ranked private, the University of Rochester, estimated that it would require an annual investment of over $112 million, in faculty salaries, scholarships and other areas, to have a chance to rise as many as 15 slots, and even then the result would not be certain. The conclusion: most institutions do not have that kind of institutional funding, and many of them are pursuing goals—better service to lower socioeconomic groups, more creative global programs—that *US News* does not reward at all (save perhaps in the purely reputational, and separate, category of "up and coming"). Of course, there will be a few exceptions to offering low priority. Northeastern University, without some of the responsibilities of a public institution, is resolutely moving up. A few state schools, probably brashly, proclaim higher rankings as a strategic goal. For most of us, however, let's do our thing well and simply suffer a few annually embarrassing questions about why we haven't cracked the top 50.

One further caution, however, though on balance it does not contradict an explicit low prioritization. Global rankings are gaining ground, and to the extent that many American institutions seek more international students, or simply in general like to bask in an international sun, they may warrant a bit more thought.

The global standings involved a variety of emphases. Shanghai Jiao Tong places a premium on research, including Nobel Prize winners; Q4, one of the British systems, is (dangerously) subjective and reputational; still others are giving greater attention to percentages of international faculty. The number of ratings grows by leaps and bounds, with Saudi Arabia and the European Union recently getting into the act, and the indefatigable *US News* has now offered a global entry (which conveniently projects the supremacy of the Anglo-Saxon university world). This very variety may be a saving grace, giving different institutions different opportunities to brag (highlighting some offerings, downplaying others) or simply wearing out the welcome of rankings of any sort; there is at least as much reason to be suspicious of the global rankings as of the established domestic ones. Besides the attention paid by international applicants, the stakes are going up, as more and more governments—like Russia's—explicitly plan to evaluate their own top institutions through rankings position and seek to invest in order to break into the top group. In this process, inexorably, American institutions will begin to lose ground, particularly given current public disinvestment. This may turn out to bother us and affect us. Again, not a big enough issue to crack the priority list but also impossible fully to ignore.

The Lure of Technology

It would be misleading, and certainly provocative, to put the promise of new teaching technologies into the lower priority list because the need for careful and imaginative expansion is inescapable. But technology is not, of course, itself a priority, and only those innovators dazzled by the latest shiny toy would ever think it so. It's a tool, and it fits into the priority scale as a tool. It is actually helpful to step back and take a look at the online reality, and the online potential, through the demands of budget stabilization and greater student success, setting directions through those priorities.

Lurking near the surface of many of the most strident critiques of higher education—particularly the external blasts but sometimes internal fulminations as well—is a sense that new technologies provide the solution to our greatest woes, delivering cheaper but more effective education than the world has ever known. Further, most educators are simply too tradition-bound to realize the great promise before them—which is why the whole system needs massive disruption and new leadership. It's important to say clearly: whatever may occur at some future point, this ambitious claim is simply not true now and will almost certainly not be true for quite a while. New learning technologies are helping us in some crucial respects; they also, predictably enough, cause some new problems. They also don't directly address some key issues one way or the other. They are part of our present and future. They will not, by themselves, resolve our greatest dilemmas.

In truth, we already know quite a bit about online technologies in this regard, with the obvious caveat that greater experience and further innovations may dislodge what has been learned to date.

First, as against the most obdurate traditionalism, online courses can work as well as, and sometimes better than, conventional classroom experience. They can, obviously, reach student audiences for whom conventional attendance is difficult or impossible, and they have served many students admirably. They also appeal to students, even resident students, who look for greater schedule flexibility or who want to continue their studies during periods like summer break. Purely online opportunities or, even more often, hybrid combinations of online and classroom experiences are gaining ground and will surely expand still further in the future for good reason. Online and hybrid development have clearly become part of a fairly standard academic framework.

Second, online expansion does not usually do much to address the budget crunch, and this is where some of the disrupters have misled or been misled. The technologies cost money. Online delivery often increases the faculty time needed to address student concerns and offer prompt response (this can be a plus from the learning side of things, but it doesn't come cheap). At least for some time, preparing online or even hybrid offerings frequently requires additional training and expert guidance. This cost may decline with greater faculty experience, but it looms large now. Again over time, there may also be some measurable savings in capital investments—as needs for additional classrooms are modified by technology delivery. In the short term, however, classrooms suitable for serious technology initiatives require new funding. Online expansion, in and of itself, is either irrelevant to the budget priority or adds at least some further burden if the courses are to be delivered responsibly, with appropriate attention to maintaining academic quality. In addition, to be competitive in what is a national or international market, tuitions for online delivery are normally well below standard out-of-state rates—no significant boost to revenue to accompany often higher costs.[16]

There is one exception, which is where the confusion begins. Online expansion, IF coupled with the employment of more inexpensive faculty—part-timers, graduate students—can reduce costs. It's the change in the labor mix, not the technology that does the trick. Perhaps this is indeed part of our future, but this must be taken up in our larger discussion of faculty resources and decisions about faculty categories. It's not directly a technology issue.

Finally, online delivery almost certainly does not improve retention—individual exceptions aside, where the flexibilities in location and timing may help some stay in school. This is a crucial point, again at least for the foreseeable future. I hope we can expand some online offerings, even MOOCs, to provide some remedial, self-paced instruction for adults returning to college, but even here we must couple this with active, in-person mentorship for any real hope of success. Overall, the undergraduate populations most at risk for dropping out simply do not, in the main, fare well with online delivery. Even more generally, online offerings notoriously see higher incompletion rates than classroom experiences, as the for-profits have abundantly demonstrated. The point cannot be overstated: online programs work best with student audiences that have already established successful learning patterns and appropriate motivations, and for them it can be a splendid resource—for example, at the graduate level as in many professional masters programs. We can and should always be open to further experimentation, but—toward the priority of improving graduation rates and successful learning—caution is essential, not out of misplaced conservatism but in the interests of responsible advancement for the goals we claim to espouse.

There's every reason to build technology into any future plans for teaching and learning. Information technology already addresses important opportunities for innovations in teaching. It provides unprecedented access to data, and we have only begun to tap into the implications here. It helps faculty diversify their modes of presentation—a direct link to the imperatives of good teaching discussed in Chapter 6. It also raises some really interesting educational challenges in working with students to develop greater ability to evaluate the reliability of unfettered information—applying critical thinking to the Internet. For all these reasons, technology will loom large in our further discussions of the major academic components, from faculty adjustments to global outreach, but these discussions will not reverse the essential preliminary: technology will not create shortcuts in meeting the priority challenges going forward.

Finally: Bring It On!

Addressing the key priorities—the necessity of stabilizing budgets and the more enjoyable if demanding task of promoting greater student success—is and will be no easy task. The challenge runs through the further exploration of the key requirements in guiding the contemporary American university. Other, if slightly lesser, priorities will add to the complexity.

The need to tackle the priorities does suggest one final, early emphasis: the desirability of making our commitment clear and accepting responsible external measurements of results.

Following on the recommendations of the Bush administration, President Obama has advanced the idea of a new national rankings system, with emphasis on relative affordability, student debt, graduation rates and job placement. (The issue is not, yet at least, clearly partisan.) Some implementation was slated for 2015, though plans have been scaled back. Many, perhaps most, academic leaders have voiced strong objections; the council of presidents in my own state of Virginia has publicly disapproved, and the Harvard president expresses grave concern.

Yet—with a few caveats—the approach is eminently reasonable as well as probably unavoidable, at the state level if not the federal (although the feds, as dispensers of rising levels of Pell Grant funding, do have a legitimate stake). Many other countries already link funding to performance measures—for example, Ireland and Denmark, both with higher education systems that are functioning better than ours at least in terms of production of graduates.

It's quite understandable that some American institutions will demur. Most of the for-profits, with deplorable graduate rates and huge student debt, undoubtedly want to hide, though at last it's probably too late for them. Some liberal arts colleges (a few of which are regulars on the 25-worst list) and more public institutions than one would like are in the same boat, with poor retention and, in some cases, high cost. The prestige institutions, which will do well enough, probably see little to gain, particularly the ones (including a few public flagships) that enroll shockingly low numbers of Pell Grant students.

Most of us in the publics that serve the majority of undergraduates should both applaud and help shape the effort. The result will actually be far more salutary than the favor-the-rich *US News* approach. The project is reasonable in providing useful information both for our government funders and for the public at large, prospective students included. What university leaders should be doing, instead of objecting, is participating—urging, for example, that a ratings system set ambitious goals but ones that also reflect institutional diversity; we're not all going to start graduating 92% of our students in four years. The need to develop better systems of measuring graduation rates to capture the growing number of students who start in one place and finish in another, is imperative. Universities also can legitimately warn against too much emphasis on first jobs, which is arguably a poor measure and often yields unreliable data. We should most definitely ask for more attention to learning quality than the federal proposal yet suggests—a crucial reason for the kind of emphasis on institutionally driven assessments discussed in Chapter 4. Accreditation requirements already help here in insisting on outcomes evaluations, but at the least these should be explicitly acknowledged in the ratings system. We should also insist that the ratings discussion include a more explicit public commitment to funding in return for high or improved performance. On the other hand, we should also urge the addition of provisions that guard against watering down standards or overemphasizing exclusivity in the interests of easier retention.[17]

The main point, however, is that we should be willing to embrace an approach that—contrary to most existing ratings system—accurately reflects our top priorities. Ratings that measure greater budget stability and tuition moderation, while encouraging a public climate that will contribute to this goal, and that highlight at least some key aspects of student success clearly push American higher education in the right direction. They can be yet another indication that we have recognized where we need to change or recommit and are confident in our ability to produce solid results. There's no reason to shy away from this aspect of the contemporary academic agenda.

Further Reading

For basic critiques and comments: Derek Curtis Bok, *Our Underachieving Colleges: A Candid Look at How Much Students Learn and Why They Should Be Learning More* (Princeton, NJ: Princeton University Press, 2008); Jeffrey J. Selingo, *College (Un)Bound: The Future of Higher Education and What It Means for Students* (Boston: New Harvest, 2013); Richard

Arum and Josipa Roksa, *Academically Adrift: Limited Learning on College Campuses* (Chicago: University of Chicago Press, 2011); and William Deresiewicz, *Excellent Sheep: The Miseducation of the American Elite and the Way to a Meaningful Life* (New York: Free Press, 2014).

A recent statement on costs, resulting mainly from the funding reductions by state governments, and the impact on students including the exacerbation of social inequalities: "Inequity on the Rise in Higher Education," a 2015 report issued by the Pell Institute for the Study of Opportunity in Education and the Alliance for Higher Education and Democracy.

On the vexed issue of rankings: M. Yudkevich, P. Altbach and L. E. Rumbley, eds., *The Global Academic Rankings Game: Changing Institutional Policy, Practice and Academic Life* (New York: Routledge, 2015); B. M. Kehm, "Global University Rankings: Impacts and Unintended Side Effects," *European Journal of Education* 49 (2014); M. Kunter, "How Northeastern Gamed the College Rankings," *Boston Magazine* (2014); M. D. Shear, "Colleges Rocked as Obama Seeks Rating System," *New York Times* (May 25, 2014).

On current enrollments challenges and responsibilities, John A. Douglass, *The Conditions for Admission: Access, Equity, and the Social Contract of Public Universities* (Stanford: Stanford University Press, 2007); and Christopher Newfield, "The End of the American Funding Model: What Comes Next?" *American Literature* 82 (3) (September, 2010). See also Crow and Dabars, cited in Ch. 1.

On characteristic disruptive proposals, largely assuming that current university structures are on their way out: Ryan Craig, *College Disrupted: The Great Unbundling of Higher Education* (New York: Palgrave, 2015) and Kevin Carey, *The End of College: Creating the Future of Learning and the University of Everywhere* (New York: Riverhead, 2015). See also a constructive approach to change in: Susan Aldridge and Kathleen Harvatt, *Wired for Success: Real World Solutions for Transforming Higher Education* (Washington: American Association of State Colleges and Universities, 2014).

Finally, a recent study explores accountability efforts and their vicissitudes, including American states that earlier introduced performance-based approaches only to pull back—and, in some cases, more recently return to the charge: Kevin Dougherty and Rebecca Natow, *The Politics of Performance Funding for Higher Education: Origins, Discriminations, and Transformations* (Baltimore: Johns Hopkins University Press, 2015).

Notes

1 For various comments, New America Foundation, both Higher Ed Watch and the newer Ed Central (www.edcentral.org); Clay Christensen et al., *Disrupting Class: how disruptive innovation will change the way the world learns* (New York: McGraw-Hill, 2008); Jeffrey Selingo, *College (Un)Bound: the future of higher education and what it means for students* Boston, Houghton Mifflin Harcourt, 2013), esp. ch, 2.

2 American Institute for Research, *Delta Cost Project* (Washington, 2013). See also Robert Hiltonsmith, *Pulling up the Higher-Ed Ladder; myth and reality in the crisis of college affordability* (New York: Demos, 2015).

3 Chinmayi Sharma, "Tuitions Rising at Faster Rate than Median Incomes," *Chronicle of Higher Education*, Nov. 7, 2011; College Board, *Trends in College Pricing* (New York, 2013).

4 U.S. Government Accountability Office, *Higher Education: state funding trends and policies on affordability* (Washington, Dec., 2014).

5 National Center for Education Statistics, *Projection of Education Statistics to 2022* (Washington, 2014).

6 Michael Worth, *New Strategies for Educational Fundraising* (Westport, CT: Oryx, 2002); see also materials from the Council for Advancement and Support of Education (CASE). Recent reports that remind us of what a high percentage of total giving goes to the top 40 institutions (with the gap steadily widening) might reasonably be taken as somewhat discouraging for the places that educate the most students.
7 University of Massachusetts FY15 Operating Budget, June 18, 2014.
8 U.S. Department of Education, *A Test of Leadership: charting the future of U.S. higher education* (Washington, 2008).
9 Richard Arum and Josipa Roksa, *Academically Adrift: limited learning on college campuses* (Chicago: University of Chicago Press, 2011). See also Arum with Esther Cho, Jeannie Kim and Roksa, *Documenting Uncertain times: post-graduate outcomes of the academically adrift cohort* (New York: Social Science Research Council, 2012).
10 Material from the Center for Assessment and Research, James Madison University.
11 Natasha Jankowski, George D. Kuh, Stanley O. Ikenberry and Jillian Kinzie, "Knowing What Students Know and Can Do" in the *National Institute for Leaning Outcomes Assessment,* January 2014; this issue is further discussed in ch. 4 and its further readings. The role of regional and field-specific accreditation agencies, often justly criticized for imposing unnecessary costs and rigmarole, will remain vital in backstopping the insistence on establishing and assessing learning outcomes, particularly as American higher education will surely face a new mixture of constructive and half-baked experiments.
12 National Center for Education Statistics, "Institutional Retention and Graduation Rates for Undergraduate Students," *The Condition of Education* report, May, 2014; Betsy Barefoot, Betsy Griffin and Andrew Koch, *Enhancing Student Success and Retention throughout Undergraduate Education: a national survey* (Brevard, NC: The John H. Gardner Institute for Excellence, 2013).
13 Organization for Economic Cooperation and Development (OECD), "Education at a Glance" report, 2013.
14 American Association of Universities, *AAU Statement on the Research and Development Efficiency Act,* July 14, 2014.
15 M. Yudkevich, P. Altbach and L. E. Rumbley, eds., *The Global Academic Rankings Game* (New York: Routledge, 2015).
16 I. Elaine Allen and Jeff Seaman, "Changing Courses: ten years of tracking online education in the United States," *Babson Survey Research Group,* Jan. 2013.
17 Douglas Belkin, "Obama Spells Out College Ranking Framework," *Wall Street Journal,* Dec. 19, 2014. For common criticisms from higher education, Allie Bidwell, "Grade G: most college presidents pan new Obama ratings system," *US News,* Dec. 16, 2013.

3

ESSENTIAL STRENGTHS

From Defense to Offense?

The need to disrupt or at least substantially adjust established practice is only part of the story—only part of the agenda moving forward. This chapter, though a bit briefer that the previous one, is no less essential. It reminds us of the many existing signs of success that must be balanced against the criticisms and the deficiencies lest we actually weaken our performance by overreacting to the loudest alarms. More important, it clarifies the achievements that underlie the more superficial acclaim. The focus is both on some longstanding strengths and more recent changes that have begun—despite the ostrich claims of our loudest critics—to respond to the newer pressures and opportunities. The result is a third top priority, closely linked to student success: preserve what is already paying off, for our students and our society, and articulate this priority more forcefully. As a few institutions are already demonstrating, it is easier to neglect existing assets than to build new ones, particularly amid budget constraints.

The basic point is clear: with all the attention to budgets and real or imagined inadequacies in educational delivery, there has not been a lot of talk lately about quality. We have already noted that this is a crucial reason universities need to take fuller, but also responsible, control over their own futures. Strategic plans are being generated that are so eager to focus on novel directions—presumably to address the newer priorities—that a commitment to appropriate standards simply drops out. Nor does insistence on quality loom large in the Obama measurement proposals. Yet quality is vital, if we are not to give out meaningless degrees, to succeed in retaining and graduating students who have in fact learned little or nothing. We will serve neither students nor society if we fail to define and maintain appropriate standards—what *Adrift* refers to, perhaps a bit too stiffly, as rigor. While some quality standards will emerge from the essential changes in educational delivery, many exist already in the core of American higher education at or near its best.

There are clear dangers to existing quality, besides the need for vigilance in any age. The current economic crisis has generated a host of proposals seeking to focus higher education on preparation for first jobs. There's a strong move to couple assertedly college-level work with the high school years in dual enrollment programs or to redefine the scope of community colleges, all in the interest of preparing for first jobs in the most economical fashion possible. The emphasis is understandable: for several years, some college graduates were having trouble finding work; even today, while outright unemployment is well below the national average, there are problems of underemployment and inadequate earnings. But to move from addressing this challenge to a narrowing of the larger purpose of higher education would be a huge mistake, for universities themselves but above all for our students and society at large. Experiments are always welcome, so long as they are appropriately assessed, but too much eagerness to find cheap solutions that need only be measured by immediate employment results will distort the process.[1]

For higher education is about careers, citizenship, and lifetime achievement—with initial jobs merely a first step. Colleges and universities should provide skills and knowledge that will help in employment, and many faculty and administrators are paying increasing attention to explicit emphasis on the capacities their curriculum promotes. Thus, history programs, clearly nervous about the jobs focus, legitimately talk about their contributions to writing, research skills and critical thinking. We are also increasingly aware of the importance of internships during the educational experience. But higher education also aims at a longer professional life, at careers that will routinely involve several shifts in direction, and this highlights the habits of mind and learning capacities that will prepare for change and adjustment. First-job focus is simply too narrow, and the point cannot be overemphasized. Further, colleges and universities also urge the skills, knowledge and values that will promote constructive citizenship, at several levels—from local to global. A bit more randomly, we also offer exposure to other types of learning that can make up a good life. Many of us can recall the breadth course we took in college, sometimes almost by accident, that opened doors that have led to lifetime interests, even though they were distant from the careers for which we were preparing and ultimately pursued.

If we do not maintain this wider mission—which embraces attention to first jobs but is not defined by this—we are not adequately serving the future. We are sacrificing preparation for lifetime careers and contributions; frankly, we are almost surely creating a system that will rigidify a social hierarchy in which a privileged few get the kind of education—at the handful of largely private "elites"—that really prepares for success, while the rest are confined to a barely disguised vocationalism. (Check out the colleges to which the well-heeled advocates of public university first-jobs training send their own kids: they'll be looking for more than employment training.)

This returns us to the central claim of this chapter: that for all the imperfections, for all the need to adjust to a radically new budget reality and to improve our service to student success, American higher education overall has a pretty good start on the future because of how we have defined ourselves in the past. Change and adjustment are essential, and in some cases already underway, but they should not overwhelm existing strengths or the standards that emerge from these strengths.

So let's linger a moment on success and on what underlies it before returning to the essential task of wedding success with substantial reform in subsequent chapters.

Testimonials

We've already mentioned in the Introduction the high standing of American institutions in all the global rankings, despite their variety. We can add to this—while also recognizing the success of British and Australian institutions in this category as well—the disproportionate American popularity in attracting international students, despite our unusually high costs. The rankings are fickle and sometimes superficial, but they do raise the legitimate questions: why do American universities do so well? Why do institutions not at the top of our own prestige hierarchy nevertheless manage to place in the top 200 or 400 internationally?[2]

The answer pretty clearly is some combination of the following: we operate and teach in English, which gives us a leg up in the current global climate. We place considerable emphasis on critical thinking—a clear attraction, for example, to many Chinese students and educators who worry increasingly about the undue emphasis on rote learning in their own system. We generate substantial and innovative research in a variety of fields. And, admittedly, for this certainly supports the research achievement, we remain relatively well funded by international standards.

We're also appreciated at home, a fact that might sometimes be drowned out by the stridency of today's critical chorus.

A late 2014 survey of university alumni, by Gallup and Purdue University as part of their "well-being" initiative, found that 83% of the graduates of privates and 86% of those from publics believed they had already seen a payoff from their educational experience; many of the rest anticipated a payoff soon. Only 12% of the private graduates and 7% of those from the publics were not sure about a payoff at least at some point. The vast majority agreed, simply, that their education was worth what they had paid for it. The approval rating of 93% for the publics was arguably extraordinary. Just for a crude comparison, these figures compare very favorably with 2014 ACSI (American Customer Satisfaction Index) rankings for key products, for example, the 79% satisfied with personal computers, the 86% with televisions, the 77–86% with their cars (American higher ed is thus way ahead of the Acura and even beat out Mercedes-Benz, though this gives us more of a run for our money). Critics might legitimately argue that colleges *should* win higher ratings, given their cost—but the fact is, they do.[3]

One other straw in the wind. Though college enrollments are down a bit right now, thanks mainly to the lower numbers of high school graduates, American universities have been an overall growth industry for quite a while, with an undergraduate enrollment increase of 140% over the past 40 years. Public universities have been particularly successful, with a 20% growth rate in the past decade and measurable gains in the share of students served. Perhaps we should have grown still more rapidly, given the desirability of college education, and certainly we should have done better with retention. But the system has been and remains widely attractive to its most obvious clients. Even today, with enrollments slightly less robust, it's the community college system, not the four-years, that have taken the clearest hit, which suggests again considerable drawing power despite rising costs.[4]

Beyond the Applause: Our Core Strengths

International kudos, alumni satisfaction, substantial recruiting appeal—these factors do not constitute a blueprint for the future, but they do add up. Even without fully evolving to address the challenges of tuition/budget and higher levels of student success, the American university clearly has important existing assets. What these strengths are would clearly be a matter for debate, but let me suggest four lead elements that create the combination reflected in the positive reactions around us.

Concrete Results

First, though sometimes obscured by the hue and cry, there is no real doubt of the economic benefits of an American college education (not forgetting the real, if hopefully short-term, problems of some recent graduates in the lingering economic recession). Surveys vary, of course, but the basic results are quite consistent. Here's a recent one (based on 2013 data): college graduates over age 25 earned an average of $1,108 per week, compared to associate degree holders at $772, "some college" at $727, and high school graduates at $651. The college graduate unemployment rate, at 4%, contrasted with high school graduates' 7.5%; by 2015, it had dropped under 3%, about as low as it can get.[5]

Arguably, differentials of this sort make it clear that even from a purely economic standpoint, and allowing for some foregone earnings during college years plus the frequent need to repay loans, college is going to pay off in income fairly quickly. The figures also highlight, of course, the desirability of finishing rather than simply starting college, so they emphasize a current strength but also the importance of assuring greater student success.

The Liberal/Professional Fusion

At their best, American colleges and universities—at various prestige levels; this is not a monopoly of the top schools—offer a combination of specialized training (sometimes in a liberal arts discipline, more commonly now in a more professional major) with exposure to a wider array of methods and insights and to analytical skills that go beyond the specialty. This is where we most explicitly address the several purposes of higher education, from first jobs to the capacities that will serve a long professional career to the types of learning that contribute to constructive citizenship and a fulfilling life.

We must, of course, adjust for changes in student taste and in market demand. Professional majors, headed by business, have long been rising more rapidly than enrollments as a whole. Currently, STEM-H (science, technology, engineering, math, health professions) draw growing enrollments; while this places some strain on the system—training in these fields is more expensive than average and assumes levels of student preparation that are not always robust—we can adjust here, too. It's important to remember that other majors still have validity, even in crude first-job terms—for example, in fields like government service or the range of nonprofits or the myriad of arts organizations. We can actually improve our guidance for students in a variety of majors, helping them identify how their training connects directly with the world of work, even as we react to shifts in demand.

Above all, however, adjustments to fashion must not obscure a continued commitment to the larger goals of a liberal education—the goals that provide breadth and perspective beyond specialization. Three criteria, at least, capture the core purposes here: freedom of inquiry, with no topic or approach out of bounds; commitment to critical thinking, by which assumptions are routinely tested (not necessarily to be rejected, but not merely taken on authority) and through which skepticism and analysis precede acceptance; and breadth of inquiry, a commitment to the exploration of numerous subjects and approaches.

Specific definitions can capture the main points in different terms. A recent *Lumina* report makes the case effectively for what it calls "broad and integrative knowledge":

> U.S. higher education is distinctive in its emphasis on student's broad learning across the humanities, arts, sciences and social sciences. . . . [Students should be able] to integrate their broader learning by exploring, connecting and applying concepts and methods across multiple fields of study to complex questions—in the student's areas of specialization or other field-based settings and in the wider society. . . . Broad and integrative knowledge, at all degree levels, should build larger, cumulative contexts for students' specialized and applied learning and for their engagement with civic, intercultural, global and scientific issues throughout their academic careers and beyond.[6]

This is grand language, I freely admit, but it does pick up on commitments that many American academics have cherished and attempted to further for a long time. The commitments are under siege (as has been recurrently the case, particularly during economic downturns). They are often belittled or ignored by those who want a laser focus on essentially vocational preparation. They also come under attack from those who talk of cheapie shortcuts for what they dismissively call "commodity courses" in the general education programs that most clearly reflect liberal education goals.

This means, in turn, that we need renewed defense of the wider scope of American higher education, the need to expose students to a variety of perspectives and to further training in modes of expression and critical thinking beyond the confines of a single major.

Liberal education is itself a changing framework, and it needs constant attention. A decade or more ago, it was vital to insert some training in Information Technology as part of the basic skill set, and this was widely done. Currently, we have opportunities to do more in training students to evaluate the quality of the plethora of information now so readily available—this is a vital current application of the broader category of critical thinking. We can certainly clarify the connection between liberal education and new global goals. Any basic agenda in global education includes the need to understand and appreciate cultural difference and exposure to the emergence of global systems; this means, in turn, an appropriate redefinition of the contributions of key humanities and social science disciplines to the liberal education program. Many would push farther still to make sure that students, whatever their specialized interest, gain exposure to interdisciplinary discussion of some set of global problems as part of balancing personal goals with a wider appreciation of societal needs. The idea of a conventional major itself may be rethought, with more of the curriculum devoted to a problem focus that would reduce the gap between liberal experience and specialization. There's ample room for additional experimentation without sacrifice to the core. The newer directions pose their own challenges, but they also illustrate the vitality of the basic commitment to breadth of view. Liberal education is a living curriculum, which is precisely the point: it must not be sacrificed to a narrower purpose. The goals involved constitute one of our great assets.

The Research Pursuit

If American universities cannot make a collective commitment to research *expansion* in the current fiscal climate, they must maintain a commitment to research itself. The reasons are obvious, but the priority needs emphasis in a climate that is clearly reducing the percentage of faculty with research opportunities. Research generates greater understanding, producing new knowledge in a variety of fields. It provides solutions or partial responses to an array of social and economic needs, from health to technology to policy and beyond. It measurably enhances the regional and national economy. And—this point is crucial to our larger argument—research contributes directly to educational quality, introducing students to the process of discovery and critical assessments of discovery, adding excitement and urgency to the educational experience.

In contrast to the liberal education framework, of course, the research university is not an American invention. Indeed, research advances are vital to the competitive posture of higher education in the world at large. At the same time, the linkage between research and education, including undergraduate education, can support both specialized training goals and some of the broader purposes of critical inquiry. This is why, along with internships, research opportunities are gaining increased attention in undergraduate educational programming. This can be participatory learning at its best, whether the format is a classic individual project or more collective training in research approaches and assessments.[7]

The higher education commitment to seeking and exploring new knowledge in a variety of fields is necessarily complex. Most colleges and universities cannot afford the most elaborate research apparatus, and we will return momentarily to the crucial question of how many full research universities make sense. But even schools that cannot aspire to a formal research category must be open to discovery, on the part of individual faculty and students alike. They must assimilate the latest findings, and they must create opportunities for their students to apprentice in the research process. The research connection, overriding undeniable differences in institutional types, is central to educational quality.

As with liberal education, this quality is under attack. An alternative version of higher education is not only under discussion but emerging in practice, with faculties paid so little, required to teach so much, that they cannot participate in the research process at any level or reasonably guide their students in the excitement of discovery. It is becoming increasingly important to improve our articulation of the centrality of research to the educational mission.

The Opportunity to Blend Formal Learning with Experiences in Leadership and Social Interaction

In any university anywhere, students learn a great deal outside the classroom and from each other. American higher education, however, is particularly committed to more explicit promotion and organization of some of these wider experiences. U.S. universities seek to provide opportunities for students to experiment, even to make mistakes in a relatively safe space. The omission of this admittedly diffuse and informal category from their outcomes assessment was one of the weaknesses of *Academically Adrift*.

For here, as with liberal education and the connections to research, the goal is an educational experience that contributes to the full range of intended gains. Through informal and non-classroom activities, for example, students gain greater experience in the kinds of collaboration that employers currently emphasize. They also prepare learning habits that can serve them throughout a career, and they have opportunities for growth that spill beyond their professional futures. We are gaining increasing knowledge of this aspect of the college experience, thanks to the growing professionalism of Student Life folks and their (frequent, though not consistent) cocurricular interactions with faculty. The result, at our best, is another clear strength.[8]

* * *

The argument, then, is straightforward. American universities stand tall in international comparisons and "customer" satisfaction alike because, for all their problems, they provide clear economic benefits; they promote a variety of skills and learning experiences beyond professional specialization; they work on student development outside as well as within the classroom; and they promote research and its connections to student advancement. Even as we face the budget challenge and a wider commitment to student success, we must maintain and cultivate these strengths. The higher education wheel does not require complete reinvention. As we undertake serious reorientation, we can gain some real satisfaction in what already exists, which arguably offers a more constructive framework than a brave new world of disruption alone.

Practicing What We Preach

In the previous section, I deliberately returned to the phrase "at our best." We aren't always at that level. We have the framework for high performance to combine with the necessary changes in budgets and student results. Each of the strengths, however, has its own dark side, which we must learn to handle better as part of our mission going forward, often connected directly as well to the student success commitment. Agendas here will emerge more fully in the following chapters, but a first cut at this juncture is essential for credibility. This section takes a second look at American higher education's four basic strengths—jobs, liberal education, the broader student experience, and research—in terms of gaps between aspiration and achievement.

Jobs results. The advantages of college completion to earnings prospects need little further comment; the main challenge is to make sure that a higher percentage of initial student admits gain the degree completion that really pays off. As noted, we are also trying to make other adjustments, for example, in the area of internships or other types of hands-on learning, that will enhance the prospects even for the graduates themselves.

The critical-thinking goals. Liberal education is another matter. There is often a considerable gulf between genuine and valid principle, and normal execution. Too many general education programs consist of a smorgasbord of offerings, calculated mainly to assure enrollment numbers for individual programs. Many also combine introductions to the major for some students with the rather different needs of the wider audience, where breadth and critical thinking are essential. Too many programs cluster in the first year or two (with students who have little idea of the purposes behind requirements), with little or no carryover into the subsequent years of specialization. Not surprisingly, in this setting, the vibrant combination of professional training and wider analytical capacities emerges painfully if at all. The one-size-fits-all approach to general education may also be a problem; how we convey the goals of breadth and perspective to business or professional majors—particularly in their final undergraduate years—may need to differ from what's best for the liberal arts and sciences crowd (who often need time for a relevant, professional minor). Too many programs suffer from inadequate faculty commitment, with more specialized teaching in the major or in graduate programs—arguably, the easier form of teaching—winning out in professional prestige over the courses that deliver the more basic analytical skills.

> **Commodity Courses or More**
>
> The commodity course challenge for the first-year/sophomore general education offerings, which too often define the beginning and end of the commitment to the "broader learning" goals, is very real. Impressive for-profit outfits like Straighterline regularly bombard their audience with attacks on the cost of general education courses, urging their online services instead. A colleague of mine, in the same spirit, once argued that colleges should offer their entry-level gen ed courses for free, though I was always baffled about his business plan. The point is, however, a wide sense that American universities are putting so little thought and effort into the early phases of the general education program that it ought, at least, to be cheap.
>
> In fact, we actually know that what we do with first-year students—perhaps particularly in their very first weeks—plays a huge role in retention. Making sure that the gen ed courses are lively, with careful outreach to students who get off to a slow start, is actually a crucial part of addressing the priority of greater student success. (I would add: the students also should have a shot at a well-designed introductory course in their own field of interest, fit into the broader liberal education framework.) The commodity course folks are wrong, at least in principle: going cheap is not the best answer.
>
> But the challenge is real to the faculties and administrations of four-year schools. It's clear what we should be doing, with the quality of our implementation of liberal education. It's clear that there's potential competition if we don't do better. Here's a vital instance where the need for recommitment is palpable.[9]

The problems here are not new, though current budget constraints may exacerbate them. They can be addressed and are addressed with some success at many institutions, which is why, for example, students do improve in areas such as critical thinking. The challenges do not contradict the basic strength claim, but they do invite constant and imaginative attention if we are to come closer to living up to our goals. General education programs, in fact, need to be recurrently evaluated and rethought. Too often, a burst of creativity is followed by a decade of complacency until suddenly a sense of crisis looms once again. Most of us can do better in assuring that the valid and truly important goals, those of breadth and analytical capacity, gain fuller expression in reality.

The cocurricular goals. Many of the same cautions apply to the commitment to educate the whole student, not just the student in the classroom; we can point to real achievements but also serious limitations. It's easier to implement good intentions in this category with residential students than with commuters—yet most students are commuters. Students in some majors respond more readily to leadership opportunities than others. The aspirations are clear and valid; in some cases, I think we can genuinely demonstrate both quality and progress, but reality is not as glowing as we should hope.

The research agenda. Research is the most complex of the basic strengths, partly because of the budgets attached—whether directly through the costs of funded research or less directly through the support for activities other than teaching. Three aspects require comment, as again we combine genuine achievement with recognition of reality.

Current circumstances inevitably raise new urgency around the question of how many research institutions we can afford. It is quite possible that research costs may reduce the number of universities that can support a systematic research effort. It is clear—as part of budget responsibility—that our longstanding habits of institutional mission creep must be reconsidered. Schools that are not yet in a formal research category but would like to get the conventional reputation rewards of doctoral training and explicit research commitment need to think more than twice—while also preserving the broader connection to research in their educational programs. Some of the public institutions that enjoyed the conversion from state college to university with at least fringe connections to a formal research role may indeed have to retreat, as they are compelled to reconsider mission in dealing with the combination of fiscal constraints and enrollment shortfalls. Universities already in the research game but who hoped to move up to top levels may need to recalibrate as well. Collectively, higher education leaders need to defend the research mission but in clear combination with other goals and with unwonted prudence about growth.

There is no general formula here. Too much rigor, from Robbespierrian budget cutters, would also be a mistake. Regional economic growth and balance in our overall national agenda require a fairly wide distribution of research opportunities. There's a demonstrated, indeed global, relationship between reasonably proximate access to a vigorous research enterprise and regional vitality. Reliance only on the most prestigious private universities plus state flagships would be too narrow, but we must at least be willing—as higher education leaders collectively—to address the topic lest we see the climate for research deteriorate even more rapidly than is now the case.

We must remember as well that even schools that cannot reasonably undertake a research commitment must replicate some of the strengths in their educational programs—as many liberal arts colleges have long demonstrated. They will have some faculty research achievements despite the barriers of higher teaching loads. They must certainly establish links to research programs for undergraduates through a variety of mentorships within and without the college, and they must generate active participation in keeping up with new knowledge.

What's the "Right" Number of Research Universities?

The United States does not have the world's highest concentration of research universities. Switzerland and Sweden, at least, beat us on a per capita basis, with arguably measurable results in terms of greater overall economic prosperity. Too much constraint would surely be self-defeating.

An exact count of existing research institutions is not easy. The Carnegie classification system, currently being revised with its administration also changing hands, identifies about 108 "very high" research institutions, with another 90 plus in the "High" Research category. Criteria for these two elite clubs are not rigidly defined (and the revisions in classification will add some further complications, among other things adjusting more clearly for enrollment level). Generally, entry to the top category involves $250 million in funded research annually, along with high levels of postdoctoral staff to boost the effort and a specified minimum number of PhD programs and annual doctoral graduates. The second category hovers more around $100 million, with production of at least 50 new PhDs annually in at least 15 different disciplinary programs. There are a number of institutions beyond these top groups that not only boast individual scholars but several organized research programs as well.

In the current funding climate, the numbers, however defined, provoke debate. One camp seeks reduction in the number of places with systematic research commitments on the grounds of cost and distraction from teaching. The other camp sees research as vital not only to institutional reputation—which clearly remains the case—but in terms of contributions to a competitive national economy and international stature overall.

Over the past decade, to take one important example, the University of Houston has been resolutely driving toward the High Research category, arguing that every dollar spent on additional research demonstrably adds $3.62 to the Texas economy. The problem: while the state may indeed benefit, it's not currently covering the costs of adding funded research (remember, twenty cents for every dollar raised); as a result, UH tuition has risen 46% since 2007, exceeding the levels of the existing high research institutions in the state.

Available reports—aside from the ranks of the disruptive critics—aim at least for stability in numbers, while hoping that a few more schools will leap into the top category. The president of the American Association of University Professors (AAUP) in 2009, admitting the importance of the subject, expressed hope that the numbers would stay roughly constant. In 2010, the National Research Council sidestepped the numerical question, asking for reaffirmation of partnerships among states, the feds, philanthropy and private business while urging research institutions to "strive anew to be places where the best minds in the world want to work, think, educate, and create new ideas, and commit to delivering better outcomes for each dollars spent." Characteristically, a TIME higher education summit in 2013 saw university leaders urge protection and adequate funding for the research mission, with outsiders arguing for making the system more cost effective— i.e., probably less research.

Clearly, a crucial question—a research question, if you will—is not being candidly addressed. The benefits claims are not trivial; research universities spur and attract business, and a significant reduction in number would come at a cost to economic performance and competitive standing. (Virginia, for example, blessed with five high or very high institutions, nevertheless lags per capita behind the European leaders in this domain.) The costs problem, however, is real.[10]

Research quality is vital. Highlighting the university's research function requires identifying the kinds of research and creative activity that add some measurable social value, distinguishing this from the kind of scholarship that turns out to be directed mainly to a narrow, infradisciplinary and defeatingly specialized audience. I think we have some work to do here so that we can legitimately insist on the importance of research beyond the more immediately applied varieties, and we'll have to return to this aspect in exploring faculty responsibilities. Those of us committed to research in fields that are not routinely vetted by external funding agencies (which are not infallible themselves) face particular challenges here in explaining social significance.

The links between research and teaching/learning must be explicit, and I actually think that many institutions have made real progress on this score. In an individual faculty life, research and teaching do not always mesh smoothly—time spent on one detracts from the other. Yet the interaction between research and teaching can be truly invigorating, quite apart from collaborations with students on specific research projects. The opportunity to test research findings in a larger teaching context offers new perspective and contributes to testing research significance. The challenge and excitement of keeping up with new knowledge links research to quality education at all institutional levels. Above all, the growing invitation to include research opportunities of various sorts in the student experience provides a vital linkage that we need to learn to exploit more fully.

* * *

The summons to live up to the strengths in American higher education can be met and is being met in many cases. Seeking more consistent excellence in the four basic areas, from jobs preparation to quality research, blends the priority of defending our established educational assets with that of recommitting to student success. The effort provides a familiar set of directions for some of the changes we need to advance. Higher education will need additional innovation, but the future must not be defined simply in terms of striking out into a disruptive unknown; preservation and enhancement of assets will be vital as well.

There's no need to become too defensive, even as we admit the gaps between intent and realization. Part of our responsibility, in admittedly difficult times, is to maintain the excitement of academic life and academic purpose. We must be able, through this excitement, to improve our articulation of what we strive for, to make it clear that our future evolution must embrace dramatic change with the quality provided by established standards and achievements. Here's one of the balancing acts that will define our future success.

Capacity to Change

One final point captures an important aspect of higher education's current success, again too often overlooked in the chorus of criticism. The American university not only has at its best a set of demanding standards in education and research; it has also begun to move in some of the additional directions required by a changing environment. The move may need to accelerate; it certainly must combine with other shifts, particularly in the budget arena. But unless the joy of attacking the academy preempts attention to reality, there are some encouraging signs.

Thus, quite obviously, the proportion of students majoring in STEM-H fields is accelerating rapidly. The push comes from the demand side, but universities are responding despite the additional educational costs involved—not only in expanding course capacity but also by adding programs of advising and tutorials to help STEM-minded students through some of the first hurdles with greater success, lower rates of failure or withdrawal. The trend needs watching. Not all the STEM fields are actually job-rich, despite the current fads. Some students must and will continue to seek other majors to reflect their aptitudes and to prepare for what is, in fact, a larger job market. STEM students themselves need an expansive liberal education context, and non-STEM majors themselves contribute directly to American vitality. At least for the moment the fact remains: there is real change and there is university responsiveness.[11]

Building greater student participation, as part of good teaching, not brand new in any event, is clearly gaining ground. Not all faculty require the latest injunctions to "flip" their classrooms, to modify their presumed proclivity for delivering one stale, boring lecture after another. I'm actually all for the "flipped" movement and its potential for more successful and active learning, and we will return to the promise in ensuing chapters. It's also valid to note that new technologies, in hybrid class settings and often in updated (and sometimes costly) classrooms, can add new twists to the flipping process: but the implication of the most ardent flippers, that faculty had never before figured out that nothing-but-lecture was a bad idea or that most still resist any adjustment, is both bizarre and offensive. Like many faculty, I did begin with the assumption that lecturing was the core of instruction, but I quickly learned that a more Socratic approach (how did Socrates manage without up-to-date instruction about flipping?) worked far better. Wider movements in history teaching, such as the inquiry method (classes based on interpretation and argument building from original sources) back in the 1960s, demonstrate similar capacity, and I know that many other disciplines could offer similar evidence. And momentum continues to build. Wider effort is surely desirable in focusing on student-centered learning, but let's not assume we've been standing still.

The same applies, of course, to linkages between research and undergraduate teaching—not new and clearly gaining ground systematically in recent years. Many institutions have mounted major programs for student research, with the growing vitality of national and regional undergraduate research conferences providing one measure of success. For all the problems, many general education programs have also been changing to meet new needs, for example, in developing greater global awareness. Not just adjustments but significant innovations describe key features of the curriculum over the past decade at a number of colleges and universities.

We've also made modest but measurable recent progress in student retention. Over the past few years. overall six-year graduation rates at American institutions have moved from under 55% a decade ago to about 59% of the entering student cohort (based on the fall 2006 first-year class, the latest point currently available for a six-year test). (These data do not capture students who started at one place and finished at another—the real weakness in our capacity to assess in this domain.) Major institutions with inclusive student bodies—Arizona State, Houston, George Mason and others—have moved six-year graduation figures up even more dramatically into the mid- to upper 60%s. Overall, the advance is modest, to be sure, as critics will quickly note; we are not where we should be. Developments here will be gradual at best, but—somewhat surprisingly, given the spike in costs—we seem to be heading in the right direction.[12]

Even more interesting, along with overall enrollment growth in recent decades, has been the dramatic increase in "first generation" students entering four-year institutions—students whose parents did not go to college at all. In 2003, for example, 23% of Mason's entering freshmen were "first-gens"; the figure now stands at 40%, amid a larger class. Many schools can paint a similar picture. The development is logical, as reductions in the birth rate among college graduates coupled with rising interest in populations such as Latino Americans redefine the eligible cohort, but the fact that changes are explainable does not diminish their importance. As against some accusations that higher education is merely perpetuating America's glaring social inequalities, we are actually witnessing a significant surge of education-based mobility. If we can continue to couple this development with improved retention amid appropriate educational standards, we will be making a measurable contribution to individuals and society alike.[13]

The numerous signs of real and constructive change are not an invitation to complacency. We can easily admit that some of the developments should have started earlier and that higher education should be pushing for a faster pace. The fact remains that American universities in general can not only point to important core educational achievements but to a degree of flexibility and innovation that belies accusations of structural lethargy. There are reasons for concern—the new priority areas—but also reasons for pride.

Quality and Motivation

There are two reasons to emphasize the existing strengths and capacities of American higher education. The first, obviously, is to assure the basis for quality going forward. Innovations are essential to address the priorities highlighted in the previous chapter. If, however, they are not combined with recognition of existing achievements and standards, we will actually lose ground. We will risk becoming cheap rather than efficient, vocational rather than educationally sound. We may win some easy applause, but we will not be serving our students, our institutions, and our society adequately. Only the tension between breadth and professional training, the inclusion of research benefits, and the combination of less-structured experiences with formal instruction will do the job. American higher education has a good product—though obviously not a perfect one—which is why it enjoys so many clear signs of approval. Beware the innovator who at most mouths appreciation for an academic core, who does not really know what academic quality consists of. Beware the budget-cutter who will clearly sacrifice definable educational quality. The priority of articulating and defending existing strengths is not a defensive one; it is central to the mission of American universities.

The second reason to combine appreciation with the equally sincere plea for additional, serious change involves motivation. Here, I admit, there can be debate. Disruptive arguments seek to shock or intimidate or perhaps to drive out the existing academic crew so that the revolutionaries can take over. Admittedly, if

American universities were adding no value, it would be hard to resist this approach. However, higher education does have valid standards and measurable achievements, and there is every reason to credit those who maintain these strengths. It will be easier to gain faculty buy-in for change if there is wider acknowledgement of the need for balance between adaptive conservation and more systematic innovation.

One of the current conventions in college advertisements, and in graduation speeches, involves the claim that we are preparing students to change the world. It's a grandiose appeal, to say the least, and certainly one that invites some critical appraisal. On balance, however, it is probably better than no claim at all, or merely a reference to the additional money that graduates will make. It suggests awareness of the wider world, a desire to do something about a few of its problems, and a belief that higher education is already providing relevant tools. The claim is arguably a public relations version of what we are trying to do: to provide educational breadth, personal growth and durable habits of mind, linked to an appreciation for new knowledge and the research that generates it. In working to meet the priorities of budget and commitment to greater student success, we must retain existing values. Then we will, with sister institutions in other countries, increasingly change the world.

Further Reading

On the values of liberal education, several recent works advance the cause: see Lumina Foundation, "The Degree Qualifications Profile," 2014; Michael S. Roth, *Beyond the University: Why Liberal Education Matters* (New Haven: Yale University Press, 2014); and Martha Nussbaum, *Not for Profit: Why Democracy Needs the Humanities* (Princeton: Princeton University Press, 2010).

On the research function: National Research Council and Committee on Research Universities, *Research Universities and the Future of America: Ten Breakthrough Actions Vital to Our Nation's Prosperity* (Washington: National Academies Press, 2013).

For a more general assessment: Jonathan R. Cole, *The Great American University: Its Rise to Preeminence, Its Indispensable National Role, and Why It Must be Protected* (New York: Public Affairs, 2009).

Notes

1. Jonathan Cole, *The Great American University: its rise to preeminence, its indispensable national role, and why it must be protected* (New York, 2009); other work also comments on quality, but the focus unquestionably needs continued articulation and emphasis.
2. Consult rankings directly: QS, Shanghai Jiao tong, Times Higher Education, and now US News' "Best Global Universities." See also M. Yudkevich, P. Altbach and L. E. Rumbley, eds., *The Global Academic Rankings Game* (New York, 2015).
3. Lumina Foundation, *Great Jobs, Great Lives: the 2014 Gallup-Purdue Index Report* (Indianapolis, 2014).
4. National Center for Education Statistics, "Undergraduate Enrollment," *The Condition of Education* (Washington, May, 2014).

5 Bureau of Labor Statistics, "Employment Status of the Civilian Population 25 Years and Over by Educational Attainment," Apr. 3, 2015. For the continued income advantages of college graduates, Pew Research Center, "The Rising Cost of Not Going to College," *Social and Demographic Trends,* Feb. 11, 2014.

6 Lumina Foundation, *The Degree Qualifications Profile* (Indianapolis, 2014); see also Fareed Zakaria, *In Defense of a Liberal Education* (New York, 2015), which happily has made the best-seller list. There is a predictable, and predictably annoying, oscillation in approaches to liberal education depending on the economy, and right now there's a hint of upswing. Here is a case where lessons from history about the budget correlations with attacks on liberal education might usefully be internalized to save us the periodic bouts of troubling rhetoric.

7 Undergraduate research is not new, but its extension, to additional types of students and a wider range of institutions, needs more systematic attention. For ongoing information, see the Council on Undergraduate research website and newsletters: www.cur.org

8 A classic study is David Kolb, *Experiential Learning: experience as the source of learning and development* (Englewood Cliffs, 1984); see also Colin Beard, *The Experiential Learning Toolkit: blending practice with concepts* (London, 2010).

9 S. M. Glynn and others, "Motivation to Learn in General Education Programs," *The Journal of General Education* 54 (2005): 150–70; A. S. Ferren and J. Finch, "The Dollars and Cents behind General Education Reform," *peerReview* (2003): 8–11.

10 National Research Council and Committee on Research Universities, *Research Universities and the Future of America* (Washington, 2013).

11 Allie Bidwell, "Science, Engineering Degrees Grew Twice as Fast as Others," *US News,* Nov. 21, 2013; see also various National Student Clearinghouse reports.

12 *College Student Retention and Graduation Rates from 2000 through 2014,* American Council on Teaching Report, 2015; National Center for Education Statistics, *The Condition of Education: institutional retention and graduation rates for undergraduate students* (Washington, May, 2014).

13 National Center for Education Statistics, "First-Generation Students: undergraduates whose parents never enrolled in postsecondary education," *Statistical Analysis Report* (June 1998); Liz Riggs, "First-Generation College Goers: unprepared and behind," *The Atlantic,* December 31, 2014.

4
SHARED GOVERNANCE

"A university leader is like grass in a cemetery: you may be on top of a lot of people, but you can't make them move."

I really like this quip, which I heard from an energetic university president, but it's quite wrong. While leadership styles vary, and several may work in different contexts, successful universities are never run from the top down. Their momentum is much more complicated because of the extensive and appropriate dependence on faculty expertise. Accreditation agencies, as well as plain common sense, recognize this complexity by insisting on demonstrations of shared governance.

At the same time, the results are neither simple nor obvious. There is a great deal of confusion, inside as well as without the academy, concerning what shared governance is all about. Shared governance does NOT mean administrators and faculty collaborating equally in every major policy area, happily in harness; it does not mean administrators as executive to the faculty as legislators in a quasi-governmental model. The process works, but its definition is complex. It's not too hard to identify current core strengths—closely linked to the basic academic standards discussed in the previous chapter. There are inevitable gray areas as well, which is where tensions predictably erupt. There are also important policy categories where shared governance probably does not work. Beyond all this, there must be questions about the capacity of current practices in shared governance to manage the kind of evolution that is now taking shape. This chapter works on the nuances of shared governance in operation: the strong points, the limitations and messiness, and the opportunities going forward.

For the future progress of higher education—our capacity to accelerate change in order to meet the top priorities, as well as defend our existing strengths—depends on an ability to move together, to improve the interactions between administrative leadership and faculties. Ideas and initiatives from both categories will be vital, as they have been in the past; involvement and commitment will be essential for any significant combination of change and quality. Hence the need for explicit discussion of how the key components of higher education work together, including attention to common deficiencies. Shared governance is becoming a moving target, despite a solid foundation.

Responsible Boards vs. Running the Show

Most universities are officially governed by boards—trustees, regents, visitors, the title varies—that either oversee a whole system or apply to individual institutions. These boards have fundamental powers. They select, evaluate and, if necessary, dismiss presidents, hopefully then leaving most month-to-month administration to the president and his or her designees. Quite properly, they also oversee finances, approving an annual budget. They certainly, legitimately, need to approve in a general way strategic plans, major program innovations, and usually also tenured faculty appointments.

Happily, there is a considerable literature on what boards should and should not do, including a major edited volume on the subject of *Academic Leadership,* and a highly responsible institution—the Association of Governing Boards—that regularly advises on the subject. Because boards do not provide detailed administration, they need loom less large in this particular account. The potential for board overreach—for example, in evaluating individual faculty or interfering in curriculum—is real, but fortunately in most instances all parties involved recognize the importance of distinguishing between de jure powers and de facto operation.[1]

Boards, and their care and feeding, are not negligible quantities, however. They exercise—understandably and, on the whole, legitimately—a great influence over presidents, for they are his or her boss. Keeping the board properly informed and reasonably content, and trying to account for particular interests of board members, is no small job. Dealing with inconsistencies can be challenging, as board members may often pay only sporadic attention to the issues at hand. Having board members simultaneously press for budget cuts while insisting on more football or more research is not an uncommon dilemma—another reason for the attention devoted to board management. Many presidents largely take this task in hand themselves, others disperse the responsibilities for contact, but either way a good bit of time goes into the process; this is part of the president's administrative burden that faculty often do not fully appreciate.

It's also fair to say that in recent years, boards have tended to exercise a somewhat greater voice than was once the case. They are aware of problems at other institutions—responses to campus violence or failures to maintain appropriate academic standards—that they seek to avoid. They certainly register on the new budget context, often pressing for efficiencies in ways that inevitably—and again, perhaps properly—intrude into more detailed management. They, or individual members, sometimes have their own hobby horses—athletics most commonly but sometimes other areas. In some cases, picking up on the larger critical atmosphere, they feel a need to press for more rapid innovations than they see emanating from the institution on its own. In 2014, the Association of Governing Boards, normally a responsible body, issued a report urging boards to take a more systematic role in university management, arguing that universities by themselves were incapable of significant change. The claim was wrong (or at least it can be proved wrong)—it relied on the myth of irresponsible budgeting: however, it clearly reflected a wider public sense of unease about the direction in higher education and the possibility that governance could change.

At present, however, the fact remains that while boards are not intimate partners in shared governance, they obviously affect it. Also, they are not the only partially external influence. Regional accreditation bodies, responsible for certifying academic respectability on pain of loss of federal funding, and also specialized accreditation groups in some fields like business or undergraduate engineering play a huge role in shared governance as well. For the most part, they support it rather than intrude on it and can, in fact, offer some salutary balance to boards in this regard. But their decisions also have budget implications—tending to require some additional specialized staffing and sometimes insisting on a major curricular innovation as a gesture of educational good faith—so they form part of an active backdrop as well.

Faculty Roles in Governance

Tenured faculty, sometimes supported by other faculty groups, essentially run two crucial aspects of the university. They decide on the qualifications of new and existing faculty, and they determine curriculum—two huge areas in the operation of the institution. Their expertise is fundamental in assuring that appropriate standards are met in both these categories. While interaction with administration is also essential, the faculty voice is, overall, predominant. In his excellent book on academic management, John Lombardi refers to internal *guilds* that define quality, usually field by field, both in hiring and evaluating at least full-time faculty and in determining curricula. The powers involved are immense, even if faculty sometimes do not realize their own importance in shaping their institutions.

Inevitably, some interaction with administration may be necessary concerning decisions on new faculty and on the evaluation (and in appropriate cases, promotion or nonpromotion) of existing personnel. It is largely the academic side of the administrative structure, most particularly deans and provosts, that has a role here. Administrative input is essential on any budget implications—whether a new position can be established and, in extremis, whether budget constraints force adverse decisions on retaining even qualified faculty. Administrative perspectives may also place greater emphasis on evidence of a candidate's trajectory—what's the best guess about ongoing productivity—with faculty more comfortable evaluating contributions to date. These are differences of degree, however, and rarely lead to direct clash.

Other issues may require special administrative review. Academic administrators must be involved in situations where different levels of faculty disagree on a case, which is not uncommon. Most promotion decisions require two committee reviews, one from a group close to the candidate's expertise, the second at a more general level—from the school, the college or even the whole faculty. The two levels are not always in accord, and this requires sorting out. Deans have the clearest task here, but provosts or presidents above them may serve a role as well. Even more rarely, administrative intervention is essential when a unit seems to be wedded to inappropriate standards—most commonly, standards that are too lax. This is an unpleasant situation for all concerned, but it does happen. Some top-down pressure may become unavoidable until the point at which the unit picks up the clear signals and rights itself. Finally, administrative oversight may be essential to provide appropriate opportunities for interdisciplinary evaluation—hopefully, a growth category for the universities of the future—and it has been vital in some cases in prompting faculty to allow greater weight for teaching strengths.

Shared governance in evaluating faculty is thus not without potential tension, but it usually works fairly well, with faculty and faculty expertise unquestionably in the lead role. Faculty judgments prevail in most instances. Mistakes can result from the final evaluation when, for example, the subsequent productivity of a promoted faculty member does not meet expectations: these are, after all, informed predictions, not sure things. But there is no question that—in all the institutions with which I have any acquaintance—the evaluation process is taken very seriously by all parties. And, again with primary weight to standards determined by the faculty, the faculty-administration collaboration normally functions smoothly and maintains appropriate standards.[2]

Curriculum is the second vital area where shared governance leans toward faculty input. Here's the other clear case where only faculty knowledge provides assurance of informed decisions. This is true at the level of particulars: with rare exceptions, individual faculty decide on the specific syllabi for their own courses. More important, it is largely true collectively: decisions on the requirements for certificates or degree programs come from faculty, though they are reviewed by administration and (in public universities) by state boards as well. Faculty inputs and evaluations, from individual departments on through school-level and university-wide program and curriculum committees, constitute the core mechanism for program development or modification.

Here, too, there is interaction between administration and faculty. Every so often, the administration may have a good program idea—perhaps particularly in interdisciplinary areas where some external impetus proves essential. However, the idea can gain reality only if appropriate faculty groups are assembled to flesh out the requirements, evaluate the desirability and define appropriate standards and learning outcomes. Administrative involvement is more routinely essential when it comes to promoting and monitoring programs. It's the administration, not the faculty by themselves, that can best suggest political difficulties or strategies where state authorization is required. It's the administration that will be responsible for making sure that new programs have an appropriate business plan going forward, in terms of needed investments and enrollment prospects, and for evaluating them recurrently thereafter, with recommendations for closure if student numbers drift below acceptable levels. Again, the shared responsibilities usually work reasonably well.

Decisions about faculty and programs form a massive share of the university's business, and the shared governance model, with faculty ascendant, arguably serves admirably in most cases, with occasional tensions around the edges. There may be threats to the model in the future: some administrations, citing efficiency, seem bent on requiring faculty to accept single curricula and reading choices in some collectively taught courses; pressures have also developed in some community college settings where, in the interests of saving students money, administrations are pressing faculty to accept a single, homegrown textbook. Online programs loom as another potential trouble spot: bent on cost reduction, some online programs establish single course shells into which faculty are inserted without effective input. Motives behind these various innovations may be good, particularly in the current budget and tuition climate, but the drawbacks, in terms of bypassing shared governance and therefore neglecting both faculty expertise and faculty enthusiasm and in the process jeopardizing appropriate standards, risk being substantial. The rapid expansion of adjunct faculty, often hired directly by department chairs, also reduces faculty input on the personnel side. Universities may need to figure out new ways to adapt decisions in these areas toward greater faculty involvement, again toward clearer assurance of quality going forward. Shared governance in personnel and curriculum must remain part of the academic bedrock.

The system is, or should be, dynamic as well. There is no reason it cannot expand more explicitly to embrace decisions and evaluations about some of the newer kinds of faculty. It surely must continue to apply to the development of new academic programs. The pace here may slacken a bit with slower enrollment growth and budget constraints, but needs for new degrees and certificates to respond to changes in knowledge and in social demand—the recent rise of undergraduate degrees in cybersecurity offer a current case in point—will persist. Shared governance will remain vital not only in assessing program ideas but in generating the ideas in the first place. The process can remain responsive to change.[3]

Gray Areas

The model is less well defined around several other decision categories where faculty and administrative/board impulses frequently diverge. The result is usually no huge crisis, but some clearly unresolved issues exist in the shared governance approach.

Appointment and evaluation of top administrators is an obvious case in point.[3] Faculty, or at least the leading faculty representatives, routinely seek a direct voice in the interviews and decision processes around the selection of a new president and other chief university officials; but the governing board has the responsibility of naming the president, and its members may be less open to a significant faculty role (though they do usually allow minority representation in the search process). It's participation in interviews of finalists that poses the clearest and probably most increasing problem. A growing number of presidential and even provostial candidates refuse to be publicly identified; many search firms, recognizing this and seeking to make their jobs as easy as possible, press the board to go along. The result, frequently, is inadequate faculty involvement (at least from the faculty standpoint) and a residue of disappointment. Even in the evaluation of sitting presidents, boards frequently do not canvass faculty very urgently, and while faculty senates may develop their own procedures, these are not necessarily given much weight by the relevant authorities.

The situation is less dire for provosts and other chief officers, where the president is directly responsible and is (usually) more open to faculty involvement. Here, too, however, there can be questions about candidate willingness and search-firm pressure. Disagreements can also surface about ongoing faculty evaluations of administrators, which do not always win wide participation and which may not be given much weight in the formal annual assessment process within the administrative chain of command. On the other hand, in periodic evaluations of academic administrators below the presidential level where the issue centers on renewal of appointments, faculty normally constitute the majority of the relevant committee, and wider faculty opinions are widely solicited. Overall, selection and review of academic administrators may generate some misunderstandings, making it hard to assure mutually acceptable shared governance in all case, but, with a few exceptions, major conflicts are rare.

Faculty grievances form another mixed category.[4] Most faculty senates have procedures, often shared with administrative appointees, to deal with complaints about tenure decisions or other matters. These complaints are understandably on the increase: in the current jobs climate, virtually every disappointed faculty member seeks to reverse a negative verdict. Faculty representatives play an important and responsible role in sorting through this—after all, there is a close relationship between weighing grievances and the basic faculty evaluation functions—but ultimately it's the administration that must decide, in most structures; while the outcome is informed by shared input, it is not a directly consultative process; and except where there is overwhelming evidence of substantive or procedural shortcomings, administrators tend to protect their prior decisions.

Strategic planning raises issues of a different sort. No problem here at the department level: faculty do the work, guided only by administrative stipulations and timing. At the collegiate unit and university level, however, coordination becomes more difficult. Representation is not usually an issue; the larger planning units carefully include diverse faculty members. Rather, the question is effective voice. Administrative leadership is also involved, and administrative participants are typically better informed about key data—for example, enrollment projections or development prospects—and this may in turn reduce effective faculty voice. Further, in many cases, the university president seeks a plan for two reasons: guiding the university over the next few years but also establishing a yardstick for the board to measure his or her own performance. It's the president and his chief administrative colleagues that will be responsible for selling the plan to the board. The result can be a level of presidential direction that limits effective faculty input as well. Again, interested faculty are not deprived of opportunity for comment, or even the contribution of a great new idea, but the decision processes are not always carefully balanced, leaving some faculty a bit frustrated and even more often fairly oblivious to these machinations at the top.

The governance challenge extends into the strategic follow-up phase: a growing number of institutions have realized that periodically developing a plan is not enough; there needs to be consistent ensuing attention to performance and necessary ongoing adjustments. This means some kind of implementation committee if the carefully-crafted plan is not to languish on a shelf or serve only PR purposes. The committee can and should include faculty representatives, but it will heavily rely on fairly detailed data and projections from the administration side and usually on administrative leadership from convening to agenda setting, all of which will tend to reduce the effective faculty voice. The governance is not unshared, but it is also not fully balanced, and it is difficult to remedy this in practice.

As with top appointments, there is no magic resolution to these shared governance complexities. Nor is there a clear crisis in most cases. As universities need to make more daring decisions, however, most obviously in response to budget pressures, better mechanisms for genuinely shared conversations need to be sought. Here is a definite agenda item for the future.

Breakdowns in Shared Governance

A 2003 study identified 47% of American institutions as fully collaborative: the rest were more on the consultative or distributive side. This is a glass half empty or full situation, and the deficiencies warrant attention. Further, given current pressures, there is legitimate reason to worry that administrations will take a stronger role over time, reducing the shared components. Even aside from trends, there are some endemic weaknesses in the faculty's governing role beyond the areas, notably in evaluating curriculum and teaching and research performance, where their expertise most clearly counts.[5]

It's hard to involve faculty meaningfully in decisions in areas such as university budgeting or annual enrollment targets, much less in areas more distant from the academic core such as public relations or representations to state governments. Nor do faculty necessarily expect the kind of role that they legitimately claim over academic programs. But the issues are not always carefully delineated, and the result can be resentment or confusion on the faculty side—plus, arguably, a failure to elicit potentially good ideas.

The problems here are not mysterious. There are a number of differences between faculty and administrators, even those of academic origin, that complicate conversation. Faculty spend most of their time on their own research and teaching agendas and those of their departments; they do little (usually) at the institutional level. Many, also, and quite understandably, are meetings-averse. Often, their loyalties (beyond departments) are more to the discipline than to the university—and that's not a criticism, simply an inherent difference from the commitments of administrators.

Some faculty—and I confess this has baffled me on occasion—are also constrained by fear. This applies particularly to the nontenured, but even some established professors claim to suspect potential retaliation if they speak their minds. There are unquestionably a few institutions where active retaliation is a fact of life. I don't know how great a barrier fear poses to candid conversation at most universities, but its presence is troubling. For all the honest commitment to shared governance, university hierarchy is also a fact of life, and it can generate constraint.

Administrators are also, characteristically, more optimistic than faculty. A 2014 American Council on Education survey of college presidents rated over two-thirds as confident that their institutions would weather current challenges, but their faculty displayed only half this enthusiasm. Arguably, administrators need to be optimistic if they are going to endure the undeniable stress of their jobs, while faculty, partially focused elsewhere in any event, get local credit for skepticism or (as we would put it to our students) critical thinking.[6]

The question of focus is the most fundamental. Many faculty, working well at what they should be doing, know surprisingly little about what is going on in the institution as a whole. I am recurrently amazed at faculty ignorance about the name change of a major campus building or about a shift in senior personnel. Busy with their own work, they simply don't keep up with available institutional news. In this situation, rumors can run rampant—even in faculty senates, which should know enough to at least check with someone before giving credence. Careful researchers in their own fields can generate surprisingly wild charges about the university domain: one faculty member once challenged the rampant growth in administration by comparing the current university telephone book with the one from the previous year, blithely unaware that in the interim, residence hall management, previously outsourced, had been taken over directly, with a resulting 160-person staff increase that was in fact no real growth at all, just a reassignment. Administrators, dealing with information gaps and distortions, can readily decide that faculty involvement at the policy level, while essential, cannot sensibly be extended to additional shared governance categories.

Faculty Senates

Elected faculty senates play a considerable role in shared governance, but they also participate in, or have to endure, some of the limitations of the arrangement. Intelligent administrators (provosts and/or presidents, primarily) spend a considerable amount of time with faculty senates, mainly in order to prevent misunderstandings or anticipate conflicts. They do not perhaps view them as fully as constructive collaborators as should be the case.

There are many shared interests. Faculty senates want to see a strong university. They certainly help define and defend the faculty role in personnel and programmatic decisions. They can, at least occasionally, call issues to the attention of relevant administrative units that might otherwise have been ignored and can participate in remediation. They can be immensely constructive, usually in collaboration with some academic administrators, on curricular issues—most obviously, general education—that cut across departmental lines. All of this is to the good.

A few limitations affect the collaboration as well. Senators find it hard to resist the occasional poke in the eye, just to make sure the administration doesn't become too overconfident; random complaints and (as suggested) exaggerations are part of the territory. Most of this can be taken with a grain of salt. Better to tolerate some venting than to seem hostile or defensive.

More serious is the data gap, which senators largely share with the faculty at large. Faculty senates, unlike government legislators, have virtually no staff, which means that it's virtually impossible to maintain information levels adequate to make serious judgments on many university issues—including budget details. Sometimes senators reach out for roles that they could really fill only if they were willing to venture a much greater time commitment—which would risk making them academic administrators, separate from the priorities of the faculty at large. There's an inevitable imbalance in knowledge and day-to-day responsibility. Partly for this reason, senates can seem (from the administrative vantage point) to devote an inordinate amount of time to debates over relatively trivial issues.

In this context, major developments at the administrative level may slip through the cracks. I once had to urge my faculty senate to set up a committee to help evaluate the growing range of global projects—which the senate was otherwise largely ignoring. The result worked out all right; a new committee did provide some oversight around what should be a clear faculty interest, but the fact that the senate did not spontaneously generate the idea, outside its normal range of operation, was a bit of an eye-opener.

A further challenge—from the administrative point of view and that of at least some faculty—is representativeness. Senates carefully allocate slots by college or school units; that's not the problem. Rather, senates often see a fairly stable handful of members take the key leadership roles, which can improve information and experience levels a bit over time but which limits outreach. Many academic units, though represented, rarely generate particularly active senators, while one or two monopolize. Senates can also be snooty about including nontenure track faculty, which raises another representation issue of growing importance.

Senates are usually vigorous, useful bodies, but their limitations may prompt administrators to spend more time seeking to avoid serious issues rather than encouraging potential contentious problem solving. In my experience as provost, the senate periodically annoyed me, and vice versa, but generally displayed good judgment and certainly a commitment to academic quality. I was ultimately invited regularly to present an annual list of issues, which was useful to me and hopefully made the senate aware of the academic administration agenda. There were constraints, and I was frequently surprised that the topics I raised did not prompt wider or more consistent discussion.

Not surprisingly, active conversations have recently focused on how to improve senate performance, though without striking results. Urging the senate chair to work hard on information gathering, along with relevant administrators, combines with a plea for selection of committee chairs with real leadership qualities. A firmer commitment to deadlines for decisions would help, along with a more proactive claim for participation in strategic planning; better communication with the faculty at large is vital, including solicitation of agenda items. No magic here, but there might be some good ideas that make this aspect of the academic collaboration work a bit better.

For here, obviously, is another clear challenge for the future of shared governance. We must return to the question of how senates or other elected faculty representatives can participate more fully and equally in some of the decisions that face us over the next decade. Right now, in most cases, senates are helpful but not overwhelmingly significant in the life of the university.[7]

Budget issues constitute a key area where, given intense administrative involvement, shared governance is hard to claim. No question that budget decisions play a great role in determining where the university is heading. No question that the same decisions deeply affect the professional lives and opportunities of faculty. No question, finally, that faculty, and relevant faculty senate committees, deserve regular access to budget information.

Shared governance, however, is another matter. Many faculty are perfectly competent to participate in budget decisions (though not, in my experience, all; there's a definite skill set involved). The constraint is time and availability. The data demands are massive: inputs include enrollment patterns, state budget decisions (where timing is often unpredictable), unit budget experience in the recent past, and requests from nonacademic as well as academic units. Any discussion must have an eye on the need for ultimate board reactions, not just internal preferences. The time required to establish a constructive working group is considerable, entailing frequent meetings. Further, while key decisions may concentrate a few months before a new fiscal year, subsidiary issues occur literally throughout the calendar—including summer. It's not easy to envisage a working faculty role beyond periodic receipt of information and the opportunity to raise questions.

Small wonder that the leading study of university governance (Hendrickson, Lane, Harris and Dorman) leaves the shared governance aspect of budget decisions virtually untouched, save for mentioning the possibility of an annual institutional budget summit in which faculty representatives would participate. There is, to be sure, a vague reference to a "more democratic process" than most corporations require, but not much by way of implementation.[8]

The same limitations apply to a number of other areas. Campus safety is a case in point. Here's an issue of growing concern, increasingly shaping campus life and budget allocations, undeniably affecting faculty (who want guidance, among other things, about how to identify and handle students of concern), but requiring the kind of expertise and frequent deliberations that pull most decisions out of the shared governance orbit.

Shared governance is, in practice, a mixed bag. It normally works really well in some key areas where faculty expertise is essential. It can survive some periodic confusions in the gray zones, though with occasional bitterness. It applies less clearly to other policy domains where even faculty senates, despite the balance-of-powers title, rarely establish active and consistent collaboration. The overall result can be functional, but it can also generate misunderstanding. Administrations can become impatient with sometimes unfocused faculty concerns and with the sheer amount of time required to deal with faculty groups. Faculty can easily find administrative decisions arbitrary. The system harbors unavoidable tensions.

Channels of Communication

When shared governance does not seem fully applicable, misunderstandings may be reduced (though hardly avoided) by other methods of mutual communication. The key here, from the administrative side, is considerable openness, a willingness to listen to criticism and a commitment to raise issues of importance before firm decisions have been taken.

The success of periodic forums on university budgets was already noted in Chapter 2. Faculty and staff need and deserve periodic explanations of state budget mandates or other budget categories, including implications for salaries. Confusion will surface. Many attendees will not fully understand distinctions between capital budgets and the operating side. A new residence hall, to be covered by student rents, may draw fire when the operating budget is not expanding, yet the investment is not (at least necessarily) irrational. Recollections of what was covered in the last forum are not always clear, which may encourage administrator-presenters to err on the side of oversimplification. But the communication is vital, and it really does improve the institutional atmosphere, even in tough times.

Other issues deserve similar airing, at least periodically, and some will present even more opportunities to learn from faculty than budgets do. A major new global project, for example, should be laid out even in the conception stage, for rumors fly otherwise; at the same time, inputs are particularly valuable before firm commitments have been made. The result could be a wall of resistance that thwarts administrative hopes, but this risk is worth it, as opposed to even greater resistance after the fact, plus a legitimate sense that administration is simply flouting any pretense at shared governance.

At least an annual opportunity for an open review of administrative regulations pays off, again both to clear the air and to benefit from constructive faculty ideas. Administrations are, or should be, quite good at knowing relevant federal or other regulations about human subjects review, safety or sponsored programs. They are not necessarily very good at knowing how their well-meaning responses actually affect faculty, so it's important to listen, to solicit ideas about alternatives, even to endure some pointed criticisms—as well as to offer explanations of ineluctable realities. As with budgets, there's no pretense of systematically shared governance, but there is some mutual learning that can really improve the institutional climate and, often, generate mutually acceptable policy modifications.

In general, despite the time and nuisance involved, administrations do far better to err on the side of open meetings, in advance of a new policy that will clearly affect faculty life, than to have to backpedal later. It's not an easy lesson to learn, for it's so much simpler to promulgate what seems to be an essential new step. Worried about campus safety and public perceptions? Let's introduce systematic background checks for all new faculty hires. It may be a good idea, and it may even be essential, but talk to faculty first, see if the rationale can be successfully explained, listen to possible modifications in interest of palatability—even when the ultimate responsibility for a decision will rest with the administration. The same applies to the growing concern about cybersecurity. Administrative responsibility is essential, but let's make sure faculty have a chance to react to policies that might affect them (as well as consulting those faculty who have clearly relevant expertise). Areas of genuine shared governance can be supplemented by commitments to communication, and the investment is more than worthwhile.

The results will not be perfect. Staging too many forums will become tiresomely self-defeating. At many of the open meetings that do occur (depending on the issue), staff attendance will surpass that of faculty (who are, after all, on campus more irregularly and may actually have a class to teach). Faculty, even faculty senate members, may blithely ignore a crucial session and its subsequent report and insist on treating a subsequent policy as a complete as well as unwelcome surprise. Getting relevant campus news out is always a challenge, but there are responsibilities on the other side as well. The administrative commitment must be genuine, not only to take the time to present to the university audience and to listen to sometimes emotional or inaccurate complaints but actually be open about what's being decided and when. Concealment, for example, about big budget categories will rarely work. Administrators must also resist the temptation of using public forums primarily for public relations purposes; to restate the institution's strengths and ambitious goals and brag about what's currently braggable; they need to be willing to talk about problems and resolutions, which can be hard.

On the whole, however, a policy of shared communication can be a vital supplement to actual shared governance. The combination can create at least a common atmosphere of mutual involvement and responsibility, while taking advantage not only of faculty expertise but creativity as well.

Expanding the Approach

Universities should also be aware of opportunities to extend shared governance to additional areas where institutional involvement must grow but should also build on faculty standards.

Athletics is ripe for additional faculty involvement. Recent examples of preferential treatment of student athletes or, even worse, outright academic fraud in certifying student work that did not actually occur make it clear that existing control mechanisms are inadequate. Publicity and revenue stakes in bigtime athletics may render largely administrative oversight inadequate; this is what faculties at the University of North Carolina have belatedly realized. Greater faculty involvement has its own challenges. Faculty are usually already represented on some relevant committees, but the committees may lack adequate responsibility or the faculty themselves may be so co-opted by the athletic programs that their voice is inadequate. Drawing in a larger number of faculty, including a few constructive skeptics, may be essential, putting more genuine shared governance in action to deal with a clear challenge.

Academic assessment offers an even larger field for a formal elaboration of the shared governance model. This is an area of rapid change and, arguably, measurable progress. It no longer depends on faculty alone—which can be a jolt to some older faculty types—but it must build on the faculty's responsibility for curriculum and appropriate quality standards. It also has additional promise for the future.

Assessment used to be solely a faculty issue, and many of us older timers readily remember a simpler past. We graded student papers and exams for our courses. Occasionally, groups of us would get together to help set standards in a multisection course or to evaluate an honors thesis. We worked hard at this task and tried to apply appropriate criteria. If asked, most of us would have argued that the student grade record testified reasonably accurately to academic achievement.

This system is still in place, of course. There has been little interference with the professorial grading prerogative (once in a while, as an administrator, I really regretted the resultant inflexibility, but it does reduce the opportunity to meddle). Grades, despite inflation, still do provide a key part of the measurement of what students have learned.

But now only part. Administrative involvement in assessment has increased for basically two reasons. First, for well over a decade, external accreditation agencies have been insisting on more careful and collective evaluation of student learning than the accumulation of individual course grades provides. This movement involves the regional agencies—the Southern Association of Colleges and Schools, whatever its other faults, has been particularly active in this process; there is regional variability still. Even more, key professional specialties—notably education, nursing, undergraduate engineering, and business—have developed elaborate assessment requirements, and the process has spread to some extent to additional areas such as the arts. In all cases, accreditation now involves the generation of appropriate learning goals for whole degree programs, not just individual courses, and a clear opportunity to measure student achievement toward these goals through a sampling of student portfolios.

The second reason for inclusion of assessment as an administrative as well as faculty responsibility simply results from growing expert knowledge in the assessment field. While institutions vary, most now include a professional assessment group—for good reason. This is the staff that deploys the growing body of experience on what kinds of learning outcomes make sense, on what kinds of student work can demonstrate progress or lack of progress, on what kinds of reporting mechanisms can serve both external accreditors and internal audiences and on what kinds of sampling are feasible and adequate. Experienced experts can also insist on the inclusion of alumni, and their achievements, as part of a larger evaluation process.

Faculty contributions remain essential, which is where the shared governance comes in. Faculty committees in disciplinary programs, general education clusters, and other areas do the work both of generating the learning outcomes and of evaluating the student work. They also populate the committees that oversee the periodic review of other units. Administrative staffs prod, guide and register results, but they do not usurp the faculty role.

The result—and this is important—is a substantial extension of faculty effort, and frankly some faculty are still reluctant to do more than a token job because they resent the whole process. There is real additional work involved, which faculty in the past did not have to perform, but the response of many faculty, not only in their own program work but in helping to evaluate the efforts of other units, has been truly impressive.

Where institutions have moved seriously into this process—and again, there is variety still—the result has been a measurable improvement both in the ability to certify student achievement overall and to use assessment results to fine-tune particular academic programs, where additional progress toward satisfactory learning outcomes is both possible and desirable. Again, the faculty set the goals: usually some combination of critical thinking, writing, oral expression, data analysis, ability to evaluate literature in the discipline, ability to generate and respond to a research question and capacity to apply core methods in the discipline. Faculty teams themselves assess a sample of student reports, oral presentations and the like and evaluate the portfolios selected, usually in the senior year, though some similar evaluations may apply earlier to general education categories. Periodically—every five to seven years—each program reviews the record, adjusts learning outcomes and educational strategies and then submits the results to an external faculty committee with participation from relevant administrators.

A side gain from this growing process, not inconsiderable, simply involves the benefits of the initial self-study by the program faculty involved. The necessity of collectively defining desired learning outcomes and reviewing the state of the program overall can be eye-opening, often stimulating additional demands for resources but also spurring positive measures that can occur internally even without further funding. This is not full assessment, which requires the larger apparatus, but it can be a real step toward improvement.

Overall, this quiet minirevolution in university assessment procedures sets up some clear additional next steps, again based on administration-faculty collaboration[9]:

- First, there is still work to do in some regions, apart from the units like business and engineering whose accrediting agencies have successfully moved to the use of assessment on a national basis.
- Second, there is an obvious challenge in making existing achievements clearer to a wider, critical public. There are limitations to what we can claim: we do not check every single student, if only because of the costs involved; here, grades still serve an important measurement role. We do actually know, and can demonstrate, that the majority of our students do make progress toward responsible, relevant learning outcomes, even though our portfolio tabulations are more complicated than reporting jumps in test scores. University leaders need to do a far better job at explaining student gains, and the shared governance responsibility for determining and measuring the gains, than they have managed to date. Many institutions can now actually prove, through established assessment results, that the critics' claims about a near-majority of students who learn nothing of importance are incorrect, and they should put more energy into publicizing the process. Indeed, higher education should be encouraging its constituencies, from politicians to students and their parents, to explore more carefully what assessment is all about and how it is being used to improve the educational process.
- Third, along with continuing the ongoing work of assessment, we need to insist on our responsibility and capacity to extend the evaluation procedure to some of the newer initiatives in the higher education field. Further attention to assessment and to institutional reporting will allow universities to greet

calls for new flexibility and experimentation with a responsible approach. We can consider students with lots of high school dual enrollment credits, or competency-based credits, so long as it is understood that we will monitor their progress according to relevant learning standards—standards set by our faculties and measured by faculty through the most current assessment procedures (grade performance included). Even the priority that I think we must embrace—graduating a higher percentage of students while maintaining quality—involves active assessment and candid utilization of results where additional educational strategies are called for. Here's where shared governance—data and procedural guidance provided by administrative staffs, criteria determined and evaluated by faculty—can push to maintain quality even amid change.

Assessment is not sexy. It's hard work, including lots of meetings, and its results are complex, yet it will become steadily more important as universities react to budget pressures, changes in student composition, insistence on experimentation with new preparatory paths. What we have achieved through shared governance in this area, including a remarkable pattern of change and improvement over the past decade plus, offers real hope that we can respond to the challenge.

Shared Governance Reviewed

A recent survey of university presidents revealed that, among the majority of those from public universities, primary reliance rested on the faculty as the key determinant for change. (Private university presidents, interestingly, listed themselves in the top slot, with faculty second; I don't know why.) The judgment is realistic, and it reflects the extent to which shared governance, for all its warts, operates successfully. It reflects core academic traditions and strengths, and, as the expansion of joint efforts at assessment demonstrates, it also can be responsive to newer demands.[10]

Two final points deserve attention. The first involves the relationship between shared governance and institutional agility. Many faculty worry that administrations are becoming ever more bureaucratic, responding to outside pressures through more and more rules and regulations, and there may be some truth to this, not all of which falls within the institution's ability to control. Many administrators worry that too much faculty consultation will doom new initiatives to time-consuming delays and negativity. Actually, however, while the dangers warrant consideration, shared governance at its best actually offers some remedies. It is compatible with an entrepreneurial readiness to seize on opportunity. Through shared governance, faculty can help guide appropriate correctives to an excessive regulatory impulse. Through established trust and communication, administrations (or faculty) can present new ideas for relatively quick consideration. The process, properly guided on both sides, does not doom initiative. It can enhance action through shared commitment, and it helps assure maintenance of appropriate standards.

The second point is tougher: are the existing mechanisms of shared governance adequate for new demands in the future? The next chapters will suggest areas where really substantial adjustments need to be considered. The challenge imposes on administration and faculty alike, which may encourage discussions within a shared governance framework, but some changes will be both difficult and contentious and may necessitate the need for some additional formats for faculty-administrative representation—formats that go beyond strategic planning mechanisms in allowing a more active faculty voice but that also go beyond characteristic exchanges with faculty senates in engaging issues of greater substance. Shared governance should work well enough for the priority of greater student success; there are issues to discuss here, in terms of teaching strategies, but the mission is easy to recognize. Budget adjustments may be another matter; they don't follow as readily from what most academics are interested in or knowledgeable about, and they may require substantial concessions. How, for example, can we adapt shared governance to take a more constructive look at the challenges posed by the rise of adjuncts? It's worth beginning to discuss how our governance structures might be adapted toward the priorities we have to face.[11]

Shared academic governance has a solid record of achievement. It is complicated—hard to explain to outsiders—and in some ways fragile. It does not depend on equal faculty-administrative inputs in all major policy areas; the relationships change with the issue involved. It does require mutual respect and openness, a sense of common purpose. It does encourage mutual generation of good ideas; it does promote motivation. These are the qualities that explain why shared governance deserves serious attention, and these are the qualities as well that hopefully can carry through some of the additional strains in coming years. The spirit, as well as some of the specific mechanisms, of shared responsibility will certainly apply to the discussions of administrative and faculty issues in the ensuing chapters.

Further Reading

On basic governance: Robert M. Hendrickson, Jason E. Lane, James T. Harris and Richard H. Dorman, *Academic Leadership and Governance of Higher Education: A Guide for Trustees, Leaders, and Aspiring Leaders of Two- and Four-Year Institutions* (Sterling, VA: Stylus, 2012).

On shared governance and further ideas: William G. Tierney and Vicente M. Lechuga, *Restructuring Shared Governance in Higher Education: New Directions for Higher Education* (San Francisco: Jossey-Bass, 2004).

On specific issues: Peter Ewell, *The Academy in Transition: General Education and the Assessment Reform Agenda* (Washington, DC: American Association of Colleges and Universities, 2009); Sherrie Trump and Brent Rubin, *Strategic Planning in Higher Education: A Guide for Leaders* (Washington, DC: National Association of College and University Business Officers, 2004).

On assessments: Alexandra Tinsely, "Faculty Discusses Ways to Improve Effectiveness at AAUP Conference," *Inside Higher Education,* Oct. 29, 2012; Association of American Colleges and Universities, "Our Students' Best Work: A Framework for Accountability Worthy of Our Mission," Washington, DC, 2008; George Kuh and Stanley Ikenberry, *More Than You Think, Less Than We Need: Learning Outcomes Assessment in American Higher Education* (Champaign, IL: National Institute for Learning Outcomes Assessment, 2009); and Natasha Jankowski George, Stanley Ikenberry, and Jillian Kinzie, *Knowing What Students Know and Can Do: The Current State of Student Learning Outcomes Assessment in US Colleges and Universities* (Champaign, IL: National Institute for Learning Outcomes Assessment, 2014).

Notes

1. Robert Henrickson and others, *Academic Leadership and Governance for Higher Education* (Sterling, VA, 2012).
2. Michael Theall and Raoul Arreola, "The Multiple Roles of the College Professor," National Education Association, 2015; C. E. Glassick and others, *Scholarship Assessed* (San Francisco, 1997).
3. American Council of Trustees and Alumni, *Selecting a New President* (Washington, 2008); M. E. Posten, "Presidential Search Committee Checklist," American Association of University Professors (Washington, 2010).
4. I know of no systematic study of grievance procedures or trends; data are readily available from university handbooks on websites. It would be good to have more information on trends—the increase in grievances against adverse tenure decisions is clear enough—but my sense is also that faculty members of grievance committees increasingly side with the complainant, often rejected judgments by fellow faculty closer to the field in question. The result, unless administrators unwisely simply decide to cave in, will not be a boost for shared governance.
5. D. Gaskill, "University and Industrial Partnerships: Lessons from Collaborative Research," *International Journal of Nursing Practice* 9 (Oct. 2003); see also Gary Olsen, "Exactly What Is Shared Governance?" *Chronicle of Higher Education,* July 23, 2009.
6. American Council of Higher Education, *Survey of College Presidents* (Washington, Oct. 2014).
7. Kenneth Sufka, "How to Make Faculty Senates More Effective," *American Association of University Professors Report,* Nov.–Dec. 2009.
8. Hendrickson and others, *Academic Leadership.*
9. Natasha George, Stanley Ilkenberry and Jillian Kinzie, *Knowing What Students Know and Can Do* (Champaign, IL, 2014).
10. American Council of Higher Education, *Survey.*
11. William Tierney and Vicente Lechugo, *Restructuring Shared Governance in Higher Education* (San Francisco, 2004).

5

ACADEMIC ADMINISTRATION

"Dark Side" or Positive Force; or Both?

Ben Ginsberg, a Johns Hopkins political scientist, offers a common faculty view with unusual vigor in the *All-Administrative University* and in many presentations. He highlights the growth in the size of academic administrations, outstripping expansions in faculty and in student numbers by a considerable margin. He explains what he sees as a really ominous trend through three factors working in combination: the result of sheer creep—bureaucrats like to expand their domains as a matter of course; a weakening of faculty clout due to the overproduction of PhDs—oversupply makes it easier for administrators to override, believing that if faculty don't like it they can lump it; and a failure of faculty themselves to take on administrative tasks. He particularly laments the expansion of assessment apparatus (and thus obviously would disagree with my take on this in the previous chapter), though in truth this is not a big part of administrative expansion overall. He's especially resentful of the growing role of administrators from nonacademic backgrounds, which gives me at least a bit of comfort in my own credentials. But he doesn't trust my type too much either, for he ends by appealing for a more oppositional faculty role. Overall, it's a Luddite approach that deserves attention, both on its merits and because many faculty would surely be inclined to agree. Casual (and inaccurate) references to budget problems resulting purely and simply from administrative bloat show how widespread mistrust can be.[1]

Larry Nielsen, a former provost, offers a different slant under a provocative chapter title, "Faculty Bark, Provost Bites." Nielsen also sees a huge gulf between faculty and administrators, but while respecting faculty intelligence, his money rests entirely on the latter. Faculty, to him, are trained in skepticism and debate, which may be great for teaching but constitute lousy qualities when it comes to running a university. The faculty role is to criticize and delay; everything, to them, requires further study. This is the administrator's—the provost's—nightmare. He or she is "responsible for making things happen"—with a focus on the art of the possible, not the art of the perfect. The goal is action, avoiding the risk that we should have done something but failed to do anything at all. Faculty want to talk about decisions, not make them—this is their barking role. Administrative leaders, and particularly provosts, have to do the hard calls: what programs to cut, what people must be fired, what student requests must be denied; "the provost is the person who is paid to bite." Deep down, particularly in a bad budget climate when so many decisions must veer toward the negative, faculty really want administrators to do the tough stuff, reserving the right, fairly passively, to complain. The quip here is: how many faculty members does it take to change a light bulb? The answer: change?[2]

This is not another chapter on shared governance, though obviously I find each of the above extremes inaccurate and misleading, both about what exists now in university governance and what must be built for the future. Rather, I'll be trying to weave both perspectives into an account of what higher education administrators do and what they should do in the future. It is unquestionably true that administrations have grown, with a host of issues resulting not only in terms of faculty reactions but through sheer budget demands, yet it is also true that administrators have to carry out some tasks that faculty will not and sometimes cannot do and that the nature of administration has been changing with an additional set of challenges as a result.

Ultimately, the focus is on what we need from higher education administrations in order to pursue the top priorities—with costs/revenues, student success and preservation of strengths front and center—but it's also important, within this framework, to clarify a number of specific administrative tasks and options and to evaluate the plusses and minuses involved. This chapter will briefly review topics like the training of administrators, mutual relations within higher administration (a muddy field sometimes), characteristic administrative styles, growing trends around reliance on consultants and partnerships, the thorny question of public relations and more. These topics are important in their own right, and they require attention if we are to deal with concerns about the expanding administrative purview or budget share. The chapter will get to the topic of costs, around the now-popular concept of bloat, but this issue simply cannot be handled without a fuller sense of what contemporary administration involves in terms of relationships and demands on attention as well as core functions. The underlying questions follow from the previous discussion: what do university administrations do that is essential to greater budget stability, protection of academic quality and enhanced student success (but with a bow to the research role and to the process of shared governance as well); and what, arguably, needs to change?

Not surprisingly, given my own record, I have a lot of sympathy for academic administrators. I'm impressed with the dedication and expertise most bring to the task. But questions and options are always useful, so this will not simply be in praise of the status quo. Most important: in the following chapter, we will be discussing some changes that I think faculty simply have to consider, again with higher education's top priorities in mind. I don't think we can make those requests without pledging some significant reforms in administrative ranks as well, and this involves not only some shifts in policy but some adjustments in current culture. Shared sacrifice, and the commitment to clarify what the sharing is all about, will be crucial going forward. This chapter has to talk about some potential pain.

Defining the Beast: Infrastructure and Academics

Administering a university or college may seem to divide roughly into two categories, both under the oversight of the president. Infrastructure legitimately commands substantial attention; in this bailiwick fall facilities, personnel or human resources, information technology, safety and risk management, budget and accounting. The second great domain involves core functions of the university: the academic side. In point of fact, however, academic organization is not so conveniently delineated, and explaining the overlaps and the demands of coordination offers a first cut at understanding what administrators actually do (or fail to do) and why they sometimes feel hard-pressed.

In most cases, the academic side of the overall structure is rather cleanly defined. The provost serves as chief academic officer. He or she has some central staff but also oversees the hiring and evaluation of deans, who in turn administer the key academic units, with department chairs and center directors largely under their purview. Occasionally, some interdisciplinary institutes may rise to a level of importance that merits direct report to the provost's office.

Infrastructure functions can be variously organized. Almost always, a senior vice president or chief financial officer oversees a large chunk in this category, and sometimes most of the relevant units report up. However, there may be separate vice presidents and reporting structures for certain categories, such as information technology. Various arrangements can work.

Even this brief outline should suggest some gray areas, where a variety of structures can accommodate with more or less tension. Institutional research and reporting, an area of growing importance given data demands and opportunities, overlaps both the academic and the infrastructural. Sometimes, a dual reporting arrangement is a constructive response. Where do libraries go? For a while, there was enthusiasm for linking libraries with information technology, as there is a close relationship particularly given the growth of electronic resources. Increasingly, however, libraries have been put back in the academic orbit, and the growing involvement of library staff not just in information acquisition but in active information retrieval collaborations with students and faculty makes this a sensible adjustment in most cases. What about athletics? Often, this looms large enough to report directly to the president or the chief of staff. The function has huge budget implications (which may or may not be reflected in close collaborations with the CFO), and increasing concern about student athlete academic performance suggests a strong working relationship with the provost's side as well—though in many athletic hotbeds, provosts and other academic officials are warned to keep a distance, a problem in its own right that may be getting worse. Human resources constitutes another vital category, with its own dynamic amid a host of state and federal regulations, operating in some potential tension with the academic responsibility to hire and evaluate faculty where deans, provosts and faculty themselves claim sovereignty.

Two or three other functional areas don't clearly fit either the academic or the infrastructural and commonly are headed by vice presidents that report directly to the president. Public relations is one such category, and development is another. Most universities now also need an equity officer; while there is a close relationship here with the human resources division, some separation is essential, which may mean another presidential direct report.

The question of student life is another maverick category. Overseeing students, including potential problems with student behavior, is such a sensitive and potentially publicity-rich area that a vice president in this category may report directly to the president. On the other hand, as we will argue in Chapter 7, student life activities increasingly link to academic responsibilities, particularly under the cocurricular label, which suggests some formal organizational relationship to the provost's side of things.

Who runs budgets? Obviously, financial issues constitute a leading infrastructure category, and a huge amount of effort is essential to provide professional budget analysis and accounting responsibility. Normally, over half of the operating budget of an institution—often, upward of 60% not counting student life and library—goes to academic endeavors, which is also where the institution's key priorities sit. In some institutions, provosts actually chair the budget committee as a result. Public universities, because of their accountability to the state, normally feature a larger CFO role. Whatever the on-paper arrangements, coordination is absolutely essential.

Admissions and financial aid form another complex component—again, in some structures, reporting directly to the president but possibly with oversight as well over university life (relevant because of the student contact and retention function). But the operation also requires tight coordination with the business side, for success or failure with enrollment targets plays a growing role in the institutional bottom line. There's a vital academic link as well, for ultimately this operation generates the clientele for the whole educational endeavor.

The same applies, finally, to information technology and facilities. The growing importance of online or hybrid educational operations requires close links between academic offices, faculty and the IT operation. How, for example, is the course design function for online offerings administered? Academic representation is also vital in facilities planning, particularly given the growing interest in more responsive teaching spaces. Here, too, what may seem like a well-defined set of reporting lines on paper must blur substantially in practice. Coordination—with its sad bedfellow, frequent meetings—is essential in far more areas than might be imagined, whatever the in-principle tidiness of a bifurcation between infrastructure and academics.

The organizational structure is further complicated, particularly on the academic side, by decisions about degrees of centralization or decentralization. (I leave aside here the potential additional challenge of branch campuses and whether they gain a full administrative apparatus of their own—for example, with multiple deans and provosts—or whether there is a greater investment in overall coordination. The proliferation of branches, designed to facilitate student access, unquestionably contributes to recent administrative growth, so it should not be forgotten.) Deans play a vital role in the governance process, for while provostial offices must bear responsibility for the overall operation, including such crosscutting areas as general education programs, it is imperative to have a strong second administrative tier closer to key academic specializations. Degrees of decentralization vary. Some institutions have a central graduate office; others leave key graduate decisions to the academic units with only modest provostial oversight. In some cases, a faculty departure returns the line to the provost's office, where an explicit decision is made about reassignment; in other instances, this kind of budget control is looser. There are numerous variations on the theme just as, within units, allocations of power between dean and departments can vary considerably.

Putting the Puzzle Together—or Not: Complications in Working Relationships

The coordination mantra cannot conceal a number of key issues. The reference to frequent meetings is no joke. The calendars of most academic leaders are simply chock full of scheduled gatherings. The president convenes his top vice presidents regularly, normally at least once a week. Provosts must meet with deans collectively at least once every few weeks, in addition to frequent individual meetings. Budget coordination requires frequent sessions with CFO and academic representatives, regardless of who presides. Major facilities planning and updates constitute another fairly regular chore. While some enrollment issues may be handled within a budget committee, the decisions involved also require a separate set of meetings with deans or their representatives, plus relevant folks from the student life and business sides. If there is no graduate school, another regular committee—this one mainly but not exclusively in the academic domain—is essential.[3]

And so on. One of the reasons—to be more fully assessed below—for the proliferation of administrative staff, both academic and otherwise, simply involves the need to identify enough representatives to keep the coordination train on track. Even with staff, the calendars can remain dangerously full.

Several differentiations also complicate coordination. They do not necessarily prevent smooth working relationships—again, there is no systematic crisis in academic management—but they can cause recurrent friction or misunderstanding.

Most obviously, officials on the academic side almost uniformly come from academic backgrounds—including the provost. We were trained in research and, to an extent, in teaching, and almost none of us entered our profession with an explicit desire to become an administrator. To be sure, provost offices are increasingly dotted with some folks who have considerable training but not a fully academic background; I include here people like admissions leaders, institutional research and assessment experts. But the lead—deans as well as provosts—falls into the unintended career category.

This means that academic leadership can be expected to have a vivid sense of the core educational values, strengths and weaknesses. The newer members of the club have emerged only more recently into the wonderful world of budgets and human resources. They are often faced, as well, with rising expectations in other novel areas, most notably fundraising; this is a common redefinition in the criteria for deanships. Initial unfamiliarity may (or may not) create tensions with the infrastructure leaders, who have more specialized training and experience from the outset and who may sputter about academic bumbling. By the same token, academic leadership may recurrently worry about the lack of full understanding of the academic mission on the other side of the house.

It is also vital to remember that most academic leaders have tenure, and the infrastructure folks do not. The academics serve "at will" in their administrative role, but they are not, normally, at risk of losing a job outright. Facilities and budget people do not have this protection. In practice, I'm not sure this makes a great deal of difference in relationships; the differences and background and orientation are more important, but it's another interesting variable.

Recruiting and Retaining Academic Leaders

As noted, academic leaders initially offer nonadministrative credentials; they've been successful enough in research and teaching to inspire confidence among their colleagues. They may or may not have administrative chops, and they will certainly have a lot to learn. Happily, there is a number of guidance programs available, as well as relevant publications. The Council of Independent Colleges offers an annual institute for provosts, and the American Association of State Colleges and Universities and the American Council on Education are also active. Several available mentorships can also help prepare for a new leadership role in the future.

Many institutions are also becoming increasingly energetic in organizing leadership training for "regular" faculty and lower-level staff, both to inform them about key issues and to give some the opportunity to consider and prepare for entrance to a higher level of administration. Here, on the academic side, is a potential source of department chairs and deans. Judging by participant testimony, the programs can be quite valuable.[4]

Preparation is also affected by recruitment practices, particularly degrees of preference for candidates coming from other institutions. Department chairs are normally homegrown, emerging from faculty ranks, but dysfunctional departments may absolutely require an outsider, and there is always a chance that no suitable insider can be identified even in a smoothly functioning unit. Ordinarily, however, it's a waste of resources (outsiders come with a higher price tag) and a needless risk to recruit externally at this level. Deans are another matter. An Ivy League leader once noted, I think correctly, that insecure universities tend to prefer to go external for new deans, seeking someone with a fresh eye, while other places prefer the predictability of an internal candidate (even if, as is usually desirable for credibility, such a candidate emerges from a genuine national search). Some of the same factors apply to selecting provosts, though here it is clear that the schools that are comfortable with looking to an internal candidate are far fewer in number. The temptation is to go outside to avoid internal bad feelings among unsuccessful rivals and to get the fabled quality of new blood. Yet when outside origin combines with short average tenures—what can someone get done in 4.5 years when it's going to take at least to year to begin to get secure bearings?—it is possible that some recruitment preferences should be rethought.

Duration of service is another issue, from department chair on up. A number of reports have called attention to high turnover, with faculty members serving as chairs much like people who are forced into extended jury duty, with the hope to get back to personal normal—that is, to return to the faculty—as quickly as possible. Some people end up finding real satisfaction in multiple terms as chair, dean or even sometimes provost. It's not uncommon to find academic administrators with 12 or 15 years of service. Obviously, there can be downsides to that kind of duration (though also some advantages of familiarity and of clout in dealing with equally long serving infrastructure leaders).

In truth—as Ben Ginsberg points out—it's actually hard to find faculty who want to serve in administration. This is one reason those who do serve are sometimes viewed with suspicion, as having gone over to the dark side. It's a clear if partial explanation for why administrator salaries have pushed up so high; more on this below. And it's a reason many authorities welcome long service as chairs or deans: the task of finding replacements is so difficult. Even a few blemishes, including faculty complaints, can be overlooked. Any serious institution, of course, subjects chairs and deans to periodic formal evaluations, with lots of faculty voice (interestingly, the infrastructure leaders, though reviewed annually, get no such careful and participatory canvassing). Durability is not automatic, but reasonably successful academic administrators, if they remain willing and pass muster, may chalk up considerable longevity.

> Questions of recruitment, training, duration and evaluation loom large on the academic leadership side. Various responses are reasonable, and typically an overall administrative team displays some diversity in points of origin and length of service. The challenge of interesting more qualified faculty in at least periodic administrative service is both serious and tantalizing and has not yet been satisfactorily addressed.

Durability prospects also vary as a function of types of administrative service, though systematic generalizations are challenging. Some academic administrators do not plan to stay in their jobs for more than a single term or at least make this decision early on in their role. Provosts, on average, currently last about 4.5 years, which is frankly not very long. Turnover results from several factors: ambition for a presidency is one element, particularly at some of the higher prestige institutions, but so is unexpected distaste for the job, for folks who never get comfortable with budgets or the rapid pace of decisions, and the lack of time for extended academic analysis. (In one survey, unappealing aspects of the job accounted for 76% of all decisions to step down.) Provosts are also vulnerable to dismissal, particularly if a new president arrives in the midst of their terms. Deans and department chairs can also be fairly transient, though here, too, there is great variety. The point is that, in many situations, infrastructure leaders, who are professionals in their fields but have no academic home, often outlast the academic administrators, despite what is on paper a lack of job security. When this is combined with their legitimate claims to expertise in increasingly complex domains—fiscal matters, personnel and so on—the result can complicate conversations when academic priorities require active commitments on the infrastructure side.

Quite apart from disparities in background, effective interaction among top administrators can also be skewed by the nature of the standard joint meetings. The most formal efforts to coordinate the various major players also have characteristic drawbacks—not fatal but at least interesting. Most presidents form cabinets composed of the leading vice presidential reports; as noted, these meet frequently. Typically, the provost is the only strictly academic leader present. Unless she or he raises pressing issues, this means that most meetings are devoted primarily to other topics. This helps the coordination effort, obviously; the provost is free to comment on the implications of IT or PR decisions for teaching or for research, but it does risk, collectively, a somewhat unbalanced agenda—and it's this agenda, individual meetings aside, that the president hears most frequently. At the least, this puts desirable pressure on the provost to make sure key academic priorities are recurrently reviewed. Less frequent are meetings of VPs, deans and a few others, often in a gathering called the President's Council. These sessions offer some opportunities for exchange of news or announcements from the president or other attendees; they are typically too big and infrequent for a serious airing of policy matters, much less decisions. An annual retreat may improve the connections involved, but overall coordination remains a challenge. Much more successful are issue-focused meetings around a particular topic like the scheduling and design of a new teaching facility or the bases for a new development push for student scholarships.

> **Budget Delights**
>
> The fundamental budget issues are clear: revenue sources are tight, which requires careful decisions about expenses in relation to basic priorities. There are two other aspects to the budget situation that must be noted that impinge directly on academic leadership, particularly in situations where, initially, budget experience is limited.
>
> *Process.* Detailed budget schedules need to be developed that pinpoint the timing of key decisions; the basic framework should be laid out over a span of several years. Planning in other key areas, like enrollment or facilities, must link directly to this roadmap. This may sound prosaic, but it is vitally important. The Society for College and University Planning (SCUP) even ventures (with a bit of exaggeration): "It is not the plan that matters most, it is the process."
>
> *Models.* Recent efforts to review and often change budget models complicate the field. The needs are understandable: key leaders want to be sure they have the best system to identify revenues and particularly expenses and to motivate units to improve their delivery in areas like enrollment and retention. A further goal, again quite reasonable, involves tackling the knotty problem of incentivizing interunit collaborations, as in interdisciplinary research projects or shared degrees. A host of models vie for attention: zero based; incremental; performance; responsibility centered. From the 1990s onward, performance-based structures gained ground, both in overall state systems and in individual institutions; this seemed a clear way to encourage and reward units that, for example, took on more students. More recently, because of pressures for greater accountability and the drive for efficiencies, responsibility-centered systems have gained the most attention, promising to blend systematic cost data at the unit level (including even facilities use) with incentives. As a result, a number of systems have formally dropped the performance approach.
>
> The current churn in the budget field—creating ripe opportunities for external consultants—may be entirely desirable, but it does introduce yet another demand on staffing and often, in the short run, additional expenses as well. In practice, most institutions use, and will probably continue to use, some blend of different models; there is no holy grail. Keeping up in this

> field unquestionably presents some new challenges, particularly for the academically trained administrators. It is vital to remember that, in the end, new models do not create new resources and do not substitute for careful and hard decisions about allocation. SCUP again: No budget model, not matter how fashionable, "replaces the good leadership required for academic administration to succeed."[5]

In practice, close and mutually sympathetic working relationships between provost and chief financial officer (CAO and CFO in ingroup parlance) become crucial, both to patch over some of the complications in the larger relationships among various elements in the higher education house and to acknowledge their mutual responsibility for the top institutional priorities. A former university president noted, correctly, that having an academic leader who understands budgets and a financial officer who grasps the academic game is a true blessing. At least an equal blessing is a reasonably candid relationship that sees neither party jockeying for a definitive upper hand in the eyes of the joint presidential boss. Obviously, effective coordination varies in fact with circumstance and personality. The current budget severities may alter the balance a bit, giving greater voice to the finance leader, greater temptation to see an additional financial cushion as an end in itself. This is another relationship where the provost must be very clear that, although his priorities are a bit more diffuse, less perhaps a matter of this-year urgency, the success of the overall relationship depends on joint commitment to the academic goals.

> **Administrators and Teaching**
>
> One way to further core educational values among university leadership is to urge administrators to teach, at least one course a year. A two-course annual load remains a standard expectation for most department chairs, who sit right in the middle ground between faculty and management. For deans, provosts and the infrastructure leaders, customs vary, but—except in the liberal arts institutions—teaching is probably not the norm. This pattern really should be reconsidered, both to provide some extra teaching power and to give administrators a more active sense of what the educational enterprise is all about—beginning with regular contact with real, live students. A few administrators with unpredictable schedules or frequent travel needs may have to bow out here—the assignment might be hard for a vice president for development—but most others, very much including the technically nonacademic crew, can and should develop a course, even if it's only on some aspect of higher education or leadership. They would learn as well as contribute, and their experience would help bridge some of the most

common divides—between the academic and infrastructure groups and between administrators overall and the faculty; at least in small ways, this participation would help tie students to the institution as well. It's not only doable—I taught one course a term every year I was provost—but frankly a welcome alternative to the issues that consume the rest of the week.

And it's fun. Putting this initiative into the should-do category risks demeaning it. There's more involved than setting a good example or modestly relieving the teaching budget. The contrast teaching provides with normal administrative duties can be truly welcome, despite the time investment involved. The chance to talk about a subject area, even to do a bit of grading, offers a refreshing and even invigorating complement to the normal week. Teaching also, for administrators from academic backgrounds, helps keep options open, making transitions less difficult when the administrative assignment ends for whatever reason. Above all, the interaction with students is particularly rewarding (a few occasional problem cases aside). It gives students a greater sense of access to institutional leadership; more importantly, it provides a direct reminder (whatever the administrator's specialty) of why we're doing this work: the chance to help move students along and the chance to enjoy how stimulating many of them are.

President and Provost

Obviously, the interaction between president and provost is particularly crucial to the successful implementation of the priorities in higher education. On a day-to-day basis, the relationship here looms less large than collaboration between provost and other key vice presidents. In the long run a sense of shared vision is essential.

Presidents, obviously, are in charge. Boards and the outside world often think they run the show in the most direct sense, though this is not actually fully true; real academic administration is far more collaborative than that. There is no question that presidents have primary responsibility or that they select, evaluate and retain or dismiss provosts. Furthermore, currently, presidents are likely to have longer service than provosts, which gives them another leg up. A couple of decades ago, there was greater concern about presidential turnover; there is anxiety today about the prospect of accelerated retirements in presidential ranks, wondering where the successors will come from. But right now the average president lasts for 8.5 years, almost double provostial longevity. Presidents do get paid considerably more, which can both reflect and cause a sense of differentiation; when they are offered bonuses on top of salary, they enjoy another opportunity that provosts (and other vice presidents) lack.[6]

The two officials share a great deal as well, and additional mutual dependency develops. Both, normally, have academic backgrounds, and the backgrounds here can be quite diverse. Many presidents had prior experience as deans or provosts, though a few come through other academic channels such as admissions; a small number are not academics at all but selected from the business or political world. Far more commonly even than provosts, presidents tend to be brought in from the outside. Selection committees almost always tend to believe, rightly or wrongly, that achievements elsewhere, with prestige and a fresh viewpoint attached, are essential attributes. This can make a homegrown provost seem particularly desirable, at least for a transition period, in knowing the local ropes.

Most importantly, as is widely known, presidencies, except at the smallest institutions, have been steadily evolving away from deep involvement with internal and academic management. The presidential face is outward: toward the community (for a variety of reasons), toward donors, toward the relevant political establishment. The president may have a deep commitment to an academic vision, may indeed occasionally dip into an academic unit, and may teach a course. But the opportunity for systematic attention is rarely available.

Which is, of course, why God created modern provosts. They do, on the academic side, what presidents lack time for—not only administering but providing at least a large slice of the leadership vision, including involvement in the academic aspects of strategic planning. The division of tasks may not always be spelled out, which can cause some confusion but also creates some leeway for informal overlap. Presidents rarely renounce their academic role as explicitly as often turns out to be the case in practice.[7]

We've already noted some possible tensions, even aside from disparities in power and longevity. As a matter of daily fact, quite apart from their external duties, presidents spend more time hearing about internal nonacademic issues, from sports to the latest facility, than about the academic side. However, it is vitally important that when a president-provost team first forms, there is an opportunity to probe mutual approaches to the key educational priorities—the need for innovations toward greater student success, the need to identify and preserve existing strengths in teaching and research, and the imperative for budget decisions that support the academic framework. The president must have confidence that the provost is on the right track, and the provost should be able to count on the president to help press the appropriate priorities should there be any challenge.

Putting Out Fires

There's no more common phrase in adminispeak: virtually everyone, from deans on up, has a batch of fires to put out every month. I am not sure presidents face as many as their reports do—there's a certain shielding involved—but blazes that reach the presidential level are usually doozies and have lots of people racing to find extinguishers.

This is an obvious, unavoidable aspect of administrative life, and while it's odd that more attention isn't given to the topic in most available university management manuals, there's no reason to dwell on it unduly. A brief mention is important, for it adds a clear complication to the effort to commit administration to higher education's top strategic goals. Devotion in principle may be partially waylaid by the pressures, and very real tensions, of the moment.

Putting the case simply: in most higher administrations over the past four years, far more time has been put into mock exercises involving a campus shooter than into systematic discussions at the top about student retention strategies and their implications. It's not just a matter of time. A plethora of crises or anticipated crises adds to the attention burdens of university administration, arguably reducing effective strategic commitments for the longer haul. There's no question that crisis response has added to budget burdens, fostering new staffing in risk management and expanding PR departments at the very least.

I can't claim to be sure that the crisis atmosphere has intensified in recent decades, but I think it has—it certainly did during my fourteen-plus-year stint as provost. Several factors are involved. First, some crisis issues have objectively become more menacing: the campus shooter, though not a 21st century invention, is a clear case in point. Second, the general intensification of criticisms of higher education increases sensitivity in response: more care seems to be essential to avoid yet another black mark. Third, the media have changed. Overall coverage of higher education (except for college sports) has shrunk. Newspapers have reduced their education staffs, and television is not as good a medium for dealing with higher education except for human interest stories—the dean who brings puppies in to soothe students during exam time—or, of course, crises. Sensitivity to media rises accordingly. A standard criterion at my institution—would you want to see this in the *Washington Post*?—was a proxy for genuine concern about administrative ethics, but it also revealed a sense of fragility.

A final preliminary is essential. I do not at all wish to imply that attention to crises is wrong or that other, longer-term priorities must somehow take precedence. One can quibble around the edges. I am still not sure that all our half-day table top exercises, in anticipation of bad news, were quite worth the time, but I may be wrong. It is certainly true that no amount of attention to student graduation rates would compensate for a single mishandled shooter incident or some other safety failing. So the crises—at least many of them—do deserve response. It's just that there can be so many of them (at least potentially), and they can create so much distracting frenzy and expense.

Some crises, or potential crises, crop up pretty directly on the academic side. When I became provost, and this was before crisis thinking had reached its current state, I tried to imagine what big eruptions I might face and wondered whether I would respond successfully. In fact, happily, none of the really huge ones materialized for me, including several cited below, but there have been plenty of smaller embers.

Here's at least a partial list on the academic potential side; some of the items, though probably not all, will greet any provost or provost staffer who survives more than a few years. The result, beyond a real love-hate relationship with emails (particularly late at night or on weekends), can be an unexpected level of ongoing anxiety:

- The big student protest or student pranks that get out of hand. For someone who entered academe in the 1960s, this category looms large, though actually (unfortunately?) issue-based student activism remains at a fairly low level. We spend a bit of time thinking about the boisterous student rally that escapes control, much less about student protest itself.
- Student suicides or other actions by troubled students, including the potential for violence against others. Unquestionably, attention to identifying and dealing appropriately, and hopefully preemptively, with students of concern has mounted.
- Substantial plagiarism cases involving students but also, in some instances, embracing scientific misconduct on the part of faculty as well. Some attention to plagiarism is, unfortunately, routine, but unexpectedly large cases, or again misbehavior on the part of faculty, can certainly jolt administrative aplomb. This has probably been another growth category, and not just on the student side.
- Violations of some compliance or safety requirement, particularly when federal grants are involved. This can generate all-consuming inquiries and potentially huge penalties.
- Enrollment shortfalls. Particularly in a period of fragile budgets, miscalculations on this score can have massive consequences and prompt an agonizing series of meetings and compensatory planning.
- Assaults on academic freedom. Any active university is periodically going to bring in a speaker who touches off outrage from the local public or alumni or more. And sometimes a faculty member will set off the storm. Systematic efforts to educate the public about university responsibilities for openness, about how hosting a speaker does not represent an official institutional viewpoint, have not done the trick. Administrators can usually weather the storm, or simply outlast the grievers; in the meantime, there's another distracting crisis every year or two.

The list gets even longer when the largely nonacademic realm is pulled into the mix. Major weather events, in their impact or potential impact on facilities but also on campus life, require planning and in-course adjustment, and these are arguably increasing in frequency. Accounting errors or delays in building completion are two other categories that can come into play, as is the IT system that nears collapse or encounters an unusual spate of external attack. A rash of crimes on campus is another unwelcome entrant, in substance and potential publicity alike. The big donor who reneges on his commitment is another charming possibility. I leave aside real or imagined crises that may emerge from the athletic arena.

Of course, there's the most recent entrant to at least a near-crisis list, the mounting concern about sexual assaults on campus, where student life and security teams take the lead but where the whole upper administration must be involved to some extent. As with other crises, there's nothing artificial about this one; the problem is serious. There's also no question that bad management will spill over into unacceptable harm to individual students, to bad publicity and ultimately to damage to the longer-term priorities. It's also true that this is the latest in an expanding list, with demands on time, emotional energy and—at least to a modest extent—budget. The competition between immediate pressures and more basic priorities becomes steadily more difficult to manage.

And recurrently, whether for academic or infrastructure administrators, there is the urgent personnel headache. This, I confess, was the category that particularly got me down—not a constant but always a possibility—and at certain levels personnel clashes will kick up to higher administration ranks collectively. I'm talking about situations of deep conflict within a unit (whether academic or not), where it becomes difficult to know where the truth lies and even more difficult to figure out a reconciliation. Human resources specialists can help, but often there is no alternative to frequent fact-finding meetings, with antagonisms that may continue to crop up despite best efforts. When asked about what caused me to lose sleep, this was my primary response.

Different emergencies press different buttons, depending on the individual administrator involved. The list above may be too narrow; clearly it would be interesting to keep an ongoing tally.

The point for this section is not to pretend there is some magic formula that will put out all the fires. As I suggested, if anything their range and frequency are on the rise, but they do risk becoming a disproportionate element in administrative life, as well as intruding increasingly on tight budgets. How many institutions, strapped for cash to maintain adequate faculties, have had to invest hugely in new cybersecurity systems or police expansions or safety-motivated campus lighting overhauls? The challenge is quite real.

Even aside from budget implications, however, there is the burden on attention and emotional energy, at potential cost to strategic focus on the long-term higher education priorities. Again, there are no full solutions, but it is clear that the current framework for administration requires the ability to maintain a certain equanimity in all but the most overwhelming crises. There is risk of a constant emotional mobilization, in which each issue—regardless of magnitude—seems to require a flurry of prolonged meetings and urgent alarums. An almost perpetual sense of anxiety is not good for judgment, and, a possibly shattering event aside, this should be a matter of conscious choice to which administrators can respond with balance and good sense. Further, too much risk anticipation may lead to undue aversion, a surprisingly cautious approach to major issues despite all the injunctions for change that surround us. For all but an unlucky minority of institutions, crises will not define our future.

Consultancies and Partnerships

Two developments involving higher education administration—neither brand new but both gaining time and attention—add to the contemporary mix. Many administrators are taking growing advantage of the clearly increasing array of external experts; consultancy contracts seem to mount with every passing year. Partnerships also win new attention, well beyond the conventional domain of farming out contracts for food service or parking. Neither of these trends presents a systematic problem; both, in fact, may turn out to help universities meet some of their fundamental priorities. Expenditures of time and money are part of the process, however—particularly on the consultancy side—and both trends arguably complicate shared governance with faculty.

The growing fascination with outside consultants is intriguing. It reflects the escalating need for expertise, on a range of subjects, in an obviously challenging time for universities. Does it also reflect some leadership uncertainty? Surely so: topics that once would have been handled internally, with some confidence, now seem to demand an additional imprimatur. Obviously, even in these days of straitened budgets, a host of firms, many surprisingly pricey, are ready to serve both substantive and psychological need.[8]

It's always been important for academic administrators to get advice, obviously within the institution but also without. It's not hard to become somewhat isolated and to assume that one's daily world is the only world there is. This is why opportunities to interact with colleagues at other institutions are so important, and there are various gatherings where this can take place; among other things, sensible higher education authorities at the state level should make sure they encourage discussion among leading institutional officers and not just fill meetings with bureaucratic routine. Higher education associations provide a related venue, and they have long offered tremendous service in organizing sessions on key issues as well as offering mentoring opportunities and other services. Finally, not only conferences and informal communications but also the higher education press offer vital information about innovations and best practices at other institutions around the country. In a period of experimentation, best practices data—examples of changes that not only looked good but really proved successful—are particularly important.

All these established mechanisms, however, clearly are not entirely adequate in our current situation. They may not seem focused enough or clearly applicable to a particular institutional context. And they do take time—there are far more intriguing conferences than the normal president, provost or senior VP can possibly contemplate. So though informal information sharing remains vital and has the merit of being fairly low-cost, additional consultancies increasingly flourish.

At their best, consultancies offer a level of expertise well beyond the capabilities of a single administration. They reflect experience elsewhere, they have accumulated more comprehensive lists of best practices, and in principle they should know their field cold.

The range of available consultancies has become truly impressive. Obviously, there are the search firms, not a new animal, ready to solicit candidacies and organize materials for crucial positions. Consultations on development issues, from evaluation of an institution's staffing and structure to systematic canvassing of prospects in advance of a capital campaign, are well established. Facilities master planning is another hallowed genre, where outside advice normally calls on talents not available within a single college or university.

Obviously, there is now much more. Consultancies offer advice on recruiting students: what targets are realistic, how should financial aid decisions be tailored for maximum effect, and how can some combination of message and staffing move the needle on out-of-state recruits. They are abundantly available in the public relations field to talk about issues from basic branding to the quality of external advertisements. They have moved into the budgeting arena, assessing current procedures and offering advice on possible transitions, for example, toward a more responsibility-based model. Information technology pulls in yet another crop of experts. And the list goes on. There are also generalist outfits that, for a hefty annual fee, organize consultations on any issue that might be identified.

We even have consultants who come to facilitate meetings, an area where I would have thought most of us have abundant experience.

Regular recourse to consultancies, clearly, has become a fact of life in higher education administration. A fair amount of time goes into crafting requests for proposals, selecting the best candidate and then figuring out how to provide the data required and listening to several iterations of the expert suggestions.

At risk of swimming against the tide, I think it is important to offer a few cautions in this now-abundant garden. An obvious one is cost. I have been amazed at how liberally some of my colleagues on the infrastructure side approach consultancies, sometimes envying them the funding involved (and occasionally wondering where it came from, in this age of tight budgets). Annual outlays can rise to startling levels, involving hundreds of thousands of dollars.

Heavy use of consultancies also impacts shared governance. Of course, faculty representatives can come to the meetings where consultants report, including the interim sessions when the experts are gathering internal ideas and impressions. In some areas—for example, consultancies on classroom design—the faculty voice is essential. Overall, however, reliance on consultants pulls away from faculty availability: the data are too dense, and the meetings too frequent and interminable. Interestingly, in one of the most classic consultancy areas, many faculty clearly and appropriately resent the current tendency to overemploy the services of search firms, where a standard, institutionally guided search would suffice while giving faculty participants greater voice and saving a lot of money.

Consultants can be wrong or unnecessary. I suspect many administrators have had the experience of a consultant who brought in a conclusion that was readily available, based on internal data, experience and horse sense, before the whole elaborate process began. Or the consultant who recommended something that pretty clearly would not, or did not, work. Sometimes, I fear that consultants are now being brought in simply for the glamorous imprimatur toward a policy that had already been decided or could be decided without their help.

Above all, I worry that too much reliance on consultants reflects a lack of confidence in administrative capacity. They may consume time and resources that could be better spent, and more efficiently calibrated, on an internal inquiry bolstered by the standard information already available about best practices.

The obvious plea, again, is for balance. Consultants can be essential. Their proliferation accurately reflects the need for more expertise and focus in vital aspects of higher education administration, but their use should be deliberate, not simply a reflex action. We need to be sure that this increasing fact of life improves management, rather than burdening it. This is an area where contemporary administrative culture—the impulse in so many institutions that accumulates consultancies annually—needs to be recast.

Partnerships constitute another area where university agendas are expanding—another staple of contemporary administrative life and, in some cases, a clear source of opportunity.

The most obvious novelty is the expanding range of possibilities with for-profit organizations. Obviously, colleges and universities have long experience in outsourcing some aspects of their operation, in areas like bookstores and food service. The collaborations here have increased efficiencies by involving experienced partners; in some cases, candidly, they have also concealed or sought to conceal low-wage staffing.

The current range of for-profit offerings is different, moving more squarely into the academic realm. Three areas, sometimes overlapping, are attracting the new interest. Recruitment of international students is one. Provision of technical expertise and marketing resources for online programs is another. Assistance in offering and evaluating competency-based experiences is a third. For-profits are also claiming advantages in arranging student internships.

For-profits—often genuinely devoted to educational goals as well as interested in making some money—have several assets in these areas that can easily benefit an individual college or university. First is scope. The vast size of a potential audience for distance offerings, for example, calls upon a marketing network that few individual universities can mount (though some particularly strong units have succeeded). Few universities, flying solo, can keep up with the growing sophistication in this area. Elaborate staffing can also provide 24/7 service, another online prerequisite that individual institutions, at least in the early stages, cannot readily venture. Scope also applies to international recruitment. An outfit with several partners can afford a range of talented agents that the individual entity cannot possibly muster. Beyond scope is experience: again, in the online domain, for-profits have expertise in course design that some institutions may not be able to develop on their own (though this is a gray area; most players do have internal talent). Even in the international arena, some for-profits argue that they have experience, for example, in organizing successful transitional years, that the academic partner lacks. Finally, of course, there is capital: many universities are simply too cash-strapped to offer the risk investment that a venture in online programming or international recruitment requires for success. In a few cases, for-profits even dangle some short-term funding, in advance of subsequent earnings, that can ease current distress.

Here, as with consultancies, is a new fact of life. Sensible arrangements with for-profits can advance the cause, bringing in new resources and potentially, through shared expertise, even assisting in the goal of greater student success. The for-profit interests need not prevent mutual benefit.

Of course, caveats intrude. The first is the obvious point that any negotiation with a for-profit will be delicate and truly time consuming with (among other things) lots of lawyers involved on both sides. For any significant contract, boards must be consulted. Faculty involvement is again challenging: of course, faculty must be kept informed—open forums from the early stages of discussion onward are crucial—but introducing daily faculty representation may be difficult.

Financial benefit must be carefully and realistically assessed. Universities right now are vulnerable, and they may sometimes be willing to accept arrangements that, though marginally useful, leave them with the short end of the stick. Cases where the for-profits have insisted on 85% of the returns, as in some online ventures, suggest the possibility of an overhasty deal.

The real concern is academic control. If an arrangement is made with an international recruiter, it must be clear that academic staffing, admissions criteria and any transitional course work remain the province of the university and its academic administration and faculty. This is usually understood by all parties, but it is vital. Similar insistence in the online domain is equally important but often more difficult to implement. The online vendor, to make things work, will want to take advantage of faculty expertise and imprimatur but will also want to standardize course offerings and recruit lower-paid academic staffing; the result, in some instances, has already turned what seemed a promising experiment into a clash between faculty oversight and administrative convenience, with real threats not only to shared governance but to basic educational quality. There are some big players in the field, ready to eat the academic lunch for the sake of expanding revenues.[9]

Finally, there must in any deal with a for-profit be clear provision for careful assessment. Obviously, this applies to the business side: if the venture can't attract enough students or generate sufficient revenues, all parties should be able to agree that it must be scrubbed. But academic standards are even more important, given the chances for confusion or disagreement. Regular assessments of student progress and quality of learning outcomes have to be built into the partnership.

The criteria can be met, have been met in several important arrangements, although there are also some cautionary tales already in this domain. Clarity on goals and principles, particularly educational principles, is vital; so is openness both about the negotiation process and about subsequent performance review. It's reasonable to check internal assets carefully to make sure that a complex collaboration is essential. Here is another area where not only administrations but representative faculty need to expand their purview. At the same time, the benefits of some of the new opportunities can be quite real, when properly organized, not only financially but in terms of opening new approaches to the education of the future.

For-profit partnerships are not, of course, the only kind. Many institutions can benefit by arrangements with other organizations, where the university's academic standards and degree-granting status can mesh with a museum complex or a non-profit research organization. Collaborations of this sort do not pose some of the challenges of work with for-profits, but they do share one feature: they will demand considerable time, for blending two institutional cultures is never easy. Here is another area that can be genuinely worthwhile in expanding range and educational value but where prudent exploration is essential.

Higher education's future may also call for a wider range of collaborations with other schools. This is well established in many state systems, between universities and community colleges, where careful articulations of standards and curricula facilitate student transfer. The arrangements require regular maintenance—registrar issues alone can be surprisingly complex—but they offer demonstrable results. Collaborations among universities is a trickier matter, for there is no such obvious benefit as student transfer involves, and inherent rivalry complicates many arrangements. There are, of course, already examples of successful partnerships—feeding a few jointly operated medical schools, for instance. Many state authorities, and businesses, would like to see wider efforts, where special strengths can be combined to the general benefit. Here may be an interesting next step in the partnership domain.

Public Relations

PR operations don't have the ring of novelty that applies to current features of consultancies and partnerships, but they have some new and expanding elements that deserve attention in any overall assessment of academic administration and its support for key priorities. PR tends to get a roll-your-eyes response from faculty but surprisingly little systematic evaluation. A wider discussion is desirable.

A university absolutely needs a strong public relations program, however labeled. Five categories, at least, are essential. First, universities must develop ways to communicate to (tiresome term) stakeholders, from potential students to donors to (for the public institutions at least) politicians. We have seen already that there are huge challenges here, given the bad press currently surrounding higher education. Second, communication is particularly vital for university neighborhoods to keep town-gown tensions to a minimum and, hopefully, to develop a sense of positive partnership—including local awareness of interesting university events. Third, there are huge needs for effective internal information flow, and this requires real imagination and professional skill: simply keeping faculty relevantly apprised is a giant task, much less the student body with its changing social media preferences. Fourth, there is legitimate need to seek a wider audience for certain achievements, most obviously in faculty research but in other areas as well; the record can boost internal morale and contribute to larger reputation, despite the stubbornness of this category. And fifth, when or if some disaster strikes, given the increasingly bloodthirsty media mood, professional guidance is essential.

It's worth remembering that many core PR tasks are becoming more difficult, as university audiences become more complex and media shrink their higher education coverage. In many urban centers, competition for attention among many institutions further dilutes the impact of any single program.

It is also true that a number of forces push for further expansion of the PR enterprise, arguably beyond what may be strictly necessary, and this does warrant attention. PR professionals have their own dynamic, often measured, for example, by successfully glossy publications or advertisements. It's quite understandable that they plead for higher budgets and more extensive programs. At the same time, the universities' own ambitions—for more ample recruitment, for greater philanthropy, for that elusive boost in rankings—can reduce care in scrutiny. As with development, it may sometimes seem that any further move is a good move. Finally, hard-charging presidents may particularly welcome PR endeavors that mix attention to the institution with attention to its leader. Nothing evil in all this, just an invitation for periodic reassessment.

Case in point: the annual bombardment of brochures in advance of the *US News* reputation survey (which goes to presidents, provosts and admissions directors). The cascade is amazing: a host of slick pamphlets touting this or that institutional achievement. The proliferation nullifies any single effort. Most of the materials are tossed in the trash (recycling, of course) without any attention. Why do PR units insist on continuing this practice, and why do they get by with it?

Second case in point, though more modest: the institutional ads on televised football or basketball games. Each strives to show that the institution is a truly distinctive, world-beating changemaker. Some are pretty good, some embarrassing, but again any clear benefit is hard to claim.

PR operations are not the only administrative area that needs review, but they do present some clear targets—again, with full recognition of the essential functions. First, there is surely some opportunity to seek some savings—as in dumping the annual glossies. The money involved may be modest (and some institutions like my own long ago decided this particular endeavor was not worthwhile), but even limited containment may help the larger budget effort; and a more cautious approach to some of the bigger branding exercises goes beyond the small-change category.

PR results also require careful assessment, which is not always easy given somewhat separate professional standards, where prizes go to design and placement of materials more than actual impact. A few PR campaigns, launched with fanfare, actually have not generated any clear benefits in terms of student applications or philanthropy. A focused institution needs to be able to determine a clear payoff for investments in this (or any) area, and it must be willing to pull the plug on hollow claims.

Do universities also have an obligation to be particularly responsible in the advertising domain? We are in principle, after all, devoted to critical thinking. Yet our efforts to make each institution seem absolutely unique typically involve a level of hyperbole and oversimplification that depends on suspension of critical judgment. Again, there is no questioning the need to sell each school to certain audiences; and we obviously live in a society where commercial exaggeration is standard fare. It might be that, even in this context, a more nuanced and modest approach would actually increase effectiveness, for example, reducing gaps between inflated student expectations and university reality. It could be interesting to talk about a more fruitful relationship between the bigger PR efforts and academic values without sacrificing the industry.

Perhaps most important: it is becoming clear that fascination with PR, and all the new opportunities particularly in social media, risk confusing message with achievement. There is always the danger of coming to believe in what initially seem to be harmless exaggerations. A further risk involves allowing the unrelenting optimism of PR handouts to overwhelm the need for candid conversations about very real problems and setbacks within at least a considerable internal audience, if not beyond. Not too much threat here for faculty, whose ingrained skepticism has already been noted, but a reminder of caution for top administrators is not misplaced. Effective PR should not be outracing demonstrable educational, research, and service accomplishments or acknowledgement of some of our institutional warts—and there are cases where campaigns have taken on a life of their own, at real cost to strategic assessment.

Public relations programs are not the greatest problem area that administrations face, but some reorientation will contribute to the larger effort to deal with the core priorities. It will also help close the outlook gap between administrations and faculty as part of shared governance.

Regulation or Facilitation: What to Expect from Good Administrations

Where do higher education administrations clearly add value, and where do they risk simply getting in the way? More often than one might like, faculty simply interpret the newest move from the president's or provost's office as a needless expansion of bureaucratization; sometimes, surely, they are right. It's important, without undue detail, to remember some of the core functions that simply have to be accomplished, not just to keep the institution afloat but to move toward the basic priorities.

Responsibility for infrastructure has already been invoked, along with necessary interactions with faculty on matters such as facility design or basic budget information. Building maintenance, satisfactory annual financial audits, operation of auxiliary services, organization of whatever kind of lobbying and government relations activities seem feasible and appropriate—the list is, obviously, extensive, and most people, inside and outside the institutions, assume competence. There are decisions to be made regularly, and some have unexpected implications. A few years back at one university, the president decided that the campus grounds should be left untended for an alumni reunion, on the assumption that the impression of poverty would stimulate more open purses; wrong—giving dropped. A revealing case where assumptions of competence were unwarranted.

Several policy areas—again, not directly involving faculty input—are particularly consequential for priority goals such as budget stability or student success. The tantalizing subject of "other business opportunities" can't be avoided amid current fiscal constraints. Does the university have real estate that might be developed commercially without damage to the overall enterprise? Are there other business ventures—restaurants on the ground floor of dormitories that might attract a wider public—that could earn money without materially damaging campus life, perhaps in some cases enhancing it? Discussion of prospects here will undoubtedly antagonize some who worry about diversion from academic goals, and there is no question that time can be wasted or ideas ventured that are frankly silly or unrealistic (a Jiffy Lube in the midst of campus, once seriously discussed, probably didn't deserve airing). Figuring how much attention is available for prospects of this sort is not easy.

Technology transfer is a particularly attractive area that properly draws growing attention where university and economic development goals may coincide. Faculty are often deeply intrigued, and there is real tension between maximizing discoveries that have real commercial potential and pleasing colleagues by acquiring (expensive) patents. There is an opportunity for unrealistic hopes and examples: few universities are really going to invent the next best thing to Gatorade or the vitamin that has fueled Wisconsin's tech transfer success. However, several universities—Houston is a case in point—have managed to turn a welcome profit over the last several years by more systematic, yet hard-nosed, business effort.[10]

The dreary topic of auxiliary enterprises harbors some clearly contemporary choices. What's to be done about the bookstore, once a source of profit, now a challenging cost center for students? Obviously, it's still fair enough to try to earn some money from sales of T-shirts and other spirit icons, but course books themselves have become a serious cost burden. At the least, book lists must be thrown open to competition, including Amazon; at best, fairly soon, we should be able to develop inexpensive online options for some of the basic texts, both to save money for students and to preempt the current tendency whereby at least a few students don't buy, and sometimes don't read, expensive assigned materials. What about food service and dorm rates? Here are categories that impinge on students as consumers but also represent cost centers that can add to student debt burdens. The best food choices in terms of nutritional results are not, unfortunately, the least expensive. Dorms must at least pay for themselves—and some schools, like the University of Kentucky, have sold their dorms to for-profit operations to reduce institutional debt. But dorms also pay a key role in successful campus life at many institutions. Both food and dorm costs are frequently, though misleadingly, confused with basic operating costs or even tuition levels by public critics eager to show universities as heedless profit mongers. There's a lot to consider.

Policies on scholarships are crucial at a time of rising costs, debt burdens, and growing recruitment competition. This is a specialty area, which is one reason that external consultancies are brought in for additional advice. The trick of balancing awards to talented students as opposed to need-based cases is not new, but—given tuition costs—it has gained greater urgency. Recently, conservatives have also voiced objection to using any tuition funds for scholarships, seeing this as taking money from the cherished middle class; given median-income woes, they have a point. The case for using out-of-state tuition funds to help assist and recruit additional out-of-staters, who still bring in more than they cost, is not hard to make, but it requires some subtlety. Overall, both formulating best strategies and justifying them commands increasing attention as part of mitigating budget impacts on students.

Most of these areas fall cleanly within administrative purview, though some faculty are inevitably interested in areas such as representation to state legislatures or the push to lower textbook costs (where indeed faculty choices are directly involved). Use of facilities in vacations and summers, another subject of increasing interest where there may be opportunities for community service or revenue generation, can also impinge on faculty goals: who determines whether some rooms should be devoted to a faculty-organized conference, break even at best, or some more directly lucrative endeavors? However, in these decision areas, the basic overall expectation focuses on levels of administrative competence, combined with willingness to clarify or debate decisions publicly where necessary.

Overlap is inevitably greater where the administration is working directly to facilitate teaching and research—and confusion may be greater as well. Several areas have been noted. Administrators, particularly on the academic side, really can help identify opportunities for interdisciplinary collaborations in teaching and research around core problems that transcend departmental or college lines; interest here will surely expand in the future. The process may also tread on faculty toes, or even those of deans and chairs, so flexibility and careful salesmanship are essential. No conceivable organization of a university encompasses all the opportunities for educational programming and research, and administrative guidance can be crucial to compensate for the resultant gaps and to take advantage of growing interest in problem-based learning and scholarship.

Online programming is another area that can build on faculty interest, which is varied but growing, but can rarely depend on faculty initiative alone. Some administrative prod is essential, not to force faculty into this mold, which would be a mistake, but to arrange incentives and appropriate technical guidance. Yet here, too, boundary lines are hard to establish cleanly. Faculty, increasingly comfortable with this approach, may develop some online segments on their own, but unfortunately they must be required to report their effort to some central authority, to make sure space is being properly utilized (in cases where conventional classes meet only part of the time) and to satisfy accreditation requirements.

Administrative assistance in student retention offers a somewhat newer opportunity for overlap but a very real one. As with assessment, higher education can benefit both from new knowledge and from new technologies to help students and institutions alike improve prospects for student success. For first-year students, for example, make sure—require—that some graded work is assigned early in the basic courses so that, in turn, a software program can determine how students are doing overall and, through survey responses, alert advisors to individuals who particularly need interventions. Here, vividly, is a real opportunity for administrators, systems and faculty to collaborate for better performance, but the opportunity depends on a willingness to admit some new administrative expertise and to impose a benign requirement on the faculty involved to adjust assignments and grade promptly.

This returns us to gray areas—as with book orders, course evaluations or online reporting—where administrators think that some new rules are essential and some faculty object. (I even had a faculty pushback when, early on as provost, I mandated midterm grades in first- and second-year courses, shocked that the system did not already exist. In this case, my clumsy haste was repaired by acquainting protesting faculty with the literature on the subject, which clearly indicated the importance to student success—but the reconciliation took several months.) In most cases, careful explanation and advance discussion will do the trick, but some tensions are inevitable.

At the same time, there is no question that, with every good intention, some administrators press regulations unnecessarily far. Research compliance is a prime category. No one, of course, wants to run afoul of federal granting agencies, but some administrators—as comptrollers, sponsored programs officers, or human or animal subjects reviewers—are tempted to regulate so closely, imposing rules to cover every possible risk, that researchers themselves are stifled. Procedures that require months to negotiate or force additional accounting staff for even fairly modest grants are clearly defeating the purpose. Granting that some tensions are inevitable, here is an area where an effort to solve problems and facilitate, and to consult with the target audience, can reduce the temptation to overreach.

Human resources issues can also touch faculty (and academic administrator) nerves. The zeal to prevent problems and maintain equitable standards may prompt new rules about salary determination or hiring procedures, which can complicate actual individual negotiations. Security concerns (and worries about adverse publicity) have already greatly extended regulations about background checks for new hires. Here is another case where bureaucratic impulses are understandable, where they promote arguably desirable goals, but where they can also become too rigid, even counterproductive to basic goals of quality. Study abroad is another interesting domain where liability concerns push for stiffer rules on student programs but where excessive zeal sometimes spills over into efforts to regulate faculty travel as well.

Overall, this section has obviously argued that competent administrations and administrators play a host of vital roles not just in maintaining the institution but in promoting steps that will help address key priorities going forward. At the same time, administrations can also overextend, trying to generate unnecessary levels of orderliness or undesirable reductions of experimentation. The need for balance here is not a new one, but changes in the context for higher education, including the media delight in seizing on mistakes, probably make the balance more precarious—which is all the more reason to give it careful attention.

The Gorilla in the Room; From Creep to Bloat to . . . ?

The facts are stark, at least on the surface. Since 1987, administrative and professional staffs at universities have more than doubled, outstripping even the growth rates in the use of adjuncts and graduate students as teachers (much less the numbers of full-time faculty) and actually expanding at over twice the rate as the increase in the student body. More than 518,000 positions have been added, with the increase affecting all types of institutions but with public colleges and universities proving particularly aggressive. In all sectors, the numerical trends suggest more than slight reality to Ben Ginsberg's laments about the rise of the administrative university.

The obvious question is causation: why have administrative ranks expanded with such disproportionate rapidity? Some of the reasons for the differential rates are obvious. Faculty disinterest in—even disdain for—administrative work is one component, though probably a modest one. Some administrative growth is designed to compensate for faculty reluctance—to provide a bit more staffing, for example, for academics willing to become chairs or deans as an inducement. It's also relevant to note that relevant specialists have become increasingly available in some areas—student services is an obvious case in point, and assessment has been noted already—because of the expansion of higher education training programs.

The main focus must be on an apparent thirst for additional professional expertise, from whatever source. New areas of emphasis (as in assessment or retention) call for new administrative supplements to faculty endeavor. New functions are required by the outside world. It is really true, as administrators commonly insist in their own defense, that additional reporting requirements by accreditation agencies, states and the feds—all delightfully uncoordinated for the most part, which increases the effort required in response—do require additional staffing. Institutional research and reporting offices expand in consequence. Provosts have to add people who specialize in accreditation, even in the off years between formal evaluations. A currently proposed federal requirement to report on the gainful employment of graduates—desirable in principle—will require massive staff upgrades and is reported to threaten upward of $51 of additional cost per student.

The big categories, however, involve research and student services. At George Mason, for example, research personnel (sponsored programs, safety, and compliance) grew from 25 in 2006 to 85 by 2013. In the same period, research funding had virtually tripled, so the reasons for expansion were clear enough, but a budget burden remained because research overhead could not cover all the personnel costs involved. Many universities over the same period (until the recent essential freeze on research funding) could tell a similar story. Overall, American research institutions, whether public or private, maintain noticeably higher staffing levels, in relation to faculty and student numbers, than do other types of institutions. (This is a key reason that, without some dramatic change in public or philanthropic funding, the number of research institutions must stabilize for the foreseeable future.) Pinning numbers down for student services is more challenging, and we will return to the issue in Chapter 7, but in many institutions—at least until recently—growth rates have been high in this category as well.[11]

So is this "creep" or even worse, or the inevitable result of the nature of contemporary American higher education? An American Institute for Research study, in 2014, cautiously concluded, "whether the administrative growth constitutes unnecessary 'bloat' or is justified as part of the complexities involved in running a modern-day university remains open for debate." We do love to debate things inconclusively, yet in this case a firm determination remains elusive.

Not surprisingly, opinions vary, and so do the data beneath the surface. On the one hand, a recent faculty study claimed among other things that administrators simply enjoy hiring employees who are like themselves, as opposed (presumably) to more difficult faculty types. On the other hand, a 2013 *Chronicle* report noted that most administrative growth has involved not new managerial levels (which actually have shrunk) but the kinds of professional staff essential for more complex technologies, research and student needs. Compounding the problem is significant variance among institutional types and among regions. The University of Nebraska, for example, until recently had three more staff per 1,000 students than the national average (which stood at 17.3). Administrative growth at public institutions has well outstripped that of the privates, at least with 1987 as a base, though recent trends reverse the ratio.

There are inevitably some niggling issues of definition that add to complexity. In some systems, librarians are faculty; indeed, as they increasingly work with student researchers, this designation may make sense, but in other counts, they are simply staff.

Furthermore, adjustments are already underway, apparently particularly at public colleges and universities. One study suggests an administrative staffing decline of 5% to 9% at public research universities and community colleges between 2008 and 2012, in response to budget and tuition constraints. Several states where staff employment at the publics had risen particularly rapidly, like Minnesota and Nebraska, have undertaken careful reviews. At the publics, executive and managerial growth, at 2.5% since 2000, has not matched the expansion of student numbers, but professional workers—now up to 25% of all campus jobs—are another matter.

Here's what I think we know. Without question, at least until very recently and possibly still, administrative ranks have increased more rapidly than those of tenured and tenure-track faculty, though references to "bloat" as opposed to more precise examination of specialist categories are misleading and, frankly, needlessly insulting to lots of devoted staff. Those faculty who sincerely believe that removal of administrative growth will solve the budget problem are simply wrong. Claims that administrators are hiring simply because they like bureaucratic duplication are not in the main correct, though a few institutions that soared above national averages may have been incautious. (On the other hand, some other public universities, even before the current budget crunch, were more prudent, with administrative and staff expenses rising less rapidly than direct instructional expenses; patterns have varied even before the current crisis.) Overall, at least partial correctives are already underway in response to budget woes and demands for greater efficiency. Yet even when some administrators openly acknowledge bloat, and vow cuts, they may remain victims of a growth culture, simultaneously adding new and even high-ranking posts without fully recognizing the inconsistencies that have them trapped.

Not surprisingly, the issue of administrative size is complex. The most frivolous claims about irresponsibility, or the possibility of saving vast sums, are off the mark. Granting all this, two or three additional measures are essential in order to make sure higher education is best prepared, on the administrative side, to address the crucial priorities—budget stability at the forefront. First, though in some cases this merely accelerates the recent trend, we really do need to take a further look at staffing size to see if, at least through normal attrition, some more substantial reductions are possible to free up resources for more direct educational functions. If some of the big categories like research or assessment cannot be pared much, other areas, such as presidential or provostial staffing or public relations, may yield greater fruit. Somewhat greater faculty involvement in certain administrative areas (along with continued teaching responsibilities) may be a useful recourse as well.

Looking for efficiencies through some reorganizations or fusions is recurrently relevant as well. I was pleased, as provost, to oversee a 50% growth in student enrollment with no increase in the number of basic academic units and therefore of deans (though we shifted unit definitions several times, without expanding administrations to match). There are occasions, particularly in no-growth settings, where some outright mergers can be considered, though these must be assessed in terms of whether real cost savings result (expectations often exceed reality) and whether there are drawbacks in terms of student experience. Universities are of necessity complex and sometimes messy organizational structures, which may limit opportunities for restructuring, but the topic should never be closed off.

Most obviously, we need to pledge better and more open reporting on the administrative side. An annual discussion of changes in administrative staffing, compared to major categories of faculty, is now absolutely imperative, not just to address and perhaps alleviate faculty annoyance but to promote responsible decision making in the first place. This is where we can detail improvements in ratios or explain why some additional staffing proved absolutely unavoidable. The sad fact is that drastic administrative cuts are probably not in the cards; there is no magic budget solution here because the functions involved are not frivolous. But a commitment to regular and interactive accounting will produce some flexibility and a better campus climate as well. An invigorated and adequately informed Senate could play a key role in what should become a regular fall review. The resulting candor should promote greater discipline, where needed, and should build academic morale as well: for faculty, who deserve to know that administrations are prudent as well as competent, and for administrative staffs, for whom the "bloat" concept is not only insulting but menacing.[12]

Finally, and closely linked to more regular communication, there is an obvious standard to seek now that budget constraints are clearer and the administrative contribution to costs more frankly recognized. When a university has to cut its operating budget further, make sure that the administrative side normally takes a slightly larger percentage hit than the academic—hopefully through carefully managed attrition and not harsher measures. Seek, even when the budget is stable or slightly growing, modestly to improve the percentage allocations to the academic core. Granting the unfairness of the bloat term, and the importance of most administrative staff and function, we can commit to adjusting the imbalance that has opened over the past two decades as part of addressing the larger budget priority.

The bloat issue is not just a question of size of staff. There is also the related issue of administrative salaries at the top, where again disparities with faculty patterns have increased markedly and arguably with even less justification. Here's another area where we need to be willing to put our feet to the fire.

Administrative Evaluations

As in any big enterprise, regular assessments of personnel are a vital aspect of academic administrations. We've already talked about some of the complexities of faculty evaluations, particularly around granting tenure, and we'll return to this in the following chapter. Few decisions command the kind of effort that goes into promotion decisions, so on several key occasions, at least, faculty gain careful scrutiny. (Annual discussions are another matter, particularly after tenure, but more on that later.)

I am not convinced that comparable diligence usually goes into evaluations on the administrative side, though on-paper annual assessments, with self-reports, supervisory comments and an ensuing discussion, are normally required. Academic administrators such as deans and provosts, as a discrete category, do face the hurdle of periodic renewals—commonly, every five years—when, as with faculty promotions, a good bit of care is expended, with heavy faculty involvement.

Other administrators, including subordinates in the provost's and deans' shops, may be treated differently. Technically, they are on at-will appointments, which might seem to suggest particular vulnerability (whether they have faculty tenure or not). In practice, however, the annual assessments may prove rather cursory for several reasons. The procedures take a lot of time, and many top administrators turn out to have too many direct reports to venture thoroughness. More importantly, they introduce a jarring note within teams that must work together closely, often on a daily basis. Further, we live in an age and a society when self-esteem demands run rampant, and sensitivities within administrative ranks can be truly delicate. Hurt feelings can easily result from anything other than a superlative evaluation—it is astonishing how a single negative in a largely positive review can trigger a reaction—and hurt feelings can in turn easily disrupt the vital working relationship.

Yet accurate assessments—not gratuitously nasty, offering sincere praise where warranted—are essential. Even for a valued subordinate doing an above-average job, there may certainly be one or two areas where improvement should be encouraged for everyone's ultimate benefit. Where there are more doubts, it is important to establish a paper trail, both in hopes of correction and in case more drastic disciplinary action is required later.

There is a real dilemma here between ease of interaction and appropriate rigor. Some supervisors in my experience resolve the problem by simply avoiding the procedure altogether, even if it's mandated in principle. Many people will know at least one top administrator who established a reputation for "not liking" personnel unpleasantness and who managed to get by with shirking.

More commonly, the tension is handled by venturing a systematically positive checklist in order to avoid hurt feelings and to make the ensuing discussion as pleasant as possible. (More rarely, a similar lack of real attention, though not shaped by concern for motivation, produces an equally meaningless column of mediocre ratings.) The result of imprecision and lack of nuance can be an opportunity for clarification missed or, at worst, a later situation in which a subordinate has to be removed for poor performance even though the preceding annual documents indicated no serious problems.

This is a plea, then, for taking the risk of greater care and candor in the institutional interest and for a willingness on the part of subordinates to tolerate and discuss suggestions. Already, academic administrators offer varied approaches; there are supervisors who are routinely candid and who

> establish the kind of trust that allows them to venture critical comments without destroying a positive relationship. But I do think, as part of facing up to administrative responsibility in a time of change and challenge, we need to encourage more nuanced reports overall, rather than yielding quite so often to the impulse to keep relationships as smooth as possible. The assignment is significant.

The Pay Gap

Let's clear away a little brush first. Faculty salaries are not entirely easy to pin down. Most faculty are paid for nine months of service, and they can sometimes earn more through summer teaching or funded research (though opportunities vary by field, and sometimes the rich get richer). Administrators are paid on a 12-month basis, which automatically means their listed salaries are higher. At research universities, faculty usually get a day a week for other work—not competitive teaching (though abuses are not unknown) but consultancies or other activities; in a few fields, like business, this can boost salaries considerably. Administrators do not have this formal option. On the other hand, some top administrators have opportunities to serve on boards, which can increase pay. Presidents, in particular, normally get perks such as housing and possibly other emoluments that add considerably to effective earnings. Additionally, top administrators usually have an ethical and rather public responsibility to give money to university programs (scholarships, sports promotion, the arts), which cuts into their pay informally. Faculty can often be exceedingly generous themselves, but there is more individual latitude. Finally, faculty salaries themselves vary widely, not just by rank but by field; standard starting pay can vary as much as 300% from the arts and humanities to business, and gaps have been widening here as well. These disparities themselves generate some serious problems of equity and collegiality. There are complexities of various sorts in the tense domain of administrative vs. faculty compensation, but on balance, while some of them warrant separate attention, they need not distract from the main points.

The heart of the issue is the increasing gap between the pay and emoluments of university presidents, their cascading effects on the salaries of other members of the upper administration, and what most faculty and staff manage to earn. While there is great variety—several leading privates head the pack; only a few publics are among the top offenders—the gap problem is fairly general.

It stems, in my view, from several sources. American culture is a culprit: what's happened with university presidents mirrors, at considerable remove, what's happened to top corporate executives generally. Boards of trustees are actively complicit: composed disproportionately of business types, they have found it logical to jack up top salaries (often adding bonus provisions as well, an unwelcome innovation in university culture) because it's what they see around them—without much regard to what's going on in the rest of the institution. The role of inflated coaches' salaries—still often surpassing the presidential levels by a considerable margin in the marquee sports—deserves attention as well. It's also important to remember that current salary patterns emerged when many places were expanding rapidly, in enrollment and research alike, which might seem to justify some inflated compensation on the grounds of growing burdens—the lives of individual faculty were not changing so rapidly. (This pattern is now shifting, of course, with slower growth, which puts the salary trends in nastier relief.) Presidents themselves (and in their wake, many provosts, deans, VPs) bear responsibility, too, for what might in an earlier age be described as undue greed. Cases in which university presidents have even continued to accept bonuses in years where faculty salaries are stagnant overall merely suggest an extreme of a widespread pattern of entitlement. (The other extreme—some significant givebacks as in a 2014 move by the president of Kentucky State—can be noted as well, but they are far less numerous.)

The trends reinforce each other. High presidential pay leads others to want more. What the previous dean made clearly affects the demand of the next in line, and where acceptable candidates are few (a key problem in characteristic searches), there seems nothing to do but give in. In far too many cases, a new recruit to upper administration, with no experience at that level, demands more than his or her experienced predecessor made; too often, because the issue arises at the frantic end of a search, the deal goes through, causing the problem not only to persist but escalate.

Here's the pattern overall. The villains in the piece are most obviously the presidents of many private institutions, including some that are hardly educational luminaries; in 2014, 33 presidents in this category made a million dollars or more. On average, presidential salaries at the privates constituted .5% of the total budget, which seems awfully high; in one case, the figure soared to an unconscionable 2.7%. Of course, there is variety, which means that not all situations reflect rapaciousness and incaution. The publics, in the main, do not show similar extremes, which is a relief—only two currently have presidential salaries, perks aside, at over $1 million. But they, too, are affected by the overall climate, so levels have climbed measurably in recent years. After all, moving from public to private is a real option, which tends to put some competitive pressure on the lords of the publics. Candidates—not only presidents but also vice presidents and deans—well aware of salaries "in the industry" often insist on relatively high pay not just for its own sake but as a credential to the rest of the world, including their own faculty: if I make this much, I must be a real player. So the escalation proceeds, if at varying degrees.

Between 1978 and 2013, presidents in public universities have seen salaries rise by an average of 75% (controlled for inflation) (with provosts gaining 50%, business officers just a bit more) while full professors advanced by less than 25%. (At the privates, the figures were 170%, 105%, 127%, and a professorial 50%). Administrators, in other words, outpaced faculty at a rate of two to one. Between 2007 and 2013, presidents at public doctoral universities gained 11% (provosts 13%, financial officers 15% in an ironic reflection of the fiscal crisis)—all this while faculty salaries remained roughly stagnant and while overall inflation advanced more slowly as well. The excesses of the privates moderated slightly, though they still saw more rapid administrative gains than the publics. The American Association of University Professors not surprisingly noted the symbolic results of both the short- and long-term trend: "they serve as a concrete indication of the priorities accorded to the various components of the institution by its governing board and campus leadership."[13]

Deans' salaries vary greatly by field and institution, but they, too, have been rising rapidly. Between 2006–7 and 2011–2, salaries for arts and sciences deans rose an average of 16%, as faculty pay largely stagnated in the same units; business school deans advanced 10%, with associate deans following a similar pattern at only slight remove. Advantages over senior faculty were less great than where higher administrators were concerned, but the trends pointed to greater differentiation in the future. The administrative patterns were spreading, and the challenge of the pay gap became increasingly general.[14]

The issue is clear. Disparities in salary levels and salary trajectories have moved away from a shared enterprise, establishing a more corporate model with faculty on a lower layer. Halting the trend will be difficult, given established habits and expectations—and, as noted, the impulses of many governing boards. While the problem must be clearly acknowledged, the promise of reform should not be exaggerated. A recent New York University study, for example, noted that a 25% reduction in the pay of top administrators would net only $5 million, not insignificant but hardly enough to do much about replacing adjuncts with full-time faculty, where annual costs could range upward of $250 million.

Both current fiscal realities and hierarchical symbolism insist on the need for change. We need to return to parity in the salary trends of academics and administrators. It's hard to imagine tackling key faculty issues without this commitment, along with the urgent accountability for the sheer size of administrative staffs. Reform will bring a bit of budget relief and will work toward restoring a greater sense of common enterprise. It will require real restraint in administrative search and retention programs. It will depend on greater discipline in evaluation of colleagues and also a greater willingness by faculty to compete for administrative slots. Administrators, to my knowledge, work really hard, often amid considerable stress; they deserve appropriate reward, but they must not be allowed to form an academic aristocracy, which is where things are headed currently.

Administrative Focus: Leadership and the Core Priorities

No one has ever, to my knowledge, suggested that some kind of professional higher education administration is not essential; even faculty anarchism has not stretched this far. This chapter has emphasized the range of issues facing administrators, particularly academic administrators in practice, including areas where policy issues have become increasingly demanding or where coordination proves particularly vital.

So what, on balance, should we want from administrators? We've noted at several points the need to assume basic competence in the range of issues that administrators oversee or manage: this means, at least usually, adequacy or better in the decisions that affect facilities, recruitment and scholarships, or research compliance. Competence or better in categories of this sort means the capacity to base decisions on the soundest available data, with due attention to best practices at other institutions. We need to add ethics as well, not because there is a systematic administrative problem here—really scattered cases of corruption or mendacity aside—but because some aspects of administration must clearly rest on ethical as well as professional responsibility: personnel management and dispute resolution are two obvious cases in point, as is defense of academic freedom. More broadly, and essential to the kind of communication that bridges between administrators and others, a commitment to truth-telling is also vital. A good administrator conveys to faculty, staff and students that there is a shared ethical commitment that embraces the entire community.

Academic leaders must listen and not merely pronounce, and this is an art that requires careful preservation even as experience and confidence grow. As noted already, the willingness to take the time to interact and persuade is vital in the university context. Where the administrator is guiding change, faculty and others must be made to feel, and to be, an active component of the process, rather than serving as targets; facilitative leadership is a useful term here, basing achievements on what others can be persuaded to do. And again, in any healthy college or university, key ideas, often unexpected ideas, will come from many sources. Rewards must be available for constructive innovation from any quarter. Administrators themselves—and this is trickier than one might expect—need to be able to support other people's projects with the same enthusiasm they apply to their own.

Above all, there is focus. A plethora of issues require administrative attention, as this chapter has suggested. There will never be as much time or serenity as there should, in principle, to devote to key priorities such as budget, student success and preservation of academic quality. Yet ultimately leadership—and not just at the presidential or provostial level—needs to convey a deep commitment to defining the core priorities and seeking to move them forward. More than rhetoric is essential. The goals are tough, and they must be addressed systematically and realistically. Administrators must be able to link many of their key decisions to the basic targets. They need to be able to move new programs forward—no matter of whose devising—that address the goals, and they must equally take a lead in figuring out what programs must be stopped because their service has ended. Risk aversion won't work here but nor will a tendency to race off in too many directions at once, launching, as one Midwestern faculty member recently put it, a series of bandwagons that go nowhere. Increasingly, administrators can also help identify and defend staff segments—in assessment, advising or student life—that also, along with faculty, contribute directly to greater student success. Focus is also required, finally, to wean more institutions from the habit of mission creep, to provide a positive, enthusiastic rationale for university and college roles that do not always ape the Ivies or the flagships.

Finally, we need administrators not only ready to lead change but to rethink some of their own conventions—both substantively, in terms of freeing up some revenue, and symbolically, leading officials need to participate actively in the process. This chapter has not identified the magic bullet. Where budget stabilization requires cutting, the process will be painful, for there is no big category of obvious excess. At the same time, a mindless reduction across the board—that does not take accreditation or student success criteria into adequate account, for example—will be foolhardy. There are indeed some special opportunities: to review the PR operation, to evaluate development more carefully, to restrain the mania for consulting contracts and to tackle the unfortunate culture that has emerged around compensation. In these and other domains, administrative review will not solve our problems, but there must be a serious contribution. This means, as we have seen, a careful evaluation of the sheer size of staffs, and it means recalibration of salaries and perquisites, and in some cases it should involve a modest recommitment to teaching as well. This is, as the next chapter will insist, a challenging period for faculty; administrators have to pick up at least their share of the challenge as well.

Academic administration remains an exciting field. There are genuine opportunities to help create frameworks in which new knowledge is generated and in which students gain new lifelong capacities that in some cases prove truly transformative. The challenges are unquestionable, but there's no reason to back off.

Further Reading

For the critique: Benjamin Ginsberg, *The Fall of the Faculty: The Rise of the All-Administrative University and Why It Matters* (Oxford: Oxford University Press, 2013).

On resource allocation: Robert Dickerson, *Prioritizing Academic Programs and Services: Reallocating Resources to Achieve Strategic Balance* (San Francisco, CA: Jossey-Bass Publishers, 2010).

On budgeting: Carol Rylee, ed., *Integrated Resource and Budget Planning at Colleges and Universities* (Society for College and University Planning, Ann Arbor, 2011); and Larry Goldstein, *College and University Budgeting: An Introduction for Faculty and Academic Administrators*, 3rd ed. (Washington, DC: National Association of College and University Budget Officers, 2005).

Notes

1 Benjamin Ginsberg, *The Fall of the Faculty: the rise of the administrative university and why it matters* (Oxford, 2013).
2 Larry Nielsen, *Provost: experiences, reflections and advice from a former "number two" on campus* (Sterling, VA, 2013).
3 John Lombardi, *How Universities Work* (Baltimore, 2013).

4. There is a National Academy for Academic Leadership, with many reports as well as programs; *Faculty Focus*, issued by Magna Publications, regularly features leadership articles, there are a host of other programs. For definitions, see S. Marshall, M. Adams, and A. Cameron, "In Search of Academic Leadership," in I. Richardson and J. Lidstone, eds., *Flexible Leadership for a Flexible Society*, ASET-HERDSA Conference Proceedings (Toowoomda, Qld, 2000); Robert Diamond, ed., *Field Guide to Academic Leadership* (San Francisco, 2002).

5. Carol Rylee, ed., *Integrated Resource and Budget Planning at Colleges and Universities* (Ann Arbor, 2011) is a good introduction to the topic and a wider literature.

6. Stephen Trachtenberg and E. Grady Bogue, *Presidencies Derailed: why university leaders fail and how to prevent it* (Baltimore, 2013)—useful insights, though focused on board relations.

7. Nielsen, *Provost*; James Martin and James Samuels, *The Provost's Handbook* (Baltimore, 2015).

8. Ron Rivard, "Great Expectations, Bleak Results," *Inside Higher Ed*, Apr. 2005; Susan Pierce, "What Search Consultants Do," *Inside Higher Ed*, Aug. 2009. The whole issue of consultancies is another understudied topic. Another introduction is possible simply through website browsing on the host of eager suppliers.

9. See the Rutgers minirebellion against a for-profit partner: Carl Straumsheim, "Faculty Push Back on Online Deal," *Inside Higher Ed*, Apr. 22, 2015.

10. Association of University Technology Managers, *About Tech Transfer* (Deerfield, IL, 2013).

11. American Institute for Research, *Delta Cost Project*: see reports "Labor Intensive or Labor Extensive" (Washington, 2013) and "Think Again: administrators ate my tuition. Really?" (Washington, 2014). Jenny Rogers, "3 to 1: that's the best ratio of tenure-track faculty to administrators," *Chronicle of Higher Education*, Nov. 13, 2012; Robert Martin and R. C. Hall, "Measuring Baumol and Bower Effects in Public Universities," http://papers.ssm.com/so13/papers.cfm?abstraqct.id+2153122; Robert Martin, *The Revenue-to-Cost Spiral in Higher Education* (Raleigh, NC, 2009).

12. This idea is not totally unlike the audit proposed in Frank Mussano and Robert Iosue, "College Needs and Productivity Audit," *Wall Street Journal*, Dec. 29, 2014—though these authors, in the article and in their book, have a more jaundiced view of academic behavior than I have—*College Tuition: four decades of financial deception* (Indianapolis, 2014).

13. Public university presidential salaries rose 7% in 2014-15. College and University Professional Association for Human Resources (CUPA), *Administrators in Higher Education Salary Survey* (Knoxville, TN, 2014); these reports appear annually, allowing trend calculation. American Association of University Professors, *Losing Focus: the annual report on the economic status of the profession, 2013–2014* (Washington, 2014).

14. College and University Professional Association for Human Resources, *Administrators*; see also the parallel report, *Faculty in Higher Education Salary Survey*, similarly issued annually.

6
THE FACULTY

Faculty members will be quick to tell you that they are the heart of any university—and they are absolutely right. We are going to be discussing a number of probable, desirable, or—in key cases—essential changes in faculty life, and not all of this will be pleasant reading. Faculty conditions are unlikely ever to recover the ease of the 1970s, but we can legitimately begin with the positive. Faculty determine more about the strength of a university than any other element, though student qualities, which are linked, are not far behind.

Faculty will continue to have the pleasure—and it should be a pleasure—of primary responsibility for effective student learning and, in many cases, also for the discovery of new knowledge. In both connections, they will also play a leading role in assimilating and conveying the discoveries of others, which offers real stimulation in its own right. Several higher ed critics totally neglect this aspect, assuming that faculty can somehow magically keep up with changing fields with no time investment at all. Currently, research findings worldwide are expanding at the rate of roughly 3% per year, which literally means millions of additional articles and hundreds of new books; not all will be worthwhile, and it is a faculty's task to help sort this out, but much will need to be incorporated in valid teaching as well as new research, and more recognition and credit are due to this aspect of the faculty task. There are several fundamental ways that faculty remain central to the knowledge core and to its dissemination.[1]

Further, as we have noted, faculty have the fundamental responsibility for maintaining standards, in research, teaching and learning alike. Administrators can help, and once in a while must intervene, but the key judgments normally come from faculty. Here is the expertise that drives assessment of student learning outcomes but also guides the evaluation of teaching and research on the part of the faculty itself.

It's the faculty, indeed, who must take the lead in combining promising innovations with the protection of core quality. How, for example, are we to measure research expressed in one of the digital media? There are conservatives who simply hold out for the traditional book or article, and frankly that's not going to cut it given the new opportunities for dissemination. There are innovators, at the other extreme, who want to be able to count potentially ephemeral blogs as works of research. This doesn't register either: we will still need to arrange peer reviews for products that count toward significant scholarship and have some assurance that, however expressed, the work will have some durability. Discussions around issues of this sort, where change is combined with rigorous protection of standards, will not be easy; indeed, they already are not easy, but it is the faculty that must guide the discussions and emerge satisfied with their results.

Any good university already has a host of talented and caring faculty. Most faculty are deeply committed to their teaching as well as their research—stereotypes to the contrary. They want to improve student success (while properly insisting on careful evaluation). They contribute to discussions of pedagogy and to contacts with students outside the classroom. They show up in surprising numbers for panels ranging from classroom design to improving student note-taking. They take on individual students, undergraduates as well as graduates, for research projects. They pour energy into advancing their disciplines or, increasingly, their interdisciplinary activities. Many faculty voluntarily, and without direct reward, evaluate books and articles of other scholars, helping not only to define standards but actively to guide junior colleagues toward more meaningful work. They are also at the heart of the governance of their own departments.

However—and here's where we have to risk a genuine tension in this chapter without contradicting the real appreciation of what faculty already bring to the table—current faculty practices are not fully addressing higher education's leading priorities. They score pretty well on preserving standards, including the valuation of liberal education—though even aside from debates over innovation, there is clearly some work to do here. They are interested in better student outcomes and have already launched some promising innovations, but they have not yet managed the degree of change that must be sought particularly in areas such as degree completion. They have certainly not solved the budget dilemma. Of course, concerned faculty can quite reasonably note that they did not cause many of these problems, particularly on the budget front, and that solutions cannot be theirs alone. Granted on both counts. However, faculty are going to have to be part of the solution, and this does force more confrontation with change than has yet emerged. Necessity—indeed, the durable protection of the basic mission of higher education—not ingratitude, forces some discomfort. As with administration, some sacred cows must be put out to pasture.

The issues fall into two broad categories, and we will address them in sequence. First, we must extend the chorus of voices urging greater attention to teaching and greater commitment to what we know about good practice, while also urging—less predictably—some recalibrations in research. All this involves relatively familiar territories in which many faculty are already engaged. In category two, we must add in the budget specter, which complicates some of the adjustments urged on teaching and research while adding urgency to others.

As we have already noted, faculty life already isn't as easy as it once was thirty or forty years ago, and what we must talk about now will increase the difficulty in some respects. I see no way around this. Academic work will still remain a great calling, a tremendous opportunity to contribute to the social good and explore new frontiers in research and in the classroom. It will still offer advantages of flexibility and variety compared to many other occupations. It will still assure participation in governance, again in contrast to many more rigid hierarchies in other fields of endeavor. But it will change. As with administration, some recent trends have actually been moving in the wrong direction, and they must be reversed.

The central focus is again on the priorities of American higher education. As the previous chapter suggested, administrations must play a direct role on the budget side of the picture, with greater self-discipline as well as clearer communications a basic requirement. They can also facilitate greater student success, and hopefully they will be active as well in defining and preserving existing academic strengths. However, it's the faculty who are the front line for preservation and for student success, and unfortunately they must be asked to respond more constructively to the new budget realities as well. There's a lot to do; some of it will be fun, but some will be simply challenging.

Core Competencies

Higher education faculty are almost uniformly well trained in their field, with in-depth specializations within the discipline. This should be pretty obvious, but it is a basic strength. No one (I assume) would want teaching performed by people who lack this competence. The competence also forms the basis for faculty oversight of standards for students and colleagues alike.

Of course, competence brings a number of companion qualities. Most faculty themselves did quite well in college, which helps explain why they got into the academic game. Again, I assume no one would wish or expect otherwise, but there is sometimes an understandable gap between what faculty remember about their eager experience and what many students in their classes expect to do. The tension is unavoidable, to a point desirable, but it can cause mutual misunderstanding.

It's also fair to note that many disciplines see a clear trend toward increasing narrowness, with faculty picking more and more limited specializations. Contemporary knowledge improves largely by small accretions, with each special advance gradually building up to a larger whole. A number of disciplines report growing difficulty winning faculty interest for the broadest kinds of questions within the field. Narrower focus does not, usually, mean that faculty lack the competence to teach about larger issues—they have been trained to handle wider domains—though it can mean they prefer smaller topics around their specialty. It does raise some complications when it comes to tackling big problems or forming interdisciplinary consortia. It's a trend to keep in mind when dealing with basic priorities in higher education.[2]

Tensions, New and Old

The ideal faculty member is quite good at both teaching and research, excited about both and eager to make connections between them. This is not a new statement, but it remains at once valid and demanding. At my institution, we have a "genuine excellence" category for teaching and for research (I've always loved the term in its implication that there is a fraudulent excellence that we will not tolerate.) Each year at tenure time, we try to determine what percentage of aspirants make the grade in both major areas (only one is required for success, with clear competence required in the other), and the result is usually around 15%. The ideal, this suggests, is not impossible, but it is also not the norm, which is hardly a surprise.

Moving forward, without abandoning the ideal, we almost certainly have to try to move the dial more toward the teaching side. This is one of the cultural shifts that must be tackled; like every change in attitude, it will be hard. Teaching is the most important faculty function, however much discomfort that priority may cause some of my faculty colleagues. Most of our pay comes from our educational role, whether from student tuitions, the state or even many philanthropists. The priority of student success depends on good teaching, though more is involved. Budget health, including support for the unfunded side of research, depends on effective teaching delivery. More important, it's where our primary ethical obligation lies. We have to start with the teaching premise. I cut my academic teeth on the charming phrase "publish or perish," with its slightly ominous preference for research achievement. We can still keep the phrase but put it firmly under another alliteration: Teach it or tank it.

Placing teaching first means real reorientation for some faculty, particularly those few who see teaching as an unwelcome intrusion on their real passion. It means renewed attention to reward structure: we must be able to evaluate and compensate good teaching and become more comfortable with this engagement. Again at George Mason, we do have the teaching excellence category, but there's no question that most faculty are less confident in criteria here than in the research bucket, and a few units, though happily increasingly few, refuse to put faculty forward on this basis at all. Obviously, some institutions, without systematic research pretentions, don't have this problem, but it intrudes quite widely and requires readjustment. It's not just a matter of paying a bit more attention to teaching; it also involves figuring out how to single out those teachers who most contribute to student success amid appropriate standards of quality and to apply more demanding criteria to the faculty overall.[3]

The current challenge also demands some candid attention to the research side of the equation. High-quality research remains essential in American higher education, even if we face some new uncertainties about capacity for growth. Yet defense of research, in light of teaching needs, is no longer automatic, if only because some of the disrupters dismiss research surprisingly cavalierly. What follows addresses the research component, as well as the primacy of teaching, precisely because both elements of the appropriate relationship require some serious fine-tuning.

A contemporary take on the classic teaching-research relationship is not the only tension to address. We also face the interplay between good teaching and adequate amounts of teaching, another dilemma that, while hardly new, demands commentary. We actually know a good bit about what kinds of teaching will best promote the key priorities of student success and quality assurance, and many faculty have taken the lead in new steps in this domain; this is one reason, in fact, that student retention rates have been modestly improving. There's every reason to believe that our evaluations of teaching can not only win greater attention but that they can be based on surer measures of contributions to student retention and learning success. This is not, unfortunately, the only focus: what we seek here may war against the demands of the budget, and we have to figure out how we will face this confrontation.

Whether we are forced to use the term or not, and right now this varies state to state, there will be no getting around the issue of faculty productivity. Our own budget needs—save for a fortunate handful of really wealthy institutions—require us to specify more clearly what we mean by adequate levels of research and a suitable amount, as well as a suitable quality, of teaching. The issue is not a new one; responsible department chairs, deans and provosts have been grappling with it at some level for a long time. However, there's less margin for error, less room for the welter of individual deals that many faculty seek, than ever before. For tenured and tenure-track faculty, formal teaching loads have been moving fairly steadily downward, dropping, for example, by an average of 13% between 1998 and 2003. The trend must at the least be assessed—there are some explanations that are not merely exculpatory—and, in all probability, it must be reversed.

New attention to teaching; new willingness to talk about teaching quality and student outcomes; a semifriendly conversation about research conventions; and now the productivity issue—here is the combination that sets the demanding framework for the balance of this chapter.

There's at least one other tension, again not new but increasingly important, that must be factored in as well. American universities have quite properly been talking for some time about increasing diversification in faculty ranks. Women have gained ground, though there are still issues of appropriate inclusion in some key disciplines. Minority recruitment remains a far bigger challenge, and there is a huge gap between what institutions routinely say they want to do—and undoubtedly really would like to do—and what they manage to accomplish. Participation in graduate training programs is still unbalanced, and not only attracting but also retraining minority faculty is no small challenge. Changes in equal opportunity law—the constraints on explicit use of a racial factor in hiring—but also the budget crunch have undeniably reduced attention to this crucial issue. Yet administrations, and faculty search committees, must not abandon the pressure on themselves. Ultimately, making faculty composition more similar to rapidly changing American demography will be not just a matter of justice but a key component in attracting and retaining core groups of students who will want some ability to recognize themselves in the faculty with whom they have a chance to deal.

Training Future Faculty

Most teaching faculty have or are heading for a PhD degree, though there are adjuncts and graduate student teaching assistants with only a Masters and the occasional, often really important, contributor with a different background. But the PhD is the common currency.

The strengths and limitations of PhD training are fairly well known, and while adjustments have been mounting over the past couple of decades, the basic framework remains intact—as it probably should. Interestingly, experiments to provide alternative channels—for example, a Doctor of Arts degree for people aiming at the community college level, with more emphasis on teaching, less on research—have not caught on widely because so many people, and so many employers, ultimately favor what academics lovingly call "the highest degree in course." While different doctoral options may help on the margins, there is no getting around the need for attention to the PhD itself.

The degree—as academics already know well—emphasizes advanced courses in several major fields within the discipline, followed by a qualifying exam of some sort, and then a focused research project. These experiences generate the core competence of many faculty—and part of the competence of almost all. Some cautions must be attached. There is often a tension between a feasible research project—the dissertation—and what may prove publishable later on; some faculty mentors don't spend enough time helping candidates think beyond the degree itself, which can impose some severe professional limitations, or further training needs, later on.

More important for our purposes, though hardly a secret, is the extent to which the degree provides haphazard teaching training as well. Many PhD students do gain teaching experience as assistants. The experience is more common in the humanities than in science and engineering (where research assistantships are more abundant and carry more of the freight), which may help explain, along with other factors, why humanities faculty often score better as teachers. For everyone, formal discussions of pedagogical issues and more systematic preparation for the teaching aspect of the faculty experience are unduly limited. The current situation may make things worse, as universities realize that hiring postdocs or adjuncts is a cheaper teaching recourse than using graduate students (who require tuition support as well as some pay). Many programs have realized the basic training dilemma over the past two decades, and institution-wide or disciplinary preparations in teaching have become more common, but a further commitment remains highly desirable. (Of course, not all PhDs intend to teach, but this is a manageable complication.)

By this point, some wider discussion of academic life has also become a desirable component of future faculty training—nothing elaborate, but enough to be as sure as possible that aspiring academics know what they are getting into. This, as opposed to the more pressing issue of systematic attention to teaching, can be accomplished by an informal session or two, stimulated perhaps by some modest reading on higher education issues.

The main goal is to try to tweak the training process in order to improve not only awareness but actual capacity for the range of activities faculty perform. Training in teaching will take less time than that for research but, properly done, will help the actual transition to higher education jobs while reducing the sense—derived from many current programs—that ultimately it is only research that matters. We've made a bit of a mistake to date in assuming that field exams and original scholarship are the only necessary components in grooming future faculty; the result has left many instructors less prepared for their actual classroom work than could be the case and others confused, sometimes lifelong, about basic priorities. Some progress has been made toward fixing the system, but we need a new level of commitment—again, while preserving the existing strengths involved.

Good Teaching

Good teaching is not a recent invention. There's a danger in a section designed to remind the various higher education players, including faculty, about what goes into successful performance in and around the classroom that we're somehow succumbing to some of the most exaggerated innovation claims of the disrupters. Many faculty have long been devoted to meaningful student success as a result of their own student pleasures (suitably adjusted for a wider range of learning commitments), natural talent or a combination of training and experience. We know that many faculty are already good by the results of outcome assessments, whether these come through high-stakes testing, portfolio evaluations or some other mechanism—as well, of course, from the fact that most student course evaluations are usually highly positive. It's also true that, even where some adjustments are called for, we're already heading in many of the directions suggested in this section, with large numbers of faculty eagerly on board and indeed actively contributing to the agenda. For the most part, we need mainly to accelerate and generalize some positive trends and again pay careful attention to our reward structure to make sure that successful teaching wins enhanced response.[4]

It is true, however, that several factors are combining to expand our list of good teaching practices. Relatively new research on student learning is one component, and many faculty are becoming aware that we can actually modify some standard patterns in light of these findings. (One recent goodie, which appeals to the Luddite in me, urges that students should take notes by hand rather than on a device, as the impact on memory is measurably superior.) Hard work by Teaching Centers, now quite widespread, helps expand awareness of what good teaching is all about—one way that modest administrative expansion actually pays off for the priorities of student success and quality. Greater awareness of the importance of retaining and graduating students, and opportunities to rethink some standard expectations about failure rates, contribute strongly; even older faculty in this domain turn out to be able to learn new tricks. Unquestionably, new opportunities presented by information technology and shifts in classroom design open up important new teaching windows.

Again, not everything is innovation. Further, against some of my disrupter colleagues, I don't want to argue that a single teaching formula—the famous flipped classroom model, the fierce effort to abolish all lecturing—has to be imposed. We know from experience that some of today's exciting fads will not last; just ten years ago, key groups were insisting that tiered classrooms were actually essential for high quality instruction, and now we're trying to figure out how to dismantle most of them. While some research findings are definite—more student participation in inquiry is vital to effective learning—we can't claim a complete recipe for the future. Keeping the opportunity for experiment in mind—try it, but also assess it and be willing to admit it didn't work—is a crucial part of the current teaching climate, but so is a recognition of older strengths.

We begin with the priorities themselves: we seek teaching that helps students advance, and ultimately graduate, but with learning outcomes that reflect the existing strengths of the American university, from critical thinking and liberal breadth to a sense of what research is all about. We have lots of assets already, but it is appropriate to remind ourselves of further opportunities.

A final preliminary: I'm deliberately cheating in this section by not yet introducing the budget priority, which may greatly complicate the teaching picture. In the long run, the priorities of student success and quality should trump budget concerns, and there's enough challenge simply in winning fuller faculty commitment to quality teaching to justify a step-by-step presentation, rather than raising all possible complications all at once. We will obviously have to return to the fuller reality.

So what's good teaching, old and new but focused on student success and learning quality, all about? Any faculty member or academic administrator should have some version of a list, and there will be variations in content and ordering. Here's one effort.

1. Be sure to identify the key learning objectives of a course, from the initial syllabus onward. Most faculty are accustomed to conveying the coverage content of a course—though we still have to impress on a few that a guiding syllabus of any sort is really a prerequisite of responsible teaching. We may be less good about telling students—and being entirely clear in our own minds—what skills and analytical capacities a course is meant to promote and what students should be able to do with the data the course conveys. Upfront and recurrent discussion here is really important in guiding students and promoting the more ambitious goals of a course. In some cases, the discussion should also touch base with other institutional statements about learning outcomes, as with the general education program.
2. Teach in ways that encourage student involvement and participation. This is the core of the flipped classroom idea. It is apparently a newer injunction in some fields, like the sciences, than in the humanities—where discussion sections have flourished for a long time—but it deserves more attention across disciplinary boundaries. Get students involved in class by working on the kinds of problems you want them to be able to solve when the course is over and as they move to the next phase of learning or life. Use the excitement of participation to help motivate students to do enough work in advance to join in meaningfully. Vary the exercises to keep the participatory spirit strong. Introduce diverse materials as well, including visual elements to appeal to the strengths of the current generation.
3. Use some of the newer resources toward the participatory goals. Many instructors have spontaneously migrated to some kind of hybrid teaching, where students get materials but also analytical challenges through the Internet or where they can use online content and response mechanisms in the classroom itself. Where possible, take advantage of the more flexible classrooms that are now becoming fashionable—with at least some additional investment involved—to let students move around, work in groups (a valid learning goal in itself) and create. Again, there's no single formula here; good teaching does not have to be massively high tech, and one can still do exciting things even in fixed-seat classrooms.
4. Unquestionably, reconsider the lecture. This is not new news to some of us, but it apparently bears insistence; a class based on lectures alone, week after week, is almost certainly no longer satisfactory. It does not encourage participation (though some students like it precisely because it allows passivity). It is not the best way to provide new information—reading is much faster, where students have the capacity, and we need to make sure students know this. Even where it serves certain students who are particularly attuned to listening, we now have means, through lectures on tape, to deliver high

quality more economically than through the hallowed pattern of each faculty lecturing on her own. Whether all this means never lecture at all may still be debated (though some of my colleagues will vehemently disagree here). Once in a while, a good lecture (often within a class segment, not for the whole class) can help students grasp passion for a subject, be exposed in person to demonstrable competence and have a target for in-class questions and ensuing discussion. Beginning and ending a course with a bang-up, though brief, performance may help motivate, at the outset, and enhance memorability, at the terminus. But don't make lecturing the basic diet, unless huge class size (not the faculty's fault) preempts alternatives.[5]

5. Test frequently enough to spur students who aren't adequately motivated by more positive measures to keep up reasonably well with out-of-class assignments. I note this with a bit of sorrow—pure enthusiasm is more fun—and of course situations vary, with introductory courses requiring more attention of this sort than offerings later in a major. Quizzes can be varied by short response papers and student blogs, but we do unfortunately need some checkup, for the result really will promote learning. The grading that results is a chore, no question about it, almost certainly the least pleasant aspect of the teaching commitment. However, there's no getting around the necessity, and we probably need more reminder exercises than most of us currently undertake. This means, further, not only a hopefully varied set of instruments but also the ability to get the results back to students in a reasonable amount of time. We know, for example, where new first-year students are involved, that some assignments quite early in the course, with prompt feedback and compensatory mentoring where results suggest problems, play a surprisingly large role in student retention.

6. Make sure we don't drop writing. There's a dilemma here as budget pressures argue for larger class sizes; it's been interesting, and depressing, to note how the writing emphasis, a key critique of higher education just a decade ago, has fallen off in the enthusiasm for cheaper degrees. There are ways to use short essays and sometimes a certain amount of peer reading to ease the evaluation burden, but the commitment is vital, and it involves more than the obligatory freshman composition course or even a final senior project. Writing across the curriculum, even in disciplines less accustomed to this kind of assignment, is absolutely crucial for basic thinking skills and employability alike. Writing and testing also involve some attention to ethical student conduct—problems of cheating and plagiarism—where technology has created some new burdens—but this is not a fundamentally new challenge, and it should not unseat the larger gains involved.

7. Expect, as a faculty member, to spend time throughout a career learning more about teaching, talking about what works well and what doesn't, and helping colleagues just as we already do with research. Teaching development, in other words, should be as prominent a factor in a faculty career as research

development usually is already. Experience suggests that most faculty actually welcome opportunities to talk about teaching and teaching problems, but it is true that we need more collective encouragement and opportunity.

8. Listen to student feedback; it's a way to make courses better and to show genuine commitment to students. Taking course evaluations seriously is one step, but midcourse suggestions from students, for instructor use alone, can also be an effective mechanism here. Good teaching involves the capacity to adjust.

9. Show that you care. A 2012 report on what college students most value in their teachers showed an overwhelming preference for instructors who display this quality. This may be a generational response; I don't think I would have rated this as high when I was a student, as opposed to demonstrations of competence and passion for the subject. But, of course, I was future faculty, so I was atypical. In any event, it's a fact of life today and worth keeping in mind, among the other qualities of good teaching. Technology actually helps in reaching out to students, demonstrating concern as warranted and simply reminding them of our personal interest in their progress. We certainly need a way around those few faculty who really don't like students or who find the students they're stuck with so far below their expectations that they can't muster up even a semblance of positive feeling. Working—within reason— on pedagogical empathy is not a bad injunction, and it can relate directly to student motivation and capacity to learn.[6]

10. Evaluate learning results with student success in mind, and do not accept poor outcomes as acceptable routine. Part of this is a no brainer: all faculty know they have to give students a grade in the course, and most of them know that prompt grading really helps students learn from their work and the attendant evaluation. But we need more: courses that routinely generate a high percentages of DFWs (D's, failures, withdrawals) must now be seen as deficiencies that must be remedied. Obviously, the problems may not lie primarily with the faculty. DFWs can result from overlarge class size or from inadequate student preparation and advising, and remedies will involve better sequencing, more mentoring assistance in advance, more tutorial assistance or online, self-paced supplements—the combination can be complicated. Instructors have to take on a responsibility for leadership in spearheading compensatory action. They must keep up with best practices in this crucial area; they must trigger discussions with colleagues about constructive change; often, through, for example, promoting participatory rather than passive classes, they must modify their teaching style directly. We actually do know now, from experience at many institutions, that teaching changes, often along with other shifts, can significantly reduce the DFW results, and we need faculty generally to become more widely aware of what works and take more responsibility for positive results. We should actually want grades to improve—inflation critics to the contrary—and we should commit ourselves to figuring out how this

can happen. This commitment must also involve enhanced faculty involvement with introductory courses—the fabled commodity category—and not just more advanced and specialized offerings where the outcome problems are far less severe.

Good teaching is always about balance but of a different sort from the more familiar tensions between instruction and research. Good teachers want their students to succeed—all of them—and are eager to help them in the process, often reaching out directly to show effective concern; but they balance this priority with a willingness to evaluate with real rigor and to tell students when they're not measuring up and what they can do to improve. Success and quality constitute the dual mantra in the pedagogical version of tough love. There are few greater rewards in faculty life than seeing the student who initially struggled a bit come through with a really strong result. Good teaching does not work with every student every time, but it has long been effective overall, and we have increasing evidence that still more imaginative commitment will really pay off further around the vital priority of student success.

Teaching Evaluations

Part of the existing, and desirable, assessment of teaching in American higher education involves student course evaluations. The category has some ironic features: many faculty worry that administrations take the results too seriously, students systematically believe that their comments are ignored. (Note: some interested students often ask about administrative use of Rate-my-Professor scores; the answer is that faculty evaluations don't use them because they have no statistical validity, and the inquirers usually accept this if we can also explain that we have our own, better though not flawless, institutional evaluation system that is taken seriously.)

In fact, despite faculty concerns and recurrent efforts to argue that evaluations simply mirror good grades, course evaluations play a desirable role in teaching assessments. They should never be used alone: classroom visits by faculty peers, consideration of syllabi and other teaching materials can serve as additional evidence. Where possible, though this can be difficult, data about student performance in later sequential courses are obviously relevant: if the products of one course consistently do disproportionately well in the next step up, we can salute the instructor involved, whatever the student ratings. Administrators also have ample experience in discounting scores from big, required courses or other special factors that may push student evaluations downward; some faculty worry more about administrative savvy in this area than they need to. Against student concerns, administrators really do look carefully at the summary evaluation categories as a key element in their personnel decisions. Hopefully as well, faculty but also department chairs see qualitative comments as providing information about desirable corrections in course, quite apart from the salary and promotion process.

It is true that evaluations sometimes reflect the views of an unrepresentative minority of student respondents, for participation rates vary; getting online responses is particularly chancy, though there are devices to improve participation. There may sometimes be a clustering toward the very pleased and the clearly antagonized. However, student evaluations overall are usually pretty positive—students are generous creatures in the main—which means that repeated low scores really do warrant attention, possibly remediation, and if persistent may point toward negative promotion or retention decisions. Evaluations can also help identify unusually good performance, which will deserve recognition as well. Overall, course ratings provide an important piece of evidence when properly weighed against other components, forming part of the process of taking teaching seriously. They let students contribute directly to the teaching process. Some faculty discomfort can be registered, but it should not govern practice.

Poor Frameworks, Bad Teaching

Good teaching depends on appropriate contexts, which go well beyond what faculty alone can provide. It depends on reasonable class sizes, though definitions here will vary with subject, level and technological involvement. It depends on adequate facilities, where on the whole, the challenge right now is greater than with technology itself: we need steady pressure to generate more flexible, exciting classroom environments, though not all renovations have to cost a lot. It depends to some degree on other kinds of institutional support, including leadership and guidance from the specialized office that deals with higher education pedagogy, and some assistance as well on the hybrid side from talented instructional designers. It depends, as already stipulated, on a reward structure that identifies and compensates teaching success and not just as a second cousin to research. These stipulations can be met, are increasingly being met in many places, but they do call upon resources and they also, frequently, demand some adjustments in mindset not just from faculty committees but from administration itself.

Good teaching also depends on increasing willingness to identify, coach and in extremis discipline faculty who are not keeping up with current demands. Unless clearly supported by nontuition funds, faculty who impatiently view teaching as a distraction from what really counts, to be minimized as much as possible and attended to with as little energy as possible, simply are not what higher education now needs—however great the tolerance margins may have been in the past. Faculty who view themselves as traffic cops, eager to pounce on student lapses and proud of regularly identifying a high percentage who literally do not make the grade, need at least to be tactfully reeducated. The whole practice of curve grading, with assumptions about a standard level of failure, needs review, not to lighten standards but to improve our capacity to identify student success in meeting the standards. Most faculty are not tainted by these outdated characteristics, but a few are, and a few others may be more affected than is desirable. Good teaching requires a willingness to tackle these problem cases.

We know what good teaching is, at what goals it should aim and the standards by which it should be assessed. We simply need even more of it, and this is a joint responsibility of the institution and of its faculty. For all the undeniable problems of higher education, this aspect of the assignment is at least as exciting as it has ever been.

Good Research

Good research unquestionably requires less comment than good teaching. It's what faculty are most clearly trained in (along with related subject matter competence for their courses). It's what they most clearly value—again, even with an explicit teaching alternative, 80–85% of tenure-track faculty will choose to come up for promotion based on their research achievements at doctoral institutions. It's what the bulk of the disciplinary conferences focus on, though teaching and technology issues are getting increasing play. So what's the problem? Given a solid record of achievement, unquestionably tops in the world at least for the moment, why not just urge faculty to keep it up?[7]

Several factors—not necessarily problems—prompt some careful attention to research as part of the faculty mix. First, the deliberate initial emphasis on teaching risks make some faculty nervous—lest we seem to be dropping research out altogether. Experience suggests that even when faculty respond well enough to current teaching demands, they want the comfort of knowing that research is still valued; and as a vital element in preserving existing higher education strengths as well as for its direct contributions to society at large, it is. The opportunity to clarify the commitment to research as part of the basic three priorities is welcome. This is all the more the case given the budgetary uncertainties around expanding the research portfolio much beyond present levels; we do need to be sure we know how to keep, and clearly justify, what we have.

The second prompt is less reassuring, less focused on a maintenance task, though figuring out how to address it successfully must be part of the ongoing mission. Growing insistence on student success—reasonable in itself—plus the nagging budget concerns combine to raise increasing questions about what constitutes essential research and whether faculty judgments, at least as universities and disciplines are now organized, provide adequate bases for response. More than in the recent past, administrators and faculty need to be able to talk to a wider public, as well as among themselves, about what constitutes the kind of good research that deserves institutional support. Otherwise—we may be told—why not just teach?

There is no question, to anticipate the coming budget section, that more and more institutions are being set up explicitly without research—not just with less, as at some second-tier state schools, but with none at all—as a cost-containment measure. Western Governors' University, which has no formal faculty whatsoever, is a looming case in point, as are many of the for-profits: if you want much cheaper faculty, ditch the research, and hire people who are paid one course at a time, with no other responsibilities. This very real option, not brand new but increasingly visible, means inevitably that if an institution and its faculty want the research, they need to be able to articulate the gain—and this may involve not just more attention to persuasive rhetoric but some substantive changes as well.

Finally, we must also plug into some of the disrupters' arguments about expanding research criteria beyond the current comfort level, for while they are not as active in the research domain as in teaching, the self-appointed innovation pioneers have an agenda here as well that warrants attention. Do we need to consider how we reward research that exploits the most up-to-date modes of presentation or that deliberately seeks an audience beyond scholarly confines? Do we need a more explicit means of encouraging and rewarding interdisciplinary efforts? The answers are pretty clearly yes, yes and yes, which returns us to the need to address anew the question of what good research is all about.

Let's remember the standard arrangement for tenured or tenure-track faculty at institutions that do make research claims. Normally, the assumption is that they will spend roughly half their time teaching (not just in class, of course, but also evaluating, assessing, keeping up with the field) and half the time in research; other service requirements get squeezed sometimes uncomfortably between. Many faculty also have summers for research, though they may want or need to do some extra teaching or other work to make ends meet. However it's sliced, there's a lot of research time for the tenure-linked group, and much of it is built directly into standard salary support. At public universities, this is part of what states pay for (increasingly inadequately); at all institutions of the type, it's part of what students pay for.

Institutions are quite responsible, in turn, in their evaluation of research, thanks to faculty competence and serious engagement in the process—at least up to tenure time. We measure productivity, whether so-called or not, by asking carefully whether faculty have published enough by the (highly varied) standards of each discipline—whether articles, books or conference papers. We assess quality and visibility by asking about the standing of the outlets themselves—how many papers appeared in top-tier journals—and by assessing the opinions of reviewers, external faculty referees and others. American institutions do act on the results: whether by denying tenure or pressing unproductive faculty at an earlier stage (often, at a midway three-year review), research universities disinvite about half of the faculty they initially hire; while poor teaching is sometimes involved, research deficiencies are the more common villain. Further, the evaluative process is repeated, with equal care, for tenured faculty that seek the further move to full professorship (though note, in this case they don't have to do this, in contrast to pretenured folks who face an up-or-out situation). Higher education can legitimately argue, at least to a point: yes, research work is paid for, but American institutions are very careful to make sure faculty deliver. Without question, on the flip side, in any given field at any of the conventional institutions, the highest paid faculty are virtually invariably the closest things available to research superstars. Rewards are usually quite clear, which is, among other things, why the need to improve the valuation of teaching looms as a challenge; this adjustment aside, however, there's no particular internal pressure to reconsider the system.

It's not, of course, the internal audience that is pressing higher education about budgets and student debt, and it's not an internal audience that is likely to generate widespread concerns about research standards more generally. As more and more governments try to measure university quality to see what value their funding generates (or, in the American case, their declining funding—there is real irony in the combination of decreasing support and increasing demands for accountability, but that's the new normal), research results inevitably factor into the mix. They have become an explicit part of an ongoing conversation in places like the United Kingdom, and they are beginning to enter into the evaluations conducted by a number of American states under the heading of "performance-based" funding. Without at all claiming a breakdown in research delivery, we do need at least a willingness to step back to talk about justifying our confidence to a broader public—students included, at least in principle, since they're now paying for much of this—and possibly to admit some need to fine-tune several features in light of current realities.

Granting, then, that a completely new answer is not required, what is significant research? What research really matters enough to warrant the various forms of public support? We need to be willing to extend some of the impact criteria we apply in tenure judgments—including a recognition that some products do not measure up—to the research endeavor more generally.

The terrain is familiar up to a point, so it's already possible to indicate some of the problems that any broader discussion of research quality will entail. From the standpoint of individual faculty, the variability of disciplinary standards simply must be recognized. Some fields, and particularly those measured primarily by articles rather than books, offer careful data about citation rates, which can be of huge assistance in measuring response to output; by the same token, others—at least for the moment—do not. There are consultants willing to help with the process of assessing research impact, but their services are hugely expensive and hard to manage in the current budget climate. Artistic areas by definition produce creative works rather than research per se, and yet (I hope) we don't want a research definition that leaves them out; this means there must be some willingness to expand the category to include performances, expositions and critical reactions. On the science and tech side (which on the whole will have an easier time with evaluation), an increasing amount of research involves large teams; universities already face the challenge of identifying individual contributions in these settings, looking for indications of priority of authorship (which again vary by field) and some capacity to work with different sets of collaborators rather than relying than a single group. More generally, in most fields, much valid research is cumulative, building from smaller, sometimes rather narrow contributions into a larger whole; not every participating scholar is going to lay claim to a massive result, but their efforts may nevertheless be significant. Noting these various complexities, with which institutions already grapple in their internal reviews, is not a cop-out, but it is a plea for some wider understanding of how effective research operates.

We are increasingly realizing that research evaluations at the level of whole institutions will have their own complexities. Current debates in the UK are instructive here. Is it all right for an institution to highlight a select group of outstanding researchers to be compared to a comparable set at other places, or should entire faculties be counted against all research output? How can we allow for reputational bias: a top place—Oxford, for example—wins better-than-average research placement simply because its faculty can display an Oxford badge; does this unfairly discriminate against a possibly equally qualified but less favored scholar from Aberystwyth (where, by the way, some interesting work on Ebola is currently located)? How much agreement is there on the "tier one" journals in each field, particularly on a global scale? American scholars are hugely advantaged by writing routinely in English, the premier scholarly language by far, but this does not mean that the definitions of top tier that apply to their work are undisputed—particularly in some of the newer research areas, such as neuroscience.[8]

Even as we admit the need for a wider discussion of research output, we must note that easy formulas, easy agreements across fields, are hardly likely. Higher ed representatives must do the best they can to make sure that nuances and complexities are not steamrolled in favor of simplified accounting categories.

Still, quantity will be easier to measure than quality as we move to wider institutional reports on research. With relatively little effort, universities can tally faculty output in key fields, generate standard expectations by area (articles or books per year or other accepted products), and produce an overall matrix that could be assessed annually or hopefully triennially (it takes time to get research out) as part of institutional measurement.

It's quality that's more interesting, of course. It's legitimate to expect research that meets three usually interrelated standards on the significance side, which is ultimately what counts: the capacity to win wide and usually favorable attention from other scholars (and citation indices helps a lot here, where available; and of course placement in higher-tier outlets will factor in as well); contributions to the reputational visibility of the researcher and perhaps, by extension, that of the host institution; and products that broadly accomplish some social good, that improve the understanding or resolution of a meaningful problem or issue or, as in the arts, provoke meaningful human response. Positives in these three categories surely demonstrate significance underneath the broader output umbrella.

Agreement could easily founder on the last, and most important, point: what is a meaningful problem, issue or response? Here's the area, ultimately inescapable, where we need both vigorous assertion and an openness to critique and adjustment.

On the assertion or self-defense side: We must hope to avoid any simple categorization between funded and unfunded research categories. Institutions already measure themselves and are measured by groups such as the National Science Foundation in terms of the amount of external support they acquire. That's fine, for the factor is relevant, but it must be remembered that even funded research costs the institution money—the fabled 15–20 cents on the dollar—so while we have every reason to welcome financial support, we should not use this criterion to excuse other evaluations of significance or to downplay research in fields where external funding does not commonly play a role.

We must also insist that the undeniable variety among significant research targets does not distort the assessment process—admitting that there is some overlap here with the external funding issue. It's pretty obvious that research that promises advances in the treatment of cancer or new techniques in cybersecurity will have little trouble winning a seal of approval. Even outside the STEM fields, research in areas like criminology, which can actually lead to policies that improve police effectiveness, surely win easy acceptance. The same holds for those related kinds of research that hold promise for economic development or for contributions to corporate growth or new spinoffs that contribute directly to regional vitality. Yet other key research areas—very much including the arts and humanities—must not be excluded merely because they don't so directly address disease, technology or entrepreneurship. Some will actually link in: studies of the creative class, vital to a region's economy, show, for example, a strong direct correlation to the vigor of the regional arts scene. Research also contributes when it challenges currently fashionable political assumptions or raises questions about the functioning of the family (when and why did the helicopter parent emerge, for example, and with what consequences?). The need to engage with definitions of significance must not narrow what university faculty explore.

The agenda here is hardly obscure: the humanities, most particularly, risk being under dangerous attack because their practitioners simply can't generate the direct connections to the most obviously useful research targets and in some cases because they legitimately serve the function of raising uncomfortable public questions. We will suffer as a society, as will our higher education institutions, if our universities do not successfully show why measures of short-term utility must not define the whole research domain. I fully admit my own bias here; I am a card-carrying historian, but I think the point goes beyond individual commitments.

This said, I also think we can also admit some deficiencies in our current system of research production and evaluation as part of a more candid conversation with a newly critical public. The first point takes us back to the quantitative; the second hones in on the more difficult issue of defining significance.

On the sheer output side: until recently, universities have done very little by way of systematic assessment of faculty output after tenure. Of course, less productive faculty have usually received lower raises; of course, the really unproductive have not even tried for the further promotion to full professor or have been denied if they put themselves forward. What can be done about the associate professor who turns out little research or the full professor who has largely stopped? The dilemma, not uncommon, has simply not factored into institutional policy. As we face the new budget times, with clearer demands on individual and collective performance, this has to change, and we will note the emergence of new efforts in this direction when we turn below to the faculty-budget relationship more generally.

On quality: while insisting on a broad definition of research significance, American universities will benefit, substantively and in terms of self-defense, from a fuller recognition of the need also to guard against self-serving narrowness. It's pretty clear that, in recent decades, more and more scholars have become comfortable researching and writing primarily for an audience of other scholars not just in the discipline but within a subdiscipline, sometimes adding obscure language or theorizing deliberately designed to discourage wider interest. This is particularly visible in the humanities, where major funding is not involved and where there is no external committee system to bless or withhold blessing from a project. It actually may apply to some funded projects as well, which seem less limited because they have some money behind them but where in fact the substantive contribution is questionable. Differentiations here are tricky; we must retain peer evaluations as part of our research assessment process, but it is desirable to move toward somewhat wider demonstrations of potential value, beginning with insistence that researchers themselves generate justifications that can engage beyond the subspecialty.

Here, I think, is where we need to consider taking the risk of some modest additional mechanisms—similar to what the STEM folks have to go through with external funding reviews—to encourage and hopefully to assure attention to wider impact. The same faculty structure that is emerging to assist in the evaluation of quantity output can be asked to weigh in on the issue of significance as well, with deference—but not undue deference—to the voices of subspecialty colleagues and with enhanced capacity to guide research away from self-fulfilling narrowness. Of course, any faculty member must be free to pursue whatever research project moves him or her—to the extent the activity is not calling on wider institutional support. However, where the institution provides some imprimatur in terms of formal recognition of research vitality even after tenure (and certainly as part of tenure), we need to do better than blanket approval. The adjustment—the commitment to ongoing evaluation of significance—is part of what I hope will be a more broadly successful defense of the research enterprise and part of the type of institutional evolution that should mark higher education's next steps. It represents a tactically prudent step, in the current critical climate, to acknowledge a need for greater selectivity while maintaining oversight within the academy.

The evolution should embrace several positive features. We clearly need to reconsider aspects of our evaluation system that mitigate against some of the newer possibilities in research presentation. Online articles and e-books can and should be evaluated in the same terms as more conventional products without bias against the scholars involved. This does not mean abandonment of peer review—here I take issue with some of the disrupters, who want everything to count—but this can easily be added.

We should be considering as well—perhaps particularly in the social sciences and humanities but potentially more widely—what credit we give for reaching out successfully to a wider public, for contributing directly to conversations beyond the scholarly community alone. Academics are capable of recognizing this kind of engagement, but it is true that we sometimes react as though popularity were a sign of shallowness. Balance counts here as well; the mere fact of popularity must be buttressed by peer assessments, but the combination is surely manageable and not to be discouraged out of hand. The university research mission and, arguably, the level of public or policy discourse will improve if appropriate public engagement wins greater credit.

Above all, as we review university research operations and their defense, we need to find additional ways to motivate and to acknowledge interdisciplinary inquiry. Legitimately hot fields like neuroscience, conflict analysis or sustainability have advanced because of their facility in bringing various relevant disciplines together and by defining problems rather than hewing to the agendas of individual disciplinary components. We need more of this. Combinations in science and technology will be particularly obvious and probably hold the key to significant funding increases should these prove possible, but social scientists and even humanists and artists can be actively involved as well, particularly as they are encouraged to modify some lone-wolf scholarly habits. The artist working with the health scientist on Alzheimer's or the historian collaborating actively with a psychologist or business faculty on the organizational impact of gratitude—opportunities of this sort are surely the wave of the future. A focus on social problems, broadly construed, rather than single disciplines is the key, and we must be able to adjust institutional arrangements to provide both appropriate assessment and appropriate reward.[9]

Finally—and this helps square the circle with the preceding sections—we need to extend the vital relationship between good research and good teaching. Here again the necessary connections are not new, and here again they have been increasing. Research and teaching involve somewhat different skills; they can definitely involve conflicting time commitments. However, they also reinforce each other. The classroom informed in part by new research, including the instructor's own, has a vigor that cannot easily be matched. The research that must be presented to a student and not just a specialist audience will be more soundly constituted, with greater potential impact, than that which aims at narrow specialists alone.

Above all, direct connections between even undergraduates and the research process brings to student success one of the real strengths of higher education at its best, making the two primary faculty obligations complementary and not competitive. A host of programs have sprung up, well beyond the confines of the leading private institutions, to facilitate student participation in research projects as collaborators with faculty or as independent investigators. A growing number of forums such as the Council on Undergraduate Research (CUR) as well as regional outlets help students present their work. It's not just a matter of individual projects, though these claim the top of the pecking order; larger groups of students can be involved in discussions of research methods and the strengths and weaknesses of scholarly analysis. Scholarly inquiry and creative work can be built into many more course curricula. The primary goal in all this is not merely the creation of a next generation of researchers, though this is one vital outcome. More broadly, treating students as scholars feeds the wider goal of improving capacities in critical thinking and skills that have direct applicability in first jobs and lifetime careers alike.

Research is one of the key strengths of American higher education. It directly supports the priority of student success. It must be maintained as a key contribution to American society and as a core component of the educational process itself. Its management, evaluation and presentation can, however, be modestly adjusted as part of a greater responsiveness to social problems broadly construed and as part of meeting budget challenges head on. The result can be even better research and even tighter connections with good teaching.

Faculty and the Budget Priority

A twin focus on good teaching and on the lesser but interesting challenges of organizing successful contemporary research offers an exciting faculty agenda, one that clearly addresses the twin priorities of quality and student success. However, it's incomplete without the budget challenge—though at the same time, the challenge must not grab the whole agenda.

It's fair to say that few institutions have systematically grappled with the faculty element in the budget domain—except that cluster that posits a much narrower mission and much more limited definition of student success and seeks either no formal faculty or at least an attenuated segment. Further, few institutions have fully engaged the faculty in an overall discussion of the issue, and blame here rests both on timid administrations, which have preferred to sidestep, and on faculties that have often demonstrably preferred what might be called a whining ostrich stance—emitting occasional laments about deterioration but sheltering from a full exploration of alternatives. Yet the fact is that faculty impact on budgets, in a labor-intensive industry, is simply too great to escape reconsideration.

What institutions have actually been doing to adjust faculty and budget realities is hardly a mystery. Almost certainly, they will keep on this path to some extent, increasingly shrinking and bypassing the tenure/tenure-track component. This path, however, has clear risks, including faculty tension and disagreement, with regard both to student success and quality maintenance, and it will also bump up against limitations as a successful budget device. We need to consider alternatives or significant supplements, and possibly, through a more candid conversation, we can actually come up with a better model overall. At the least, we need to be open to changes that will limit the need to expand further some of the stopgap options that have carried us through the past decade, notably the growing reliance on adjuncts.

What has been happening. The basics here are or should be fairly familiar: to deal with budget cuts amid (often) growing student numbers, institutions have been increasing their reliance on adjuncts and teaching faculty on term contracts rather than tenure contracts. The categories are not brand new. Places like Stanford and Carnegie Mellon were experimenting with nontenure, full-time faculty several decades ago to respond to research funding (developing a research faculty category on soft money, without a lifetime commitment) and to special teaching needs. The big increase in full-time nontenured track faculty actually occurred in the 1990s, with modest increases since. For their part, adjuncts of some sort have been around for a long time, vital (to take an easy case) in music programs where it is simply not sensible to hire a full-time instructor for every instrument type in a student orchestra. However, the degree of current reliance on diverse faculty categories is arguably revolutionary. Few institutions formally adopted an explicit policy of diversification; much of the change results from decisions by deans and department chairs in response to budget stringency and the need to have key courses available for student progress. Expanding the teaching corps needed for online offerings is now accelerating the process in many institutions. It is the accumulation of ad hoc decisions that has ultimately resulted in a very different faculty array.[10]

Over the past 20 years, the number of tenured and tenure-track faculty has grown but at a slower pace than the expansion of the student body; it now constitutes about a quarter of the total faculty corps. Conversely, reliance on part-time or adjunct faculty has exploded: with a 300% growth rate, it has doubled the rate of student growth, rising from less than 25% of total faculty headcount in 1975 to about 37% today. It is obviously true that the full-timers offer more classes still, with many adjuncts delivering only a course or two, but many first- and second-years see few regular faculty of any sort. This is not entirely novel; in some cases, adjuncts serve where graduate assistants once held forth, with full-time faculty visible to entering students only as lecturers in the big introductory courses. The changes in mix cannot be dismissed, however; the teaching corps has changed, in the interests of greater institutional flexibility and lower cost, and it would be folly to pretend that no problems result.

The Several Flavors of Adjuncts

Discussions of adjuncts are often complicated by a failure to recognize that a number of categories exist, which present different mixes of advantages and disadvantages. Adjuncts are by definition part-timers; most institutions have clear rules that limit how much teaching an adjunct can do (though there are no barriers to teaching elsewhere). They are paid by the course, and often their salaries are deplorably low. But from this common base, considerable variety emerges.

There is, at the high end, the adjunct who has (or had, in the case of some retirees) a full-time job elsewhere, who wants to contribute a bit of teaching in a particular area and whose service the university values because it adds to the specialties available, particularly for upper-level undergraduates and Masters students. Music adjuncts fall in this category—the flutist who is on call from the local symphony orchestra in a situation where hiring a full-timer would be foolish. Various engineering, policy and business professionals fit the description as well. Faculty of this sort sometimes add luster because of name recognition; even more commonly, they bring welcome real-world experience, along with their specialization. Students, often unaware that there is anything unusual about the adjunct category in any event, often respond enthusiastically to the opportunities that result.

At the other extreme, where most of the legitimate concern about adjuncts centers, are the part-time faculty who are depending, precariously, on some accumulation of positions to make ends meet, usually teaching primarily in some of the larger general education courses including faculty-intensive areas like introductory writing. They are often well trained—some of them products of an overproduction of PhDs, which helps explain why there are so many people willing to take low salaries. (In some fields, PhD production has outstripped the growth in overall student numbers by 60–70% in the past 20 years, creating an obvious labor force imbalance.) They may be very good at what they do, but their dependence on low-paying slots at several different institutions (often with significant commuting time attached) raises questions about their own survival and about the effective quality they can bring to any one course. Some of these adjuncts, further, are hired at the last minute, precisely because they offer low-cost solutions to an unexpected student logjam. They do not necessarily get much training or support for the courses they actually teach and usually lack the time to stick around for much socialization once the semester begins.

In between are adjuncts who are not exactly prestige specialists but who also—for whatever reason—don't fall into the most exploited category. Some don't want a full-time job. Some simply love to do a bit of teaching, whether they have other work or not. Many adjuncts—in composition courses, for example—stay at an institution for a long time. Their teaching is evaluated as part of regular renewals of contract, but they are not in constant flux. Of course, they're serving the university's budget needs, but this does not preclude devoted and effective performance.

Adjuncts, as part-timers, are typically not as available as might be desired for interactions with students outside the classroom. They may be hard for students to track down if there's some special problem, for example, a

> confusion about an assignment or a test score. Some studies suggest that they grade more leniently than faculty in general, eager to please students in hopes of a renewal of contract or simply too busy to be bothered with student complaints and rigorous evaluation. Adjunct availability also varies crucially by region: institutions in urban centers, in the main, have a richer pool from which to draw (but also, often, more opportunities to exploit the army of the academically underemployed). Institutions like Arizona State have deliberately downplayed adjunct use in favor of relatively high student loads per full-time faculty; variations of this sort deserve fuller evaluation.
>
> There are all sorts of reasons to worry about the expansion of adjuncts and about their appropriate management and connection to the larger teaching enterprise. Reliance on exploited labor—not always the case, again, but certainly true in many instances—is always distasteful. But on a key question: do students see the difference; does adjunctness clearly correlate with inferior teaching? The verdict is actually unclear. There is some research that suggests better student persistence when involved with full-time rather than part-time faculty, and if this is true—and it's not implausible—we have a basic priority at stake. On the other hand, many talented students routinely mention an adjunct when asked to identify the most effective faculty with whom they've worked; while this is sometimes a prestige specialist, there are also adjunct-stalwarts in the general education mix for first-years. Many universities also have developed some useful programs for adjunct orientation, reducing though not eliminating the problem of lack of acquaintance with teaching systems and operating procedures at a particular institution.
>
> Even in the best of budget times, certain kinds of adjuncts would be essential for expertise and flexibility alike. The problems created by the adjunct surge are not as clear-cut as some critics (regular faculty included) may imagine. There is no question that the huge expansion of adjunct ranks is not a desirable trend and that universities should be striving both for better management and treatment of adjuncts and for a reduction in institutional dependence. We should also work harder to assure that the normal first-year student has opportunities to work with some full-time faculty and not simply an adjunct array.

Somewhat less heralded, but also interesting, is the concomitant role of purely teaching faculty (variously labeled), with no assigned research responsibilities and noticeably higher teaching loads than their tenured colleagues.[11] This group now stands at about 15% of the total headcount, up from 10% in 1975. The faculty, often on 4:4 loads rather than 2:2 and usually paid at a slightly lower rate than equivalent tenure-track folks, offer some of the advantages of adjuncts—though at higher costs—with arguably fewer of the risks. They can be dismissed fairly easily if student numbers or budget situations change or if their own teaching performance falters. Their focus on teaching alone can generate imaginative attention to the teaching process, which can affect not only their own work but that of their colleagues. It's no accident that faculty in this category are often central to the innovations that have led to better student success in science and math courses or in introducing some of the more successful online or hybrid offerings. At the same time, these faculty are at least in proximity to the research enterprise, so that vital connection is maintained to a degree. Many institutions have made great strides in offering this faculty category opportunities for advancement in rank and in duration of contracts (three-year, then five-year terms after a probationary sequence in single-year arrangements) in return for measurably good service. Some can and will build a career at a single institution within this framework.

The expansion of faculty categories outside the tenure group has brought some clear benefits, even aside from budget relief. Properly managed, it provides greater opportunities for acting on the results of teaching evaluations, both positively in terms of advancement and negatively through easier dismissal. The nontenure-track faculty often bring enthusiasms and expertise, including pedagogical expertise, that can feed back to the faculty as a whole. Their growth has been consistent with continued gains in student retention and graduation and the largely positive assessment of learning outcomes. In a real sense, they have been central to maintaining the size of the teaching operation in many institutions. However, these results should not eliminate real concerns, particularly around potentially excessive reliance on part-timers but also around the impact on research expectations and on faculty participation in shared governance. We need to consider a number of changes for the faculty as a whole, possibly to adjust a bit the current faculty mix, certainly to avoid still further heedless growth and definitely to do better with the teaching blend that has now come into being.

Online Faculty

Faculty composition is being further challenged by the growth of online operations at public institutions as well as other types. Many faculty want to experiment with online courses, and this should be encouraged. We know that for some student groups, online instruction produces equivalent learning outcomes to classroom offerings; in a few cases, larger numbers can be accommodated, thus saving money. And, of course, online offerings facilitate geographic accessibility and reductions in commuting or housing costs. However, it's abundantly clear as well that online is not suitable for everyone, either because of insufficiently established learning habits—hence, lower retention rates—or because of personal preference. Variety and dispassionate evaluation of results remain essential.

> There is real confusion about budget implications, which is where faculty types come in. Some online operations, at the Executive or Masters level, bring in good revenues, and faculty can be recruited with quality, not just budgets, in mind. But the big online operations, including those aiming at lots of undergraduates, depend on cheap labor to compensate for competitively limited tuitions and the fact that, in most cases, technology itself does not cut operating costs. The University of Southern New Hampshire, an online beehive, has a faculty composed of about 12% full-timers, none on the tenure track, and 88% adjuncts; the University of Maryland-University College is similar, with 8% full-timers, none on tenure. If, as some disrupters advocate, these are models for the future, the existing problem of faculty mix is about to get much worse.[12]

What must happen going forward. Two adjustments are absolutely essential to mesh the new budget realities with the priorities of student success and quality. Both are underway in many places, but both need more explicit recognition and attention as part of an administration/faculty commitment to constructive change.

First, institutions must work toward more systematic integration of the diverse faculty categories. Too often still, many units operate as if tenured and tenure-track faculty are the only ones that count, with not only adjuncts but also full-time teaching faculty relegated to the sidelines. Many tenured faculty take out their understandable concern about the relative reduction of their ranks in snobbish if veiled hostility to colleagues in other categories who are actually carrying much of the load in the types of teaching most essential to student retention, in the first years of undergraduate study. Often, only tenure-type faculty are allowed to vote on key curricular and personnel issues, as if they alone had a stake in the outcome. Sometimes, representation on key institutions of shared governance is also reserved for the faculty elite. This situation is now out of touch with the durable realities of faculty composition, and we need changes in both attitudes and rules to assure a healthier, more constructive framework for faculty interactions. Different categories of faculty are mutually supportive, and we need fuller recognition of this fact, more effective combination of the various strengths involved.

At the same time, administrations, from department chairs upward, must do a better job of creating mechanisms to guide the growing number of nontenured instructors and particularly the part-timers. Each unit that uses adjuncts should have a clear plan for their recruitment, evaluation and support, with appropriate participation by more senior faculty (whether tenured or not). This is part of the integration process as well.

Second, universities must move more consistently to a regular evaluation of research output AND quality as part of the determination of an effective teaching load. Here, the focus clearly is on faculty after tenure. Effectively, we need to move more consistently to a two-tiered arrangement within tenure that will result in greater teaching loads for some faculty but also a more defensible research structure for the institution as a whole. Faculty who qualify as research intensive—as reviewed by a faculty committee at a school or college, rather than merely departmental level, and with attention to significance as well as amount of output—have one teaching load (which may be further modified when external research funding permits, though never to the point of no teaching at all over any significant span). Faculty whose level of output or evaluated research significance falls below the intensive levels simply cannot continue to claim the 50–50 teaching/research split that can be maintained for the rest of the tenured ranks.

There will be problems with this new arrangement. Faculty involved in making the judgments will have to generate unwonted, if anonymous, candor about their colleagues—one reason to take the decision making out of a strictly departmental bailiwick. Research-active faculty will feel even more superior than their higher salaries now encourage; more troubling, those with higher teaching assignments may see the results as punishment. Worst of all—to be implicitly addressed in the next section—some administrators will find themselves seeking expanded teaching assignments for some individuals no longer strong in research but somewhat uncertain in teaching results as well. However, the recalibration must be attempted. Many units in many institutions have already recognized the necessity of greater rigor on the research side and greater participation in the teaching mission as part of constructive contemporary oversight of tenure, and the results have largely been manageable. This is an essential and responsible adjustment of the system as a whole.

These first essential steps aim obviously at a more integrated approach to teaching on the part of the whole faculty and at some modest increase in teaching capacity.

Poison Ivies?

Ivy League institutions, and a few colleague universities in other parts of the country, are the clear gem of American higher education. They grab a disproportionate share of the most talented students (though not all of them), including a small selection of scholarship recipients from lower socioeconomic groups. They generate research leadership in many categories, though some of the flagship publics join in here. They have the highest international visibility.

So what's not to like? (Full disclosure, I received an Ivy League degree, which has in most respects served me well.) One problem, too rarely mentioned, is the distracting role model these schools provide. They are so blessed, and above all so wealthy, that they can afford policies that are not only impossible elsewhere but undesirable.

> Leave aside the question of salaries (including in several cases presidential compensation, where some members of the group set a bad example). The bigger concern is reasonable teaching load. The Ivies and the wannabes routinely, for example, extend offers that excuse the new recruit from any teaching at all—in some cases for up to five years. In these and other instances, the Ivies set a standard that additionally complicates efforts by the rest of the field to establish the appropriate faculty commitment to instruction.
>
> Competition for faculty will remain unfair, possibly getting worse as greater gaps open between the top group of private schools and the rest of American higher education. But Ivy leaders can legitimately be urged to recognize the wider impact that their policies have and to undertake, voluntarily, more social and educational responsibility. Some competitive extremes should be out of bounds, and teaching commitments lie at the heart of academic fair play.

What probably should happen. We need to face up to a further discussion as well, though this will be more challenging: tenure itself requires a focused review.

The North American tenure system is not as recent a development as some claim, but it is not engraved in some academic bedrock. During the final quarter of the 19th century, after some fiery cases of faculty dismissal particularly for religious views, a growing number of universities in the United States developed a system of assured employment for faculty after a probationary period. The system gradually expanded in the early 20th century, spurred by yet additional cases of controversy around politically motivated faculty terminations. The American Association of University Professors promoted expansion; by 1942, the tenure system was widely accepted. A Supreme Court decision in 1972 added further support to the idea of tenure as a contractual right. For many decades, an important category of faculty have expected and enjoyed assurance of employment after a usually six- or seven-year trial period and (as we have noted) a rigorous evaluation at that point. Dismissal is not impossible—the McCarthy era cast some doubt on the sanctity of the system; program shutdowns can remove the guarantee for the faculty involved at some but not all institutions. On an individual level, really bad performance can even now call forth a post-tenure review that can lead to termination. For most faculty, however, tenure means permanence. In 1994, the end of mandatory retirement at universities added a vital codicil: tenure can now mean for the rest of one's life.[13]

This has not meant freedom from evaluation. Tenured faculty are assessed annually by deans and department heads and usually an advisory faculty committee within their unit. Teaching and research performance are both scrutinized. The results, to be sure, rarely lead to dismissal—that's a post-tenure review matter, discussed momentarily—but they do affect pay and, through this, prestige. In recent years, the lack of systematic salary adjustments has weakened the force of this aspect of the system. In principle, against some of the attacks on tenure's job security, there are some modest safeguards. A few institutions offer more intensive reviews of tenured folks every three to seven years.

Tenure has always has its critics, who are not always fully informed about its nuances; these have become more vocal during the past two decades. Many university administrators themselves harbor grave doubts about the inflexibilities of the tenure system, and concerns are even greater in the outside world. As early as 1996, the Florida legislature tried to mandate post-tenure review, designed to weaken if not undermine job security. More recently the Sunshine State has returned to the attack, requiring a link between "student success" (primarily retention) and faculty contracts in the state college (formerly community college) system. Again, the undercutting is clear because it would be difficult to measure individual faculty impacts on retention; the goal is a ploy to void tenure. Many community college systems don't pretend to have tenure in the first place. Assaults on tenure may spread more widely on the twin bases of legitimate concerns about sheltering unproductive faculty and a conservative legislative zeal to challenge liberal faculty views; watch developments not only in Florida but also in Texas and similar sites.[14]

Against these concerns, there are a few valid reasons to support the tenure system, even aside from a veneration of the established order. One factor, very real in practice, involves the tremendous difficulty and distraction a full attack would entail. The institutions best positioned to jettison tenure—the prestigious Ivy types—have no reason to take the trouble because they have no major budget pressures with which to contend, and without action here, competition for top faculty—and I mean top on the teaching as well as research side—would become next to impossible if a slightly lesser institutional set was required to drop the system.

Beyond competitive realities, tenure matters first because it helps keep some faculty salaries down. Several studies suggest that, without the prestige and job security tenure provides, faculty salaries would have to be upward of 10% higher than is currently the case. While this stricture may not currently apply to some humanities fields, given the glut of PhDs, it would still affect the vital (and expensive) STEM fields, where higher-paying jobs in industry beckon. It's not at all clear that a tradeoff—no tenure but necessarily higher pay—would actually alleviate the basic budget dilemma.[15]

More important still—though clearly contested—is the extent to which tenure still serves its original purpose: protection of academic freedom and therefore of the role of universities in challenging cherished assumptions. To be sure, most faculty, even with tenure, are not particularly interested in rocking the boat. Unquestionably, the faculty who do develop provocative ideas by definition annoy wide sectors of the public, who would be delighted to dispense with an employment system that protects them. But this is precisely the point. Anyone who has lived through the past decade or so in the United States, with the many occasions in which unpopular views have been pilloried, has to recognize that, without tenure, pressures on numerous faculty and the institutions that house them could have become unmanageable. We're at one of those recurrent moments when some faculty want to discuss issues, like security or race, that much of the public would rather ignore; this is part of higher education's role and service. Tenure in this sense at least helps protect quality.

In my view, though with some regret as an ex-administrator, I can't see the desirability, much less the practical possibility, of attacking tenure wholesale at most public four-year institutions. There are two features of the system that need reform toward promoting better research and teaching and providing modest relief on the budget equation as well. Both would also help defend an attenuated tenure system itself, which without change may simply be washed away at many places.

1. The first is familiar enough: post-tenure review. Most tenure systems do allow the faculty involved to be fired for egregious misconduct, sometimes fairly quickly though with due process procedures. They also permit a contractual challenge when, over time, faculty performance falls noticeably below acceptable levels, even with no striking misbehavior attached. This is where a post-tenure review system may come into play. The system allows an institution, through a committee composed largely if not entirely of faculty, to act on cases where a tenured faculty member can no longer attract students, experiences teaching evaluations consistently well below the unit norm, and/or offers curricula that are measurably out of date, all usually with inadequate research performance tossed in. The process is appropriately protracted: any post-tenure review should begin with clear warnings to the faculty member involved, with active collaboration in devising a remediation strategy: it's only right to begin with a positive approach.[16]

This said, however, there are deficiencies in the system that must be addressed, if within an adequate but not indefinite period of time that positive approach does not work. Even in the best of current circumstances, the system is impossibly cumbersome, stretching out over three to four years with grievance procedures usually prolonging further. The remedy? Without stripping protections for the individual faculty, and while clearly allowing time for consultation and remediation, the process should accelerate, in serious cases reducing to a two-year decision process. Of course, greater flexibility would invite the intrusion of political factors—there is risk in change, given the vultures that hover over academic freedom—but a more effective review process will actually help defend the system as a whole while offering greater quality assurance to the students involved and, hopefully, encouraging administrators themselves to venture greater rigor in their approach to seriously underperforming academic colleagues. I think we should bite the bullet on this one and meet some of the more responsible critics halfway.[17]

That's not even the full story. A large number of institutions have no clear post-tenure review system at all, at least with any defined process of dismissal where remediation fails. Almost all, in deference to tenure, sugarcoat their approach, talking about reviews as a means, as Westmount College recently put it, to "make the good ones better" rather than weeding out the bad. Many places define a first-year process, which is where the positive guidance can be established, and simply duck the question of what might happen next should the guidance not produce results. And some places—Ball State is a current though probably temporary example where the Senate is dragging its heels against trustee insistence on some defined dismissal process with suitable protections—hope to evade the issue altogether. However painful the change, higher education must do better.

We should hope that post-tenure dismissals will be rare; it is possible that a clearer system will actually provide effective performance incentives and more conscientious annual evaluations. Due process safeguards are vital, if difficult, but the possibility of removals based on consistently poor quality must be more clearly established.

2. Step number two within the tenure system involves confronting the consequences of ending mandatory retirement. Here the result, predictably enough, has been a clear increase in faculty's average age—moving from 50 to 52 between 1994 and 2006 as individuals stay on beyond 65, sometimes well beyond. Retirement rates have declined under the tenure umbrella, and this means a faculty that is not only older but also more highly paid than average: during the 1992–2003 span, the percentage of salary payments going to faculty over 60 jumped from 18 to 25.[18]

The end of mandatory retirement has been a welcome innovation in American society, universities included. Systems elsewhere—even in neighboring Canada—that cut faculty off from most productive activity at 65 are harsh to individuals and socially inefficient in terms of utilizing established strengths. I admit a self-interest here; I passed the conventional marker quite a while ago. More widely, lots of programs depend heavily on the experience and continued vitality of an older faculty component, not only in established domains but even in newer venues; in one study, faculty over 55 were more open to online activities than their younger colleagues, though that equation will surely change with time. To be sure, several observers have recently urged the desirability of accelerating retirements to save money, allow more entry to young faculty, and adjust the professoriate more fully to the programs students currently want and need. Against too much zeal, I think it would be a mistake to seek a return to a mandatory departure system.

However, the intersection between tenure and later age should be open to review; in fact, the issue should have been discussed back in the 1990s, when the retirement system shifted in the first place. While a few older faculty may still need protection for unpopular views, tenure at this level has clearly shifted to job security, pure and simple; in light of current realities and simple common sense, this aspect should now be changed.

What has resulted is not only an increased presence of faculty in their 70s and beyond but also some frankly ridiculous and expensive arrangements to try to induce expensive faculty to leave—frequently offering a final two years with massively reduced teaching loads. Further, the continuing assumption that older faculty should continue to operate at the high end of the salary scale adds needlessly to overall faculty costs. In individual cases, tenure protections have made it very difficult even to talk with faculty whose ageing has included measurable deteriorations in the classroom, including nodding off from time to time, where everyone would hope to avoid the harshness of formal post-tenure review but where there are no formal alternatives.

Again, let's admit a problem while seeking to take continued advantage of those older faculty whose capacities still contribute. Tenure should end either after a period of time (25–30 years?) or at a certain age—possibly mimicking Social Security onset. Interested older faculty can then be signed up on mutually agreed contracts—up to three years at a time or perhaps an initial five-year option. This negotiation—which admittedly will not always be easy but must be part of an updated administrative responsibility—can include some salary adjustments to modify the impact of the older faculty segment in this regard. It will obviate the publicly indefensible buyout gyrations that currently cost money and reduce teaching power. It will allow evaluation and continuance to be more flexibly aligned, making response to any deterioration that does result from ageing less painful. It also blends with the wider patterns already discussed in which the balance of research and teaching activities must be recurrently reviewed.

A change of this sort needs wide discussion—shared governance front and center—and it would only gradually have an impact on faculty performance and budgets. However, the adjustment is overdue, acknowledging tenure's continued service but making a clearer commitment to ongoing faculty effectiveness.

There's no way to keep tenure out of the spotlight where legitimate budget concerns combine with diffuse resentments about higher education more generally. The system is worth saving; scrapping it would generate both unproductive conflicts and unforeseeable consequences. However, universities should be taking the lead in adapting tenure to more responsible management, making a further commitment to faculty effectiveness around the core priorities.

What We Also Should Be Discussing

Possibly, finally, we should be discussing teaching loads—at the least to make sure that we more fully end the practice of individual faculty deals and halt the continued effort to cut teaching back further, possibly to venture a modest increase for the tenured segment.

This is a really tough category, likely to become increasingly political, so some clarity at the outset is essential. Most faculty are working very hard—a recent estimate ventured 50–60 hours a week, and that may well be true. A few don't measure up, which is a key reason that adjustments for measurable research activity are essential and that some aspects of tenure may need review, but the issues are not wholesale. Even a modest effort to increase teaching loads for most faculty—outside of the contract teaching segment—will clearly affect research and will in all probability reduce teaching quality as well. Therefore, this final section focuses on a possibility, not a desirability—a possibility with consequences that are not trivial. A few adjustments are needed at the margins, but a core change would have real repercussions on the priorities of quality and student success.

Some conversation is probably unavoidable. Early in 2015, the governor of Wisconsin, proposing a major higher education funding reduction while insisting on no tuition hikes, said quite baldly: "Maybe it's time for faculty . . . to start thinking about teaching more classes and doing more work." Not, obviously, a constructive approach from the standpoint of motivating change. The response from university officials was enlightening as they emphasized the hours faculty put in, rather than what's actually been happening to teaching loads for the tenured ranks—which was at the least somewhat disingenuous.[19]

Teaching loads for tenured and tenure-track faculty have gone down during the past two decades, even aside from faculty buyouts based on external research funding. Many middle-of-the-pack research institutions have adjusted from a 3:2 course load to a 2:2 for the tenured and tenure-track category. Some particular fields—like economics, which is high prestige though not particularly productive of research funding—have dropped below this. There is recurrent pressure for still further adjustment and lots of faculty seeking special arrangements that would create additional exceptions to standard patterns. In some cases, competitive job offers include course load reductions as part of the inducement, still further complicating faculty commitments in this area.

There is, to be sure, some misinformation afoot over this issue. A sensationalist 2013 report, *Selling Students Short,* claimed a 25% cut in teaching power; the data were later recognized as inaccurate and the report withdrawn, though not before some public damage was done. Loads have been dropping, if more modestly, largely in favor of research. The 1998–2003 data, showing a 13% drop, revealingly point to a disproportionate decline at Masters-level universities, where faculty and institutional ambitions promote mission-creep at teaching expense. There is, in other words, a trend to be discussed, though not the catastrophe that some gullible or irresponsible critics have ventured.[20]

Any resistance at all risks seeming rather damning to any outside observer—fussing over an additional three hours a week in a classroom (which is what a 25% increase in standard load would often involve) seems unnecessary. Why don't we simply jack the loads up again, maybe to even higher levels? Before we return to this understandable reaction, we must introduce several serious complications to any facile condemnation of faculty proclivities—complications that begin to explain why systematically higher teaching loads would surely affect educational quality.

Good teaching takes lots of work. Brief recollection of the desirable practices discussed earlier in the chapter should provide ample illustration of how much out-of-class time the best work entails, from frequent grading to devising participatory exercises. Most relevant experts openly hope for greater recognition of the importance of teaching but hope as well that loads will not go up—precisely because of the demands involved. The need to keep up with current findings in the field (and, hopefully, with advances in pedagogy) adds a further dimension. Some facile critics wonder why faculty can't simply go from class to class; the result, at the higher education level, would be increasingly out-of-date material that would do no one any good. Even with some recent decrease in teaching load, the average faculty member is still devoting more than 60% of his or her effort to the teaching process directly, with only the doctoral institutions, particularly the privates, really affording a 50–50 split between classroom and other duties.

Faculty spend a lot of time on essential educational tasks for which they usually get no formal teaching credit. This includes individual project work, from undergraduate research to PhD guidance. It includes at least some informal advising and mentoring. It includes participating in the activities of shared governance. It increasingly includes work on assessment activities. Quite possibly, these informal commitments have expanded in recent years, which would help explain the trends in formal loads.

Numbers of classes taught are not the only way to measure productivity. Some systems legitimately take into account class sizes, with more credit to effective teaching of somewhat larger groups. The Arizona State pattern, with high numbers of students per full-time faculty, embraces this implicitly, even as student success indices improve. This approach can be particularly important where senior faculty can be induced to contribute to general education courses. Increasingly as well, headcounts may factor into the assignment of appropriate teaching credit for online programs. Correspondingly, one of the key adjustments deans and department heads are already making toward meeting budget realities involves more strictly regulating minimum numbers of students in a class (variable depending on student level), in some cases with faculty invited, should they wish to volunteer because of a particular subject passion, to go ahead with a smaller class on top of the usual teaching load. Considerable savings can result from this move alone without the need to encounter teaching loads directly.

No sober advocate can assume that even a modest countertrend in teaching loads would not risk adverse consequences to educational quality—quite apart from the obvious fact that a huge fight would be involved, along with risks of faculty departure for sunnier (read: lower load) institutional opportunities.

It would also be irresponsible, however, not to recognize that there is a subject here that at least may need to be discussed. Tenured faculty who bemoan the growing use of adjuncts and contract teaching faculty need to acknowledge that one way they might respond effectively is to reconsider their own contributions. At my institution, a 25% increase in normal teaching loads (which for most faculty would mean a return to a 3:2 rather than the current 2:2 setup) would save a minimum of $15 million a year by reducing employment of other types of faculty. Investment of even half this amount in additional tenure-track lines would generate, conservatively, 40–50 new positions, with correspondingly less reliance on other faculty categories. Even as we urge new policies on consultants and on administrative numbers and salaries, we need to treat the teaching load issue as a legitimate agenda item. Responsible discussion—though not gratuitous insults about faculty commitment—is hardly out of bounds. At a minimum, it is both reasonable and, at public institutions, probably unavoidable to commit to ending any further trend toward teaching reduction.

Balance

These are tough days for faculty morale at many institutions. Bad budgets, unusual external criticism, real as well as imagined concerns about administrative practices and external requirements—it's a considerable list. To be sure, every period generates problems of faculty morale, something of a standard trope in Senate complaints to presidents and provosts, but there's real meat on the bone this time. Now we add the need for still-further change and difficult discussion around further and tighter evaluations of faculty teaching and research and several substantial adjustments to rewards and requirements.

There's no need, however, to throw baby out with bath. The chapter began by noting faculty strengths, and it resumes this theme in closing. As noted, there are and will be institutions that largely dismantle conventional faculty arrangements in favor of low-paid, no-research part-timers. I think they will be inferior, and I think most students will realize this. Many institutions, however, can and should maintain a recognizable faculty life and should strive to preserve its many existing qualities—beginning with basic competence and the fruitful interaction of teaching and research. Better shared governance may even generate new opportunities for faculty to participate—though often still as faculty—in leadership roles. We just need some additional elements that take advantage of new opportunities in effective teaching, new responsibilities in defining good research, new adaptations to budget stabilization—and new willingness to discuss what combination of adjustments will be most realistic. The adjustments are not inconsiderable, but they will be manageable, and they will give academics a surer voice in American higher education generally.

In the institutions that do adjust successfully, faculty life will remain recognizable. It will still offer some flexibility in daily scheduling. It will still offer opportunities to participate in genuine shared governance, contributing to policy decisions that really make a difference—indeed, these opportunities should expand. Good administrations will actually increase their efforts to make sure that faculty understand and contribute to key issues and potential decisions, ungarnished with facile PR optimism. Faculty life will also continue to offer opportunities for honors and advancement, even if the evaluations involved add some further dimensions.

Faculty roles will still generate excitement and invitations for further initiatives. Exploration of new discoveries will continue, and a growing encouragement for interdisciplinary combinations will promote further frontiers across conventional boundaries—already obvious in such areas as sustainability or neuroscience. The rewards of student success will be at least as rich as ever, and new pedagogies and teaching settings will enhance opportunities in this domain. Global frontiers—still to be explicitly discussed—will continue to expand. All this won't add up, quite, to the ease of faculty life a generation back; that's gone. However, the academic profession remains dynamic, with new vistas as well as new demands. Faculty morale deserves attention; it will be challenged, but—with good leadership and appropriate collaboration—it can rise to the occasion.

Further Reading

For the distorted or at least overblown critique on teaching loads: Andrew Gillen, *Selling Students Short* (Washington: American Council of Trustees and Alumni, 2013).

A number of recent studies deal with learning research and good teaching: See L. Dee Fink, *Creating Significant Learning Experiences: An Integrated Approach to Designing College Courses* (San Francisco: Jossey-Bass, 2003); Peter C. Brown, Henry L. Roediger III, and Mark A. McDaniel, *Make It Stick: The Science of Successful Learning* (Cambridge, MA: Belknap Press, 2014); Susan Ambrose and others, *How Learning Works: Seven Research-Based Principles for Successful Teaching* (San Francisco: Jossey-Bass, 2010).

Two books by Stephen Brookfield are important: *The Skillful Teacher: On Technique, Trust, and Responsiveness in the Classroom* (San Francisco: Jossey-Bass, 2006) and the more recent *Teaching for Critical Thinking: Helping Students Question Their Assumptions* (San Francisco: Jossey-Bass, 2010).

On interdisciplinary research and its growing promise: Robert Frodeman, Julie T. Klein, and Carl Mithcam, eds., *The Oxford Handbook of Interdisciplinarity* (Oxford: Oxford University Press, 2010); National Research Council, *Convergence: Facilitating Transdisciplinary Integration of Life Sciences, Physical Sciences, Engineering and Beyond* (Washington: National Academies Press, 2014).

On tenure and its downsides: Ryan Amacher and Roger E. Meiners, *Faulty Towers: Tenure and the Structure of Higher Education* (Oakland: Independent Institute, 2004).

Notes

1 Hugh Lander, Phillip Brown and Carl Brown, "The Consequences of Global Expansion for Knowledge," *Beyond Current Horizons,* December 2008.
2 For discussion of the narrowing problem in one discipline, Jo Guldi and David Armitage, *The History Manifesto* (Oxford, 2014).
3 The discussion of new roles for teaching is now a quarter-century old. See Ernest Boyer, "Scholarship Reconsidered: priorities of the professoriate," Carnegie Foundation for the Advancement of Teaching (New York, 1990); and Lee Shulman, "Taking Learning Seriously," *Change* (July–Aug, 1999): 11–17. At best, the results of this groundwork still constitute a cup half empty.
4 See the works cited in the Further Reading for this chapter. Also: C. Kreber, "Teaching Excellence, Teaching Expertise, and the Scholarship of Teaching," *Innovations in Higher Education* 27 (2002); M. T. Huber and P. Hutchings, *The Advancement of Learning: building the teaching commons* (San Francisco, 2005); Gloria Wright, "Student-Centered Learning in Higher Education," *International Journal of Teaching and Learning in Higher Education* 23

(2011); Cari Crumley, *Pedagogies for Student-Centered Learning: online and on-ground* (Minneapolis, 2014).
5 "10 Big Problems with Lecture-Based Learning," www.onlineuniversities.com, Nov. 2, 2011; David Kimbro, "Promoting Student-Centered Learning across an Entire University," *Higher Education* 58 (2009): 1–13.
6 National Survey of Student Engagement, *Promoting Student Learning and Institutional Improvement: lessons from NSSE at 13* (Indianapolis, 2012).
7 There is far less work on challenges in research quality than there is concerning teaching. This reflects the existing competence of faculty evaluations but probably also a dose of complacency, plus the fact that disruptive critics have either ignored research or dismissed it out of hand as costly and irrelevant. This section, then, seeks to stimulate further discussion and some potential innovations in evaluation. See for a recent and rather bitter debate in one discipline over research assessments, "AHR Exchange: On the *History Manifesto*," *American Historical Review* 120 (2015): 527–54.
8 Catrina Manville, "Measuring Inputs: how Australia and the UK are tackling research assessment," *The Guardian,* Dec. 17, 2014.
9 Robert Frodeman and others, *The Oxford Handbook of Interdisciplinarity* (Oxford, 2010): National Research Council, *Convergence: facilitating transdisciplinary integration of life sciences, physical sciences, engineering and beyond* (Washington, 2014).
10 J. W. Curtis and S. Thornton, "The Annual Report on the Economic Status of the Profession, 2012–2013," *Academe,* Mar.–Apr 2013.
11 Curtis and Thornton, "Annual Report."
12 Data from *Collegefactual.com,* 2015.
13 Ryan Amacher and Roger Meiners, *Faulty Towers: tenure and the structure of higher education* (Oakland, 2004).
14 Lisa Roney, "Florida Governor Rick Scott Takes Aim at University Tenure," *Daily Kos,* Sept. 22, 2011.
15 D. W. Leslie and N. Janson, "Easing the Exit," *Change* 37 (2005): 40–7.
16 Colleen Flaherty, "The New Post-Tenure Review," *Inside Higher Ed,* May 2, 2014; Joseph Morrell, "Post-tenure reviews: evaluating teaching," in Peter Seldin, ed., *Changing Practices in Evaluation Teaching* (Boston, 1999). Getting basic data on existing review systems depends also on reviewing relevant sections of faculty handbooks online. Great for insomnia, but the issue demands attention.
17 Flaherty, "New Post-Tenure Review."
18 Calculations developed by John Frederick, Provost at University of Texas-San Antonio, to whom my thanks. American Council on Education, "Review of Faculty Retirement History" (Washington, Apr. 2010); Robert Clark, "Changing Faculty Demographics and the Need for New Policies," TIAA-CREF Institute, conference on retirement, Apr. 1–2, 2004.
19 Lucy McCalmont, "Scott Walker Urges Professors to Work Harder," *Politico,* Jan. 29, 2015.
20 Andrew Gillen, *Selling Students Short* (Washington, 2013); for better data on an admittedly elusive subject, Rudy Fitchenbaum, "From the President: why is US higher education in decline," *Academe,* Nov.–Dec. 2013; and particularly National Center for Educational Statistics, *National Study of Post-Secondary Faculty* (Washington, 2004).

7
STUDENTS AND THEIR SERVICES

Universities are more than administrations and faculty with a surrounding chorus of boards, governments, philanthropists and chirping critics. They are also students, and ultimately their success depends on this segment above all. There's a risk, in the chapters that preceded, of seeing students mainly as passive vessel to be better filled by more good teaching and better protected by a budget stabilization that will reduce continued pressure on their tuitions and their wallets. They are, of course, much more active participants than this. Exploring student issues more directly, in the current chapter, will focus on the student role in the key priorities of higher education—their responsibilities toward the goals of success and quality, their advice on a number of budget issues, but also the additional services many of them seem to require.

One of the several problems with current critiques of higher education, and some of the "disruptive" remedies proposed, is a considerable ignorance or neglect when it comes to understanding what contemporary students are all about—and therefore what key aspects of higher education must build upon. Students vary, of course, and they are changing, and there is always room for debate. However, American universities and their faculties and particularly their specialized staffs actually know quite a bit about students and what they seem to need for success, and approaches that neglect this knowledge may prove seriously misleading. This chapter seeks to address this issue directly.

More specific topics involve the student role in learning and some current concerns about goals and work habits, as well as whether students should be encouraged to play a more active role in university governance than is currently the case and whether this would relate positively to academic achievement. We then turn to the various components of the contemporary student population, with attention above all to the obvious changes in composition—challenging but potentially exciting—and also to some special student categories that require assessment in relation to larger priorities. Next, and in clear relationship to the first two subjects, the chapter deals with student life, its role in student learning but also its budget impact, where some crucial debates must be pursued. Finally, by way of summary, we talk about some of the pressing policy issues around costs outside the classroom—what student fees should be covering, and whether there are possible savings in the larger category of services and amenities. Budget issues loom large here, but there are also questions about the role of higher education in addressing inequalities—again, both old and new—in the student groups we address.

Contemporary students are sometimes measured against a dubious nostalgia for the past. There are current changes in interests and composition that do raise several questions that must be confronted, but students were not clearly better in the past than they are now (particularly when the sheer expansion of the student population is taken into account). To be sure, what used to be acceptable gentlemen's C's—representing some real study but not too much—have been inflated a bit, but the student negotiating for an acceptable but not top grade in not a new animal. I always vowed not to succumb, in later age, to the fashionable pastime of bemoaning the younger generation, and I certainly don't propose to do this here; it would not be accurate, either, concerning contemporary data or a realistic picture of the many foibles of students past.

We also need a more balanced picture of student-life activities. These must not be dismissed in terms of climbing walls or political correctness—despite the delight of shallow contemporary critics. Climbing walls may be new, but universities have long tried to organize recreational opportunities for students—witness the now-depopulated squash courts of a past generation. More importantly, student-life ventures are not organized primarily around the student as consumer. Too many observers of higher education—even many faculty—simply ignore a range of vital activities, from learning beyond the classroom to support for students with problems.

There are policy questions that deserve debate; this is not a defensive chapter, any more than those that preceded. But contemporary studenthood wins at least its share of confusion and inadequate information. Symbols like climbing walls turn out to be far less important than several more basic problems—some new, some ongoing—that reach farther into American society than many realize. As with administrations and faculties, we need a better sense of what current students are all about and where we should be discussing some fresh options.

The images abound. The student as consumer—without doubt, some accuracy for this category. Students as accumulations of minorities, including undocumented dreamers but now also a growing number of veterans. Students as customers (they are this in part, deserving good service; unlike conventional customers, they are not always right, so we need something beyond this label). The helicoptered student—again, some reality here. But also the student as disoriented first generation—again, reality here as well. Students, obviously, are a lot of things, and their collective complexities will be increasing in the future.

Students' Share in Success

Some blasts against contemporary higher education focus unduly on the input aspects; people ask what are administrations and faculty doing, on an apparent assumption that if they would get their act together greater student achievement would automatically follow. We have already discussed obligations toward more participatory classrooms, greater commitment to more varied and interesting learning materials, even the need to convince students that instructors care about them. There is a reciprocal obligation as well; all the gyrations in the world won't matter if students choose to be idle, passive or disorganized, and while faculty must actively strive to counter these conditions, they are not solo performers. The whole concept of the flipped classroom assumes student preparation and engagement.

There are reasons to worry about these qualities, even when faculty are doing many of the right things. Of all the varied criticisms in *Adrift,* the one that concerned me the most was the claim that contemporary students are putting less time into their studies outside the classroom. Of course, the data are hardly massive for the deterioration claim, and some authorities contend that they do not capture the ways current students actually study (for example, group work), but several surveys bolster the claim, including the recurrent National Survey of Student Engagement. Institutions vary, and those who attract more academically qualified students not surprisingly see more study investment than others—whether by cause or effect or both. Individual institutions escape the trend at least briefly when they improve the qualifications of entering students (as judged particularly by high school GPA, the best predictive measure because it reflects established habits as well as aptitudes). Even in cases like this, the recorded effort usually falls short of faculty expectations. The problem may be widespread; many of the bellwether public flagships display surprisingly meager average study times.[1]

There are other troubling indicators. Recent studies of percentage of reading achieved, as in general psychology classes, find that only about a quarter of all students claim to have done all the assignments. This may reflect deteriorating reading skills. It undoubtedly responds to textbook costs, which have driven some students to shortcuts. It certainly mirrors faculty lectures in some cases; when faculty cover the same materials as the assignments, students quickly figure out that selective reading, or little at all, will suffice. Whatever the combination of factors, there is a problem, possibly a growing one.

Again, we are not ascribing academic sainthood to generations past. Nor are we ignoring the many splendid undergraduates we have today: students who work hard and display initiative and imagination offer clear rewards for effective teaching. But the averages, even if not in fact novel, are troubling. A number of contemporary factors may be involved, some working in combination, others applying to particular clusters amid the student population.

Entitlement. Some students unquestionably think that even a modest amount of effort deserves a clear reward, and possibly this category has been growing. High school grade inflation—including the schools that now bless as many as 16 valedictorians in a single class—convince many students that they are more meritorious than college faculty may adjudge. Remember, American secondary school students score best in international tests in one clear category: expectations that they will do better on tests than they actually manage. Fond parents, the national obsession with self-esteem—there are several reasons that students may decide that a small amount of work should clearly be crowned with a passing grade or better. The worst offenders are rare, but some degree of infection may well touch a larger number.

Work demands. Many undergraduates now work a lot at jobs on and off campus, and obviously the pressures on tuitions have expanded the motivations involved, at least in regions where opportunities are available. Some work relates to professional training; some actually helps students organize their time toward more focused and effective studying. Research suggests that about 15 hours of work a week actually helps academic focus, though more is deleterious. There is no question that many students struggle with the work-study balance. In some cases, they may be trying to earn more than college requires because of personal consumer proclivities or family needs. However, there is a problem here that often goes beyond student capacities to resolve, another compelling reason to seek greater budget stability in higher ed.

Consumerism and the ubiquitous media. Student consumer needs are unquestionably greater with each generation; just take a look at the amount of things students trundle into their dorm rooms. Some items relate to study, but many do not. Students regularly feel the need to watch to some top TV shows; other media opportunities include Netflix binge watching, video gaming, in many cases sporting events, and almost always music. Some of these interests are compatible with at least a gesture at studying; others compete directly. Most important is the amount of time now devoted to social media, to keeping in touch, often with communities formed before coming to college—as with former high school classmates. Again, let's keep perspective: in earlier generations, we bemoaned the students who were constantly on the telephone (I won't try to go farther back than this). Some media links actually do involve study and can be encouraged in that direction, but there is competition for time and attention, and academic work may suffer on balance. Whether that most famous distraction—partying—has gone up or not is harder to judge. We have relatively more modern concerns about binge drinking and some drugs (though these last have declined on campus), but it is remarkable how many of the party schools of a generation back maintain their position today (including some public flagships, though I won't name names). Overall, student consumer distractions vary greatly with the individual, as has long been the case. The impact on budgets—see below—may be greater than the intrusions on study time. But there is a challenge.

> **Student Housing**
>
> One area where growing student consumerism shows clearly highlights the steady upgrade of housing amenities. Dorm rooms in new or renovated facilities are unquestionably larger and fancier than in the past, often rivaling singles' apartment complexes. Some of this essential to accommodate the growing array of necessities, such as computers (not to mention gaming equipment or high definition TVs)—a far cry from when my dorm room needed only space for my quill and inkwell—but much of the upgrade simply reflects new expectations of comfort; particularly interesting is the growing insistence on in-suite if not private bathrooms. Note that American students are not alone responsible. Their parents are often fussier about dorm splendor than they are, and certain categories of international students are also surprisingly demanding. It all adds up to an interesting component in contemporary higher education.[2]
>
> I have no sense that the result contributes to academic performance one way or another, except to the extent that adequate computer space factors in, though plusher surroundings may—all things being equal—promote retention; nationally, rates among residential students are higher than the overall average. Arguably, nicer dorm rooms might reduce roommate tensions, which would be a positive, though I have seen no evidence on this; digitized compatibility protocols probably are more effective than relative luxury in any event. What the dorm trends do signal is an additional set of burdens on student budget and additional differentiations between students who can afford this choice (or think they can) and those who cannot—and these consequences flow back into divisions in the contemporary student body and the whole issue of budget priorities. Dorm costs, year to year, do not usually increase faster than inflation, but when new facilities are added, they definitely affect student budgets and debts; while institutional decisions contribute, so do the preferences of students and their families.

Disorganization. The student-life folks and advisors who deal with students most frequently on a daily basis contend that inadequate study time is much less a problem than poor use of time. They argue that many students, including lots of first-generations, believe they are working very hard, and while they may exaggerate a bit, it is ineffectiveness more than distortion that ends up holding them back. In some cases, parents have spent 18 years organizing their kids in the best helicopter fashion so that the students have never had to make serious decisions about time allocation on their own; these include the contemporary parents who ask university personnel at orientation who will be taking over the task of individually monitoring their children or those who talk with residence advisors about making sure their children simply wake up to go to class. In other instances, it's the schools that have done the job, whether they actually assigned much work or not; high school assignments are doled out in such detailed batches that again no serious time management is required. College has always been a leap in terms of time responsibility, at least in the United States. Again, many students manage the transition just fine (one of the advantages of AP programs is less what they have taught and more what they have fostered in terms of budgeting skills), but for many students, at least for a crucial initial year or two (the point at which some may decide simply to give up), the time management problem is acute.[3]

So? Whatever the combination of factors, and whether or not study time has actually deteriorated, colleges face some uphill climbs. This is why the need for imaginative and committed teaching is so compelling; this is why, as discussed below, a range of student services, and probably an enhanced range, is essential as well (with cost implications attached). Courses in time management, prosaic and annoying as they may seem, may require even further attention, for example, for first-years and often transfer students alike.

However, with all the apparatus available and desirable, a student responsibility remains. At the risk of fogeyism, faculty and administrative staffs need to emphasize this at the outset—at orientations and initial class sessions, along with our desire to make it clear that college, and even learning, can be fun and that we are all rooting for student success. Students should be presented with a sober balance sheet that demonstrates the institutional commitment to the priority of student achievement and the various measures, old and new, established to this end but that also insists on the irreducible student component that attaches as well.

A leadership element? One final factor deserves consideration in this context: if we gave students a greater role in academic governance, would this help address the need to make some students better aware of their responsibilities to their own success?

There's no question, again, that students are capable of impressive initiatives largely on their own; my university, like many others, has seen a host of student projects in recent years, ranging from policy discussion groups to cybersecurity technologies to philanthropic outreach. There's no question as well, however, that since the 1960s most American universities—in contrast to many European counterparts—have largely left students out of the academic governance arena. In general, contemporary American society has been much better at figuring out ways to protect and shelter (at least middle-class) children than at giving them new responsibilities. Thus, the attempts to provide students fuller representation on policy committees, briefly ventured during the historic student protest movement, largely died off after 1973, whereas they continued strong across the Atlantic (in the Bologna group, for example, 10–20% of university committee slots are filled by students).[4]

To be sure, American institutions have active student governments with enthusiastic meetings. They offer a growing array of leadership training opportunities.

Many also have student advisory boards for presidents or provosts and sometimes token, voteless and usually fairly silent, student reps on trustee boards. The students involved provide vital advice about campus activities, safety issues, food complaints (a hardy perennial)—but they rarely know or voice much about academics directly. Arguably, they lack the time to really become versed in teaching and research issues, which are by definition a bit more remote than parking or intramural sports; many institutions have had the experience of naming student reps to academic committees who rarely showed up or remained quiet if they did. Further, a four-year or so career may make it hard to get up to speed, even where there is student interest. Finding really representative students is another challenge: student leadership groups on many campuses are disproportionately filled with political science majors, and coaxing out the engineering or arts students is not easy. Further, many of the ablest leaders are quickly overcommitted to a variety of activities along with their own studies, complicating any effort to expand students' roles.

There may nevertheless be some untapped opportunity here, in relation to the larger issue of student commitment. My university had rare but splendid results from student inclusion on a general education planning committee, an undergraduate research initiative and a presidential search; the individuals involved were so knowledgeable and dedicated that many did not even know they were students. Should we renew an experiment with extending the practice, even or perhaps particularly at large state schools, with more concerted effort to get students involved, say, in departmental or college curriculum committees? At the very least, a number of institutions would do well to figure out ways to talk with students more directly and openly about the student responsibility component. It would be another genuine means of showing commitment, and we might learn more than we expect. Time management and devotion to study are prosaic topics—not nearly as jazzy as the latest online extravaganza or student entrepreneurship—but they warrant both serious thought and additional experimentation. Further advice from students might really help.

Certainly, any assistance more involved student leaders can provide on how both to communicate with and gain input from students more generally would be a huge boost in evaluating educational programs and improving awareness of a variety of opportunities, though this is a tough assignment. Student willingness to respond to (doubtless unduly frequent) polls declines steadily, as does their diligence in reading email. A greater sense of representation might improve this situation; it certainly wouldn't hurt.

Who the Students Are and Are Becoming

Overall patterns. Significant changes in the student mix have been a recurrent feature of American higher education, and many previous shifts have been managed successfully. A recent example, still working through, involves the surge of women into clear numerical preponderance. This has had some impact on student services and related policies; on the more purely academic side, it has challenged some of the STEM fields to recruit and retain more successfully, but it has not disturbed the basic academic enterprise. On another front, for some years now most colleges have been adjusting to the need to accept substantial Advanced Placement credits from entering students, another innovation that alters the presumably classic first year; while some issues have resulted, the academic roof has not caved in.

Shifts that are currently in the works—some, such as the rise in average student age actually began a couple of decades ago—may demand greater attention. Certainly, in combination with the prospective lack of growth in the conventional age group, they will require a growing number of institutions to evaluate their commitment to greater inclusiveness. The classic game—still possible during the early 2000s—of expanding the student body while steadily improving SAT and ACT score and high school GPAs will become more difficult for quite a while. Even some of the public flagships, where minority students still are clearly in the minority, will have to reconsider their mix.

Here's what's happening: according to the Association of American Colleges and Universities, 73% of all undergraduates are now "nontraditional" students. They are older than 23; 47% of students enrolled in American higher education are in fact over 25 (in 1970, the figure was 28%) and/or they are various kinds of non-Caucasian, as the minorities move to become the majority on campuses in advance of the nation as a whole. Particularly important is the rapid surge of Hispanic students, who are now attending college at the same rate as the population as a whole. Hispanic student enrollment increased to 16% of the total by 2011 and continues to mount. Directly attached to these changes, a growing segment of undergraduates are "first-gens"—first in their families to attend college. In 2013–14, about 36% of all entering first-years in public institutions fell in this category; obviously, the rate was even higher at some institutions.[5]

These are truly encouraging trends, giving the lie to some of the baldest criticisms about American higher education's inability to respond to contemporary social change, American colleges and universities are creating mobility opportunities for many individuals, and are helping to insure a productive labor force and citizenry for society at large. There are imperfections. Access wars against other American trends that are increasing social and economic inequalities, and there is no assurance that higher education will ever be able fully to square the circle. However, current developments at least point in promising directions.

The same developments also, of course, require adjustments if both students and institutions are to succeed in these changing circumstances. The shifting age structure of the student body links directly to the rise of "swirl," both as cause and effect—the growing pattern for many students of moving among several institutions between matriculation and graduation. A 2012 report from the National Clearinghouse Research Center suggests that a third of all undergraduates are now ultimately taking courses at two to four institutions, plus in some cases additional online offerings, before graduating. Their patterns obviously complicate assessments of retention and graduation rates—we noted their contribution to problems in American rating systems in Chapter 2—but more to the point is the challenge these peregrinations pose to students themselves and to the various institutions that greet them along the way.[6]

For their part, first-generation students have their own characteristics, beginning with the obvious fact of less personal and family comfort with aspects of college life. They are less likely than the average student to seek on-campus housing, for both financial and cultural reasons. Without compensatory effort, their retention rates will be lower than average. Latino students, as a group, are likely to seek a campus relatively close to home: again, cost and culture combine. They, and many other so-called minority students, will prefer professional over liberal arts majors more than is the case with students in general. These kinds of characteristics may fade over time. For the moment, however, they invite awareness and constructive reaction, lest promising trends yield less positive results than should be the case.[7]

Further changes may be in the works. A number of state governments for some time have been pushing dual enrollment programs in the high schools to encourage greater college participation while cutting costs. Students take community college courses combined with junior and senior year offerings so that they can enter college with a substantial set of credits under their belts; in theory, in fact, some could graduate simultaneously with high school and Associates degrees, seeking direct entry into the third year of college. There are intriguing issues here both for actual academic readiness and for college-level social maturity (whatever that is)—again, a flexibility test for higher education, at least in principle.[8]

There is no need to exaggerate. Some possible changes may turn out to be less substantial in fact than in potential. At least until very recently, liberal arts numbers have still been rising, despite the greater proportionate growth of professional majors. Advanced Placement experience suggests that many students may enter college with a number of credits in hand but will choose to stay for a full four years anyway simply to take advantage of other college opportunities. Current patterns even cast some doubt on some of the most obvious swirl possibilities. Though community colleges are cheaper, the fact that their enrollments have been declining to the benefit of direct entry into four-year institutions suggests that students are not necessarily seeking the greatest short-run savings. Obviously, federal moves to promote the two-year option could change this, but—for the moment—challenges are less great on this front than might have been expected.

Still, developments already in process, and possible acceleration in the future, have some obvious implications for the higher education enterprise.

Inclusiveness. Greater inclusiveness is happening, but it needs fuller recognition as well as appropriate support. As indicated, the eager availability of some of the new student aspirants, and the decline of birth rates in the white middle class, require some explicit decisions on the part of university leaders.

First-generation students may be fully as talented as college entrants in the past, but the idea of steadily pushing up test scores and other on-paper attributes—directly encouraged by the *US News* rewards for schools with massive application numbers but low acceptance rates—must be rethought. The principle of balance obviously applies. It is no service to students to admit the obviously unqualified for any reason—despite some of the current fiscal dilemmas that press for adjustments simply to keep revenues up. The notion of taking pride in successfully educating students from a variety of backgrounds and with some range of entrance qualifications is hardly a contemporary invention. Current patterns nevertheless suggest the importance of defining and highlighting inclusiveness over exclusivity, and taking the necessary steps to make this approach is beneficial to all concerned. Assuming adequate minima, there is far more glory is dealing with students who can take advantage of a good education, even if they lack maximum glitter on entry, than with trying to exclude as many as possible. Rankings, in this instance, clearly be damned.

Flexibility plus. More adult students and more diversity in points of entry obviously place a premium on an institution's willingness to be nimble. Many public and some private colleges already have fairly detailed arrangements with relevant community colleges. Articulation agreements spell out what students must do to be assured of entry into the four-year institution after an Associate's degree and in principle establish clear pathways for fulfillment of first- and second-year requirements. We need more of these arrangements to minimize wasted time for transfer students, and we need to expand the principle. Oregon State, for example, has seized the lead, now with several community colleges, in allowing students to take courses at a number of participant institutions simultaneously, benefiting as well from eligibility for financial aid programs.[9] Northern Virginia Community College has established a Pathways program for high school juniors, providing college advice and some college courses during the final two years of high school, with entry assured for community college completion (assuming a grade point minimum) and then in turn to the four-year institution after the Associate's degree. Many institutions are also experimenting with competency credits for adult students and with various responses to students who bring in online work (including some of the MOOCs, where assurance of results is provided). These kinds of adjustments are both vital and inevitable, even as they greatly increase the varieties of the undergraduate experience and place undeniable burdens on both registrar and admissions offices (with some expenses attached).

The arrangements must include assessment and advising as well as responsive flexibility, hence the need for flexibility plus. Institutions that dive into the variety pool should not only plan the standard evaluation arrangements for individual students but should invest in some group measurements. Even established articulation arrangements with community colleges need recurrent review under two criteria: whether they are compatible with smooth student transitions to the four-year school and whether the students collectively are performing adequately in terms of grades and retention. Evaluations of this sort are even more essential for some of the newer arrangements. We need to be as sure as possible that some of the novel preparation patterns are actually serving the students adequately, in terms of their performance and persistence after entry. We certainly need to provide key groups—like some of the adult categories, including veterans—with accessible and relevant guidance to make sure they don't get lost in the larger system and to assure opportunities to discuss any compensatory measures that may prove necessary. Again, there are cost implications here that must not be ignored. The key point is to make sure that institutions keep careful tabs both on the growing range of student categories and on the track record of the systems that generate this range.

Group cohesion. While some minority groups experience below-average retention and completion rates—reflecting differences in preparation, the pressures of costs, and in some cases family involvement—there are a number of individual institutions that stand as exceptions, where Latino and African American records match student levels overall. Obviously, given growing student diversity, we need ample discussion of best practices in this area. Without pretending an exact science, one factor stands out, along with general attention to financial aid resources and appropriate advising and tutoring services for students regardless of origin. Minority students prosper particularly when they can identify formal or informal support groups with colleagues sharing similar experiences; this is where advice can be most relevant and opportunities to see successful advancement most encouraging. Obviously, interactions with other types of students will be a vital part of the educational experience as well, but group identity matters. The same point seems to hold true for first-generation students as a category, where the opportunity to share specific problems and adaptations is particularly meaningful. Institutions and individual student initiatives ideally can combine to create this kind of supportive environment.

Online. The changing nature of the student body raises some intriguing complexities concerning online offerings. On the one hand, as some of the eager providers of online courses point out, distance learning is an obvious response to the need for greater flexibility. It can meet some of the locational needs reflected in student swirl: online may thus be particularly beneficial for various kinds of adult students who need to be able to move from place to place or who want some relevant coursework prior to formally resuming a college career. On the other hand, and admitting all sorts of individual variations, an online diet is probably not the best response for first-gen's as a category, at least for the moment. These are undergraduates who often need more individual and personal attention, not less. Their prior experience with online courses is often limited; in some cases, they actually do not have easy access to off-campus facilities that make online possible in the first place. Poor online retention rates can be exacerbated for this category. Caution in promoting online offerings too enthusiastically and ongoing assessment of experiences that do accrue are both essential to avoid a mindless connection between student change and counterproductive shifts in delivery systems. What online offerings can do for students with more established learning patterns, at the higher ed level, may not extend easily to the rising crop of freshmen and sophomores.

The mission of public higher education—not brand new but increasingly clear—must center on taking able students from a variety of backgrounds—not simplified toward artificial exclusivity—and providing an education that serves them well and adds clear value. This is where the priority of student success really counts and where academic and support operations must combine to promote steady improvements in results. The process is far more interesting than trying to maximize the number of applications than can be rejected, and it should anchor an institution's pride in its educational achievement.

Special Student Categories

A final element in recruitment and retention policies relates to the larger undergraduate population trends but requires a discrete set of policy decisions—with another set of budget implications attached. The issue is straightforward: how many distinct student categories should an institution try to maintain when some special costs are attached? Student athletes and honors groups loom largest here, but a few other clusters warrant attention as well. When budget times were good, and tuition pressures intruded less fiercely, we could conveniently avoid some of the implicit decisions that had been made about particular programs; now, at least many institutions simply must confront some choices.

The student athlete. A recent proposal in one state, to limit student fee contributions to athletic programs to no more than 50% of the total, puts this particular category into sharp relief. The proposal is well intentioned, though it probably will not work even if enacted because most of the universities involved would quietly take funds from another bucket, with no real relief resulting. But the principle is interesting. Student fees vary a lot, but they are often 25–30% as high as tuitions and sometimes more; of course, it's the combination of charges, not the separate categories, that really matters to the student-consumer and her family. At some schools, up to 72% of the total student fee budget goes to intercollegiate athletics—a whopping figure by any standard.

Athletic budgets involve coaches and personnel, equipment, and travel costs as well as scholarships to the student athletes themselves. A handful of schools, mainly state flagships or other institutions often located at some distance from big-city entertainment facilities, easily cover the costs through a combination of football/basketball earnings and philanthropy. Even here, one wonders if more of the earnings could contribute to the institution more broadly, and less to coaches' pockets, and whether philanthropy might be more widely targeted if the athletic program were better balanced. Still, this special category has to be noted. For most schools, however, there are no big football earnings, and athletic programs in general simply cost money; the burden includes many of the athletic scholarships involved—with students in general, who are rarely if ever asked directly about their wishes, bearing a considerable amount of the freight. Some sports everywhere—tennis, soccer, and so on—invariably lose money. Finally, this whole combination may become more burdensome than ever, from a student fee standpoint, with current proposals to hike the pay to student athletes, at least in the glory sports.

So it is legitimate to ask, as we confront the priority of budget and tuition stability, should we recalibrate? Some faculty senates are appropriately waking up to ask questions about costs, attendance at events, and the contributions of many if not all sports to the campus overall. Several universities, led by places like Kent State, are reviewing whole programs, with recent edicts about increased pay and stipends for student athletes in mind. The questions will surely multiply, again outside the Big Five conferences particularly. At the same time, at least for institutions with football, flexibilities are limited by NCAA and federal mandates concerning funding that must be reserved for female student athletes and concerning the sheer number of nonfootball sports required.

The sports most vulnerable to the knife, because of their costs but low spectator draw, are appealing in many ways, depending on taste; soccer, after all, should loom larger in a globalized world. Several sports like track help attract talented minority students; many sports play a key role in drawing and sustaining both racial diversity and truly talented individuals of various backgrounds, people whose abilities, personal organizational skills and often academic chops make them real contributors to the campus as a whole and potential leaders in the wider world as alumni. In many places—though aided, it must be noted, by careful tutoring setups that might be the envy of students in general—student athletes do better in grade point and graduation rates than the student body as a whole. One hesitates, for several reasons besides sheer inertia, to bring the whole house down.

However, a more critical discussion is becoming unavoidable as incompatible forces converge at least outside the Big Five conferences. Probably an additional set of schools must decide simply on cutting the number of sports, as places like the University of Maryland already have done. Discussions should also reconsider conference realignments, at least for most sports, in order to reduce now often ridiculous travel costs (and travel time, an obvious burden on the student part of the student-athlete). A number of topics need to be reopened.

Honors programs. Here's a category that has been less in the news of late. It's not novel or innovative; many of the schools that develop the most eye-catching strategic plans, filled to the brim with bold departures, may not mention honors at all. A little secret: to make matters worse for a disruptive agenda, most honors students actually want a fairly conventional education at least in terms of classroom involvements, disdaining online offerings and seeking real interaction with talented teacher-researchers.[10]

Honors comes in for inspection not only for traditionalism—which may be a real strength; remember the quality priority—but more obviously because of costs. Honors students, like talented athletes, are competed for. Their scores and high school performance make them desirable catches for many institutions, so, to a point, like the athletes, they need to be bought. Institutions with honors programs invariably offer a category of merit scholarships regardless of need, which means they are using someone's money—if not student fees, at least philanthropy or bookstore earnings or something that might go to other purposes—for some candidates whose families actually could afford to pay more. Then, like the athletes to a point, they are also getting some special treatment once they arrive, with a distinct set of usually fairly small classes, some special staffing, often some special housing—these are able students but in many cases surprisingly high maintenance.

It's no surprise that, as with athletics, though usually from different critics, honors arrangements come under attack. There's a valid and consistent line of reasoning that blasts any use of financial aid for purposes other than meeting need. Given student debts and the social gaps that beset us, how can we throw money away on students who don't strictly require it? Add the fact that one reason behind honors programs involves doing better in *US News'* eyes by boasting at least one group with high scores and clear selectivity—an ignoble motive—and it's tempting to join with the critical chorus.

Yet, as with the athletes, let's admit a problem but not go too fast. Honors students do contribute to quality. They do help set standards in areas like undergraduate research. They do provide student leadership for some of the more interdisciplinary combinations of study. Properly organized—and honors programs are increasingly moving away from isolation into an array of campus and community contributions—they provide academic colleagueship for other types of students, working directly, for example, with international students to mutual benefit. Again, in well-conducted programs, they contribute in their own way to accessibility. Good honors systems can now reach out not only to first-year students with diverse backgrounds but can also establish linkage programs for qualified transfer students, adding strength to that vital operation. They can help identify high student performance even after admission, again providing student colleagueship in ways that improve retention and highlight academic achievement more generally.

Review. Current circumstances unquestionably call for sober attention to some of the special student categories that command special costs. Honors and athletes are the most obvious groups, but students recruited for orchestra slots have some of the same features; and we undoubtedly spend more in the care and feeding of student leaders than we do on students in general. Subsidies for study abroad is another special category at some institutions. Review should not, in my opinion, lead to some costs-only standard that blithely dispenses with the programs in question. The idea of basing all the allocations to students on demonstrated financial need is compelling but, in the end, too narrow. It may be that, to meet the budget priority, we need some scaling back—the discussion must occur. There is certainly every reason to seek that holy grail—"other sources of funds"—for the special student categories, rather than directly burdening student fees and tuitions. It is also vitally important to assess campus benefit: how much does the program involved contribute to students more generally by bringing additional intellectual or global stimulation and by building a relevant sense of community? Are there ways to adjust the program toward greater results in these areas? Here is an intriguing, complex policy area that merits recurrent assessment in light of higher education's basic priorities.

Student Services

Substantial staffs at most universities, particularly the big publics, provide an array of services to the student body, especially at the undergraduate level, that fall between sheer upkeep arrangements—providing food—and academic life. They are variously organized. Sometimes, most if not all activities fall under a single vice president who reports either directly to the president or to the provost. In other cases, certain services, such as advising, are separated out in terms of reporting structure. Variations matter little so long as there is some overall coordination—after all, services to students should interrelate—and, crucially, a clear link, formal as well as informal, to the academic operation.

The services do cost money. Most student-life operations run on funding that comes from a mixture of student fees and revenues from auxiliary enterprises (such as housing or bookstores), with some special, usually optional, fees attached for particular activities like family weekends. They are a very definite part of the overall budget structure, and this affects students as well as the institutional bottom line.

Further, the costs have been increasing. Between 2002 and 2012, expenditures on student life broadly construed have been growing between 2–5% annually, more rapidly than any other category except, in some cases, adjunct faculty. The result represents a substantial component of that bugaboo, administrative costs. It also invites assessment as we heighten the focus on core priorities.

Partly because of in-between status, partly because of the sheer variety of operations, but partly now because of the critical climate and budget concerns, student-life operations risk some mixture of neglect and attack. They do include activities like climbing walls, designed in part to entertain students and to attract new applicants to the university on grounds of consumer quality of life rather than academics per se. (There are, at this writing, 269 climbing walls at American universities, with the Lone Star State leading all states for better or worse and introducing another feature, explicit competitions for Highest Wall.[11]) Student-life operations also do help organize groups like African American or Latino or LBGTQ students, therefore running the risk of seeming to cater to political correctness. Their practitioners are not always esteemed by faculty themselves; they usually lack full academic qualifications, usually boasting Masters degrees in the field rather than disciplinary PhDs. They are supposed to be peppy and cheery and/or warm and fuzzy (in contrast to faculty?), and they seem to enjoy sharing activities with students that some faculty—even those talented in outreach in other respects—find beneath them.

It is also true, and fascinating, that American universities have developed a commitment to student-life staffing that is unparalleled in the world. This means, of course, that in principle there are alternatives to our current arrangements that might leave more responsibility for out-of-class life to students and cut costs for the institutions involved.

As with all major aspects of the university, student-life programs merit review. Some probably must be cut somewhat, as part of overall administrative response to budget realities, but some are literally indispensable at something like current levels, partly because of special requirements—unfunded mandates on disabilities for example—but mostly because of their direct contributions to the priorities of student success and of quality properly construed. It's also worth noting that many student-life activities provide work, pay and experience for a range of students themselves as employees—a benefit that does not automatically justify the status quo but should not be neglected. Overall, the whole category unquestionably reflects American culture about what we owe our middle-class children—but that hardly means it's dispensable. Above all, student-life activities also provide an array of functions that invite wider appreciation and more explicit evaluation in terms of higher education's goals.

There are a few obvious dilemmas. Many American universities were established in ways that cried out for some special attention to students; in contrast to the preponderant European or Chinese tradition, lots of schools were set up in the countryside near the farmers (and often the farmers' daughters as potential teachers). Entertainment was sparse, and American schools, even now the urban ones, have worked hard to compensate (a reason, among other things, for the disproportionate attention to spectator sports). Add to this the current generation of students accustomed not only to constant entertainment but, often, to elaborate adult attention, appealing for more, not less, "high touch" from faculty and staff. Some student-life services can still be adjusted; we may need a different calculus of what should be provided undergraduates as opposed to what they should choose to pay for directly (or do without). We should know, going in, that there's an uphill road to prune even some of the entertainment entries, and most of the categories are dead serious. Indeed, in several sectors, some responsible campus leaders are actually urging still more investment, not less.[12]

The Fun Stuff

Debate can start with the most vulnerable category: what student-life folks do to arrange entertainment for students. This is a large rubric. Most campuses organize special entertainment nights. They provide some popular movies. They arrange encouraging breakfasts and snacks during exam weeks or the onset of classes. They distribute endless arrays of T-shirts. They provide fairly elaborate amusements, complete with student as well as professional staff, around orientations. They orchestrate special events such as International Weeks that have some clear educational content but are dominated by costume shows, vendors and dances. At a time when some of us worry that students are not working hard enough, they seem bent on making sure that play options abound. Some activities, to be sure, rely on special charges rather than general budget support—parents' weekends and orientations are cases in point—but they add to educational costs nevertheless, and they can seem almost obligatory.

Should we be doing all this? Are we setting the right tone? Are we using student and family funding for activities that, often, only a minority of students actually participate in? Do we really need to bring big-name concert acts and comedians to campus? Answers will vary, and the questions are legitimate.

But against too facile a budget ax, building a sense of community and a set of enjoyments undoubtedly contributes to student retention. It's impossible to say how much or for how many students, but as a number of campuses have moved to a greater sense of student engagement and higher graduation rates, new investments in student life have clearly played a role. Probably we could safely cut a few expenses here; probably it would be valid to offer a bit more at cost rather than gratuitously reduce obligatory pressures on student wallets, but the category is not as frivolous as it may seem.

Leadership

Facilitating and guiding student leadership is another student-life category that goes way back in the United States but that has unquestionably expanded. Universities devote considerable facility space, and considerable staffing, to encouraging a wide variety of student organizations. They also provide increasing opportunities for student leadership training, on the boundary line between academics and cocurricular enrichment. Under this umbrella, a host of group identities can be fostered and supported, including some of the politically correct operations that do at the same time provide clear benefits to academic success for a variety of minorities. Groups also sustain special recreational interests, community service, policy debates, artistic expressions—the range is truly impressive. In this category, student volunteer leadership unquestionably does most of the work. Could more of this array be left to students themselves? Do we need so much formal advising, for example, around student government? Here, too, are we investing money in activities and leadership experiences that in fact benefit only a minority but derive funds from students whether they participate or not? No easy answers here either. Given the leadership development involved—often from students who did not on admission show clear promise in this direction—and the clear academic importance of group support and identity, this is another category where at most some fine-tuning is called for, not a chopping block.

Health and Fitness

This is a fascinating area that involves no small amount of funding. American (and some other) universities have long sponsored playing fields and indoor recreational outlets, and modernization has clearly expanded the range to include gigantic fitness centers. Staff time is essential to monitor the spaces and to help organize specific activities like intramural sports. Unquestionably, expansion has not only fattened the cost ledger but has reflected growing student consumerism: exercise facilities are a prime attraction for applicants and a clear area of admissions competition—perhaps more than the far more expensive intercollegiate sports, that actually have less to do with application rates than many imagine.

Should this be scaled back? Should interested students bring their own ladders so we can tear down the climbing walls? Again, ample room for debate. But against too much puritanical zeal: basic commitments here, to the *mens sana in corpore sano* pairing, are not new at all—we've always wanted students to have a chance to take care of their bodies. Given current health concerns about child and youth obesity, it might be really foolish to make exercise opportunities harder or more directly expensive to come by. In fact there's a move afoot, for better or worse, actually to expand university commitments in this general area. Linked to the Gallup Organization, bent on selling evaluation services, several universities, including Purdue and George Mason, are now beginning to call themselves well-being centers. The label goes beyond fitness, but investments in exercise and better (and more expensive) diets as well as a variety of self-assessment and advice services figure strongly. The venture is too new to evaluate fully, particularly in terms of degree of student interest (staff may turn out to be more engaged, for the programs are institution-wide). More than with fun or even leadership, this intriguing category is now raising questions in both directions: are there things to cut? Are there additional goals to fund? Should students be left more to their own devices or more actively shepherded toward better physical and mental health and habits?[13]

Placement and Internships

The questions we can legitimately be discussing—with active but hopefully broadly representative student participation; not just the campus eager beavers—about fun and games begin to drop off when we talk about helping students with job seeking and what we fondly call experiential learning. Staff investments here are essential. To be sure, we might wish that some students would take more initiative in learning how to prepare effective résumés and organize employer contacts; we may now be compensating for some of the parental overinvolvement that goes into college applications in the first place and leaves student insufficiently able to fend for themselves. However, the basic category is inescapable. Institutions can and should help students by organizing job fairs that bring employers to campuses as no individual student effort could manage. They can and should increasingly be helping to arrange internship opportunities. Individual academic units can offer contributions here as well—the art history links to museum experiences, for example—but an institutional effort is fundamental. At least in the foreseeable future, and particularly for some of the crucial disciplines that do not surge into job slots as readily as others, more effort, not less, is essential.

Mental Health and Disabilities

Essential student-life services have long been devoted to assisting students with special needs as a fundamental contribution both to accessibility and to improving conditions for academic and personal success for a considerable body of undergraduates. Demands in this area have been quietly but inexorably soaring over recent years—one of the many ways that contemporary American colleges and universities touch some unexpected rough spots in American society more generally. Certain kinds of mental health issues have been growing among young people; better treatments allow some youth to attend college whose problems once would have been insuperable, and greater awareness increases reporting rates. It's a potent combination, and the result constitutes one of the leading reasons student-life staffs have been growing rapidly. A 2015 *Inside Higher Ed* study indeed argued directly that the emotional health of American undergraduates was at an all-time low—one of the reasons students truly believe they are working extremely hard, to the detriment of social contacts, whatever the objective reality may be.

Several specifics are involved. Federal definitions of disability, and requirements on universities to accommodate, have been expanding with some unexpected results (should a school with a branch abroad be required to set up services for an individual hearing impaired student?) Eleven percent of all American undergraduates now officially report some disability. How should colleges be adjusting to the growing number of students with food allergies? What about the rising rates—57% increase in recent years—in Autism Spectrum Disorders in American youth and the growing number who show up on campus offering potential problems both to themselves and to classes and classmates, requiring special support to integrate successfully in courses and residence halls alike? (Reports of occasional disruptive classroom behaviors have been going up.) On some specific campuses with particularly good maintenance options, Autism Spectrum rates have grown several hundred percent just since 2010, from less than ten to nearly a hundred. What about the growing rate of depression among students—from 10% to 15% of the total since 2000—along with recognition that many other depressives are not formally tallied? Here both better diagnoses and, surely, some real increase in the problem combine. What about the massive increase of the number of students entering college with prescriptions for some psychotropic mediation, from 1.4% of the undergraduate population in 1987 to 3.9% already in 1996 and far more since? Here is a huge improvement in college access, based on more effective treatments, but a huge challenge for the students involved and for student-life staffs, amid the various pressures of college life—including financial worries and, sometimes, new drinking habits—along with the absence of more familiar adult supervision over behavior in general and medication in particular.[14]

The cumulative impacts of these trends are daunting. More students seek counseling services, with often whopping annual growth rates in appointments involved. Some institutions report a 20% surge in counseling appointments just since 2009, even when total student numbers have not increased at all; crisis interventions, including those involving students with suicidal thoughts, have risen even more substantially. More faculty need some training in how to identify and assist troubled students; rates of third-party consultations about seemingly troubled students have risen particularly rapidly. Overall, thanks to the expansion of counseling, more students can make the grade even with some impairments—contributing directly to the overall priority of student success—but they need the additional help. Add in the needs of some other special but vital groups—the rise in the military veteran population, with particular requirements for advising and support, is the most obvious recent development—and the pressures on the student-life category broadly construed become almost self-evident.

Suicide: A Standoff

Student suicides sit high on the list of campus tragedies. They constitute the second largest cause of student deaths after car accidents—well ahead of homicides that, for youth as a whole, loom larger in the United States. About 1,100 students kill themselves each year nationwide, or .07% of the relevant population (with Caucasian rates noticeably above those of key minorities). Understandable concern about the problem increasingly preoccupies student-life personnel, including dorm counselors, and spills over into faculty awareness of "students of concern."

There are some positives. Student suicides are 50% lower than suicides for the age group as a whole, which races against stereotypes about college stress. The rate has not worsened since the 1980s—though it also has not improved, even as the overall national suicide incidence has declined. Actual suicides take place against a backdrop in which 18% of all undergraduates say they have seriously contemplated suicide at least once in their lives. Overall, it is hard to avoid the conclusion that the problem could be much worse and that the increasing skill and range of student-life services have made a positive contribution in one of the darker aspects of middle-class life in the United States.[15]

The Cocurricular

This is the most amorphous student-life category but arguably the most important beyond crisis interventions. It embraces some elements already discussed, such as contributions to internships. It assumes a deep connection between staff members, increasingly expert in their fields and normally more knowledgeable about students than most faculty are, and the teaching corps. It assumes as well a substantial connection between what students learn in class and what they learn outside. It reflects, finally, an undeniable recent change in the self-definition of student-life professionals toward a more sweeping commitment to student success and the orchestration of all available resources.

Through advising, day-to-day contacts and programming, student-life staff hope to help students mediate between their activities and university rules and regulations so they do not get lost or needlessly entangled. They want to encourage learning experiences that bridge between class and what we used to call the extracurricular: for example, a global emphasis may combine some course requirements with internship work for an international NGO or formal interactions with international students. They want to encourage self-regulation with activities—even formal "badges"—that give students recognition for various measurable achievements. Along with faculty, they want to be able to reach out to students, not depending on notorious student recalcitrance to show up on their own, and, again with faculty, they want to mentor. They see their efforts as fundamental to effective student learning, retention and success, and there's a wealth of evidence to back them up. Student-life leadership would admit the tension involved: they're trying to guide students to become more self-directed, but they have a solid argument that this is precisely what many current students need.[16]

Three specifics of the cocurricular are obvious and again increasingly important. Many institutions have found that staff-faculty collaboration around Living/Learning communities in the dorms can be extremely effective around themes like sustainability or leadership and community engagement. Here are opportunities for students to combine classes with activities that additionally provide special opportunities for students to educate each other.

Voluntary or one-credit classes on academic skills or related issues—like financial awareness—are not new but again warrant expansion. Students who volunteer for these courses may be self-selected for greater success, including higher retention, yet the results at least fulfill the prediction.

Above all, advising is essential, a service that students routinely complain about, often underutilize, but clearly require. Faculty have an advising role, formal or informal, as part of constructive contacts outside the classroom. This is particularly true for declared majors in academic programs, but professional advisors are also essential, whether under student-life or academic direction. They will have expertise and, often, a detailed knowledge of requirements that many faculty cannot provide. They can assist with career advice. They can also help students use the increasing array of technological aids to chart their progress toward fulfilling requirements. They serve that large population of students who don't yet know what they will major in or who change their minds—another category vital to ultimate overall student success. Above all, the professional advising crew can help reach out to students when grades, dorm counselors or some other source suggest a difficulty.

Student-life staff tread a fine line between overintervention, when students should be left to work more out for themselves, and appropriate guidance; in this, not surprisingly, they replicate dilemmas of many contemporary parents themselves. There are no easy definitions of boundary lines, no easy decisions about the level of budget investments required. Whatever the disputes around the margins, the direct contribution to university priorities is beyond dispute.

A Final Challenge: The Scorned Commuter

The evolution of the undergraduate student pool, and what we increasingly know about the role of student services, raises a basic question about one other familiar but poorly discussed divide: the relationship between residential and commuting students. There is, of course, an intermediate category, the "resi-muter," who moves out of dorms during college but does not live with family, but this is a very different population from the real commuting group.[17]

Over the past decade, a number of institutions have put a lot of effort into expanding their dormitories and residential student populations, and many of them found an eager audience. More residence halls were essential in growing the out-of-state population with its tuition contributions, and the establishment of a more residential campus also facilitated the development of the many activities and services that link classrooms with wider learning opportunities. The residential student raises some challenges—we have to care about his drinking habits, for example—but there's no question that this kind of student is more identifiable and easier to integrate than the commuting counterpart; probably, in most cases, this student is a potentially more enthusiastic alumnus as well. Finally, residential schools enjoy a demonstrable reputation boost over their scorned counterpart, the mere "commuter school."

Yet the commuter has not gone away, and the numbers are likely to increase. Dorms are becoming more expensive to build, and university borrowing opportunities are diminishing. More important, a disproportionate number of first-gens, swirls and transfer students don't want to reside on campus anyway or can't afford it. They may have cultural preferences that keep them with families. They may quite sensibly greet the challenge of affording tuitions and avoiding undue debt by simply bypassing the dorm rent component—even if, in some cases, they would really prefer the on-campus experience if all else were equal.

Hence, many institutions should be candidly facing a renewal of an old issue: how to be as sure as we can that we're providing commuting students with as full an educational experience as possible. It is probably not feasible to erase the public bias against the commuting school, though there is reason to actively contest the stereotype rather than wiggling around it by overemphasizing residential numbers. A handful of publics will still be able to attract a largely residential population, including those located in places where fully off-campus rental opportunities are limited; but lots of good public universities must re-embrace their commuter segments. Student services operations have a crucial role to play here—though they also face their own challenge in moving away from the disproportionate attention paid to making the residential student feel at home.

We need, obviously, to figure out new ways to facilitate commuter participation in activities, including fitness and counseling opportunities. We need to devise some equivalents to the Living/Learning arrangement and to make sure that qualified commuters have access to the honors program. We must help generate more active mixtures of student types, residential and nonresidential alike—and probably some facilities modifications, with more accessible lounges, figure into this combination. We need to make sure advisors maintain active contacts, perhaps particularly when commuting combines with the first-gen experience. We must talk more extensively with commuters themselves about what will work for them (it's distressingly easy to find student advisory panels composed exclusively of residentials, who are around anyway and easiest to recognize; here, a special student contribution to governance may need to be identified). Universities may well have developed some services for residential types with which commuters simply can dispense, but still others should be expanded; this includes not only the cocurricular array, where services to commuters may be particularly important, but the counseling and fitness activities as well, where the population's needs can be unduly neglected. We also need to charge both student-life professionals and student leaders themselves with responsible assessments: if student organizations do not, for example, successfully reach out to some proportion of commuters, they may need some special guidance or admonition.

The task is straightforward enough but easier to state than fulfill; a growing number of public institutions need to figure out active ways to minimize the effects of an undeniable divide, around the overarching commitment to common learning goals. While we surely won't bury the commuter label, we can hopefully place the real emphasis where it belongs: on the successful student, pure and simple.

Back to the Budget: Some Palliatives on Student Costs?

Exploring student needs and student services makes it obvious that there is no disproportionate contribution to budget stability emerging from this source. If cuts are essential, they should certainly be no greater than in the overall administrative and faculty categories; except around the margins, they will risk impact on student success.

It may, however, be possible to discuss a few other, and frankly modest, cost adjustments on the student side. Three related approaches are already under consideration and will warrant greater attention in the future. Two would create new differential payment patterns, while the other, though outside the services category proper, focuses directly on the burden of book costs. None of the categories offers easy decisions, and it's worth remembering that—through no fault of their own—instate undergraduates at the publics already pay far less than the actual costs of education. However, the stone should be turned at least briefly.

Fees

This discussion has already made it clear that some students, without question, pay for services they are never going to use. Graduate students, most obviously, subsidize athletic events that probably interest very few of them (on the other hand, they also benefit from smaller classes and more senior faculty paid for in part by undergraduate tuitions, so perhaps fair is fair). Should we create further adjustments for off-campus students who are unlikely to participate in clubs and organizations or even for those undergraduates in general who dislike sports? There are limits here: students might want to avoid fitness facility or counseling expenses, but they probably should not be allowed to make these fine distinctions that would affect access and opportunity in ways they cannot fully evaluate. Commuting students, in particular, might make some cost-saving choices that would come back to haunt them. In general—intercollegiate athletics largely aside, if only because they loom so large on the fee side in many cases—one hesitates to encourage further barriers for easy student interactions in a range of activities and particularly to promote still further, potentially invidious distinctions between residentials and commuters.

One differential is already under exploration: at some institutions, students with unusual counseling or disability needs are now paying extra, or their parents are. (Several institutions, for example, have autism services for as much as $3,500 per year.) The result, though burdensome, is arguably only fair to students in general, though it does raise questions not only about invidious distinctions but about availability to students in the lower socioeconomic categories. Tough times may well require some tough options.

Tuitions

Students have long paid special course fees to cover unusual costs, for example, in laboratory fields or the arts. These have almost certainly gone up faster than tuitions in general, as colleges try funding ploys that are not widely noticed—or that do not require public approvals. Increasingly, differentials have also been applied to undergraduate tuition rates themselves—a pattern well established at the graduate level, particularly for Masters students where educational costs and career opportunities both vary with field. Again, somewhat desperate times make for unpleasant measures. Engineering education costs more than education in general, and students seem willing to pay an overage because their job prospects are reasonably bright. So a tuition plus may seem a no brainer. What about nurses? Again, expensive education is involved (several very small practicum classes are mandated, with high faculty costs) and usually fairly good job opportunities—but not, in fact, very high salaries, so is a differential both feasible and fair? Or should we be taking an alternative approach, as some conservative state governments have advocated, and charge humanities majors more even though their education is much cheaper than average— on the grounds that what they are studying is next to useless if not positively dangerous politically? Again, various tuition differentiations are happening around us, so my obvious concerns about the choices to be made, and the clashes among diverse alternatives, may be beside the point. Yet too much tuition differentiation risks punishing students who get trapped in a major they don't like but can't afford to switch; we have abundant evidence that students themselves, no dummies fortunately, game the system and switch into more expensive programs at the last possible moment. Again, there's no avoiding the tuition differential topic, and necessity may require decisions that harm both fairness and flexibility, but we should at least be sure to keep student success, and basic quality, in mind along with the budget games.

Books

Book costs loom large, and they have been going up faster than inflation. They add to student burdens and potential debt and so must be considered along with more directly institutional policies; their impact on student reading adds to the urgency here. More and more libraries are stepping in to ease the problem by providing widely assigned textbooks on reserve, though limited borrowing times constrain actual utilization. More and more instructors (some of whom were slow to wake up to the problem, preferring maximum latitude in selecting best readings) assign materials largely available online. There are also promising moves among university consortia to provide online textbooks independent of costly, often downright greedy publishing companies and to offer captured lectures as a partial alternative as well. We must hope that these patterns will spread, creating real cost savings for students in the process.

Inevitably, there are downsides. It's fine glibly to talk about providing online textbooks directly, but investment funding is essential to motivate faculty authors and to oversee reasonable production and periodic revision costs. (We can, however, avoid the frequency of commercial textbook revisions, designed less for updating than as fairly blatant attempts to undercut the secondhand market, so there are definite potential gains here.) Also interesting is the fact that students, by a current margin of 80–20, prefer books with real pages to the electronic alternative. This bias may change with time, and in any event, even in this chapter, students can't get everything they want. It's reasonable to hope for further progress in this area, recognizing that the resulting relief, while real, is not massive.

Conclusion

Changes in student composition create exciting opportunities for higher education in serving contemporary society. They also require thought and, in many cases, will reward additional funding to assure best possible results. Already, student habits suggest some additional needs for guidance and personalized attention; while novel educational delivery technologies will help in some cases, they may not usually be the best solution.

Student-life staff, and those who make decisions around them, face some tough choices in the years ahead—at least as difficult as those involving other administrative domains and the faculty itself. Debate is warranted, but preservation of most of the services involved seems essential for student success or for the sense of community that links to this success. To be sure, as noted, costs in this category have been rising disproportionately rapidly, and unquestionably present some margin for review, but for the most part the reasons lie not in mindless bloat but in measurably, sometimes distressingly, mounting student needs. Though it is hard to be absolutely precise, quite apart from basic health concerns, we know enough about the importance of student service and advising activities to enhanced retention to be truly cautious about cutting back. This does not mean immunity—some cuts may have to be shared with other sectors of the university—but neither disproportionate pain nor disproportionate protection is called for.

Assuming sensible funding does stand, with student life not destructively singled out, there are still some special budget decisions to face. Almost certainly internal reallocations will be essential, possibly to help deal with the continuing counseling surge and certainly to invest more heavily in the support of first-gen students and the commuting population. What are the most prudent tradeoffs, and should more of the other activities be maintained only on a special fee basis?

A few other adjustments may help. It may be possible to combine some teaching activity with student-life expertise to aid in coordination and provide greater efficiency. It is certainly valid to urge faculty—along with more constructively integrating the different categories in their own ranks—to work more equably with their student-life colleagues, rather than privileging their own superior knowledge and contribution. As more and more faculty realize the benefits their students gain from cocurricular offerings, internships, or in dire cases counseling assistance, we can hope that a sense of shared endeavor will become increasingly pervasive.

One final point: the chapter has already evoked the desirability of considering new ways of benefiting from student input in governance and new ways of using student opinions to help guide the challenging process of allocating student-life resources themselves. It is also vital to remember how much students educate each other in any vibrant college or university. They are the most widely credited source of advice for their peers (sometimes a scary thought but inescapable), but they are also sources of knowledge and motivation. This is a key reason for making sure that the student body includes not only conventional diversities but also diversities of interest and accomplishment—athletics, to a reasonable point, included. As institutions continue to build their student-life efforts and adjust to changes in student characteristics, they should proudly highlight what students do, and can do in the future, for each other. Whatever their particular sets of strengths, students contribute not only to their own success, framed by appropriate institutional support, but to student success more generally.

Further Reading

On students: Harold Ladd and others, *The Differentiated University* (Boston: Parthenon Group, 2014).
On residence life: Lauren Schudde, "The Causal Effect of Campus Residency on College Student Retention," *Review of Higher Education* 34 (4) (2011), 581–610.
On student-life services: Peter M. Magolda and Marcia Magolda, *Contested Issues in Student Affairs: Diverse Perspectives and Respectful Dialogue* (Sterling: Stylus Publishing, 2011); and Ashley Tull and Lina Kuk, *New Realities in the Management of Student Affairs: Emerging Roles, Specialist Roles and Structures for Changing Times* (Sterling: Stylus Publishing, 2012).
On the vital issue of community colleges, crucial in so many transfer sequences: Thomas Bailey, Shanna Smith Jaggers and Davis Jenkins, *Redesigning America's Community Colleges: A Clearer Path to Student Success* (Cambridge: Harvard University Press, 2015).
For an overview: George Kuh, Killian Kinzie, John H. Schuh, Elizabeth Whitt and Associates, *Student Success in College: Creating Conditions that Matter* (San Francisco: Jossey-Bass, 2010).

Notes

1 National Survey of Student Engagement, *Annual Results* (Indianapolis, 2014)—obviously, annual reports can be traced over time; see also other reports on the website: www.nsse.iub.edu; Richard Arum and Josipa Roksa, *Academically Adrift* (Chicago, 2011).
2 Probably the best source in the *Journal of College and University Student Housing*.
3 Maria Pescucci, "5 Time Management Tips to Calm College Student Stress," Campuscalm@www.campuscalm.com/tiome_management.html
4 Perhaps the best study is, revealingly, an old one, when the topic was hotter: Mary Meehan, *Role and Structure of Student Government* (Chicago, 1966); see also materials from the American Student Government Association. There is much more on student leadership development; see "Student Leadership Programs," NASPA (Student Affairs Administrators in Higher Education), www.naspa.org/constituent-groups/kcs/student-leadership-programs
5 American Association of Colleges and Universities, *America's Unmet Promise: the imperative for equity in higher education* (Washington, 2015).
6 Jeff Selingo, "The Student Swirl," *Chronicle of Higher Education*, March 8, 2012.
7 National Center for Education Statistics, *First-Generation Students: undergraduates whose parents never enrolled in post-secondary education* (Washington, 1998).
8 "Dual Enrollment Programs: the pros and cons," Studypoints, www.studypooint.com/ed/dual-enrollment
9 "Oregon State Degree Partnership Program," oregonestate.edu/partnerships/students.
10 "The Benefits of College Honors," National Collegiate Honors Council, nchchonors.org/hs-students-counselors . . . /the-benefits-of-college-honors. See also Lynn O'Shaughnessy, "The Pros and Cons of College Honors," *The College Solution*, Feb. 22, 2013.
11 Data derived from Google searches. Knowing that this finding is one of the most important empirical contributions of this book, I have to admit that the calculation may be slightly inexact.
12 George McClellan and Jeremy Stringers, eds., *The Handbooks of Student Affairs Administration* (San Francisco, 2009).
13 This is an aggressive program, too new for results to be clear. "Gallup Student Poll," www.gallupstudentpoll.com
14 Daniel Eisenberg, J. B. Hunt and N. Speer, "Mental Health in American Colleges and Universities: variations across student subgroups and across campuses," *Journal of Nervous and Mental Disease* 201 (2013): 60–7. See also http://www.thinkcollege.net/topics/

opportunity-act; Matthew Barnes, Z. W. Davis, J. G. Dean and K. R. Letcher, "Increasing Need and Decreasing Availability: supply and demand of counseling services in higher education," *Journal of College Student Psychotherapy* 21 (2009): 1–25; and annual reports, National College Health Assessments, over the past decade.

15 David Drum and others, "New Data on the Nature of Suicidal Crises in College Students," *Professional Psychology* 40 (2009): 213–22.

16 On the competency movement, Deborah Everhart, F. M. Hurst and Ellen Wager, "From Badges to Breakthroughs: unleashing learner potential through competency-based achievement," *EducauseReview*, June 2, 2014; individual campus living and learning programs can be followed up on the web.

17 George Kuh, Robert Gonyea and Megan Palmer, "The Disengaged Commuter Student: fact or fiction?" nsse.iub.edu/pdf/commuter-pdf. See also John Welty, "Resident and Commuter Students: is it only the living situation?" *Journal of College Student Personnel* 17 (1976); Barbara Jacoby, "Why Involve Commuter Students in Learning?" *New Directions for Higher Education* 109 (2000).

8
BEYOND THE CAMPUS
Regional and Global Roles

American higher education institutions have wide orbits, in the locality and well beyond, that can relate strongly to basic priorities. The broad reach that results may enhance funding opportunities and educational quality, including student success. It may also distract and compete. Figuring out how to address regional and even global opportunities and pressures has significant implications for administration, faculty and students alike.

As in so many aspects of higher education, the outreach field is changing. Regional service is measurably expanding in many cases, though the category itself is not new. Most institutions take pride in extending their educational mission beyond the formal student body, and they often serve as anchors for economic development and cultural life. The global area is even livelier as international contacts widen. It is a legitimate to talk about a substantial new component of quality education—though precisely because of its novelty, amid so many other pressing issues, there is considerable debate over both the nature and the degree of engagement.

The Regional Mission

Colleges and universities usually loom large in their communities broadly construed. Often, particularly in the United States where so many centers sit in smaller cities, they are the largest single institution in the area. Big public universities can claim this distinction, perhaps in competition (or conjunction) with a major hospital system, even in larger urban environments. Add to this the fact that colleges and universities sincerely embrace at least some elements of a wider educational mission, seeking to enhance learning beyond a particular student audience, and a significant outreach function is an inevitable result. Healthy universities depend on various kinds of community support and provide various services and advantages to the community in turn.

Much of this mutual interaction is unproblematic, requiring no particularly unusual commitments or decisions. A brief review to round out the record will suffice. But two issues, at a minimum, push beyond this framework. Current university challenges may suggest a deliberate enhancement for some aspects of community outreach, where we can hope for a bit more assistance in meeting basic priorities while in turn improving the articulation of regional benefits. At the same time, some community expectations may need to be modified in light of the costs and distractions involved. There's no broad crisis here, but some fine-tuning may be desirable in light of higher education's basic, and somewhat beleaguered, priorities.

Staple items: economic impact, philanthropy and town-gown. Higher education institutions make significant economic contributions to their regions. They maintain substantial personnel rosters; they attract students with at least a bit of buying power; and in many cases, they directly pull in research funding, some of which may also bear a potential for local commercialization. Claims that major research institutions contribute two or three times the size of their overall budgets to their home regions are both common and plausible. Land grant institutions have even more extensive obligations in research and training beyond the campus base. Several large public universities—including North Carolina and California—are currently increasing their investment in economic development projects in hope of profit but with regional benefit intended as well. Without inflating a public relations apparatus, there is every reason for institutions of various types—and not just the big players—to make their contributions clear to the local population. Given recent economic flux, and the wide expectation that future prosperity will depend even more heavily on new technologies and health systems, universities have every reason to consider further contributions in this area, in consultation with other regional leadership segments. Collaboration in regional economic planning, facilitation for entrepreneurial startups, and more focused attention on opportunities for technology transfer all constitute areas where some additional push may be warranted, with benefits to institutions and localities alike.[1]

Maintaining and hopefully accelerating a regional philanthropic base is another obvious relationship, sometimes with direct connection to universities' service as an economic engine. In many cases, regional "friends" of a university, cultivated through a variety of outreach activities and recruited to advisory and trustee boards, will prove more philanthropically significant than actual alumni. The result, among other things, is a clear source of support for attractive outreach activities, like varsity sports or artistic performances, that may particularly motivate donors, in some cases generating rewards that go beyond the activities themselves.

Regional issues inevitably include relationships with immediate neighbors. Town-gown interactions are almost certainly less problematic now than they used to be. Some universities have used their capital power to restructure neighborhoods, ultimately resulting in less local protest potential. Cities and even neighborhoods may have become more aware of the advantages of a college or university, despite some traffic and occasional student conduct problems. Institutions themselves have properly become more conscientious in keeping localities informed about relevant plans and even compromising with neighborhood concerns once in a while; this is a legitimate PR function broadly construed. There is no systematic current problem in this category, but obviously administrations will need to continue to devote some attention to maintaining constructive relationships.

Beyond special foci, like economic stimulation or town-gown harmony, the basic priorities of the contemporary university have obvious regional relevance—deserving attention but again requiring no particularly challenging adjustments. Even the most prestigious schools provide some opportunities for local students to seek more education, sometimes simply as commuters. And Masters and certificate programs play a great role in enhancing the skills of a regional labor force; this has fueled the substantial numbers of Masters institutions that have such a striking place in American higher education overall. Communities have a direct stake as well in student success, including higher graduation rates. On average, two-thirds of all college graduates stay in the area, though the figure varies greatly with type of institution and local economic conditions. In many cases, the outcome is little more than a function of origin: many public universities have a student body that is strongly local and simply stays put after graduation—though with stronger economic and civic capacity in the process. Some schools with a wider recruitment base measurably feed the strength of the regional labor force, as even out-of-state graduates stick with the area. Good graduation rates, when combined with a commitment to quality education, have important local ramifications.

Additional connections. Institutions, and even more their faculty, staff and students, have a variety of opportunities to add to regional benefit through individual, largely voluntary activities. In turn, local community members and alumni groups add strength to the operation of the college, again with no extraordinary adaptations involved.

Any school worth its salt, for example, will maintain some kind of speaker's bureau that provides local organizations with names and topics that will add to the regional educational climate, and in principle build greater support and understanding for the institution in turn. There's a small cost involved but probably not worth great debate. Many institutions also arrange for opportunities for alumni to maintain both social and educational contacts with faculty, and while there's potential philanthropic payoff, the effort is a worthy extension of professional services without a major commitment of resources.

Many colleges and universities now play host also to retiree learning groups, including the Osher Lifelong Learning network. They offer some access to facilities during lower-use times of the day. More importantly, a variety of faculty and graduate students voluntarily contribute to instruction, simply finding it rewarding to address a really interested, experienced audience (that has the additional merit of not requiring grades or grading). Opportunities to test some new topics or explore ramifications of a research project for a wider public may factor in as well.[2]

A decade ago, before the contemporary pressures on higher education became entirely clear, I would have predicted a more robust "lifelong learning" commitment from colleges and universities than has in fact materialized. Formal degree and certificate programs do part of the job in return for payment: their variety and range have expanded, particularly at the Masters level, in response to needs for further training and retraining in a rapidly changing economy where careers must prove adaptable. Televised and online offerings also contribute, though as noted earlier the business plan basis for some of these operations is not always clear. However, current conditions make it hard to envisage a more systematic regional commitment for educational service, particularly in liberal arts areas that many adults find interesting but not directly job-relevant. The current patchwork of volunteer offerings for regional and alumni groups is unlikely to change greatly in the near future—but it does contribute value.

In turn, individuals, as alumni or local residents, put constructive time into colleges and universities by serving on advisory boards, mentoring students in various ways, and building support for programs in athletics or the arts. Networks of reciprocal relationships involve surprising numbers of individuals.

One other connection, growing until a recent slight downturn, deserves mention: for at least two decades, contemporary undergraduates have been scoring high in their wide interest in community service—even as formal political involvements have often declined. While 2004 was the peak year for student volunteers, 26% of all undergraduates were still engaged in 2010. A 2015 poll found that, along with concern about first jobs, finding service opportunities constituted the top items of interest among the current student population, with altruistic motives topping the list. Universities contribute a bit to this surge through some of the student activities structure, sometimes now under formal labels of "social entrepreneurship," but much of the impetus really comes from the students themselves. Student outreach—as tutors, health assistants, advocates for the homeless, food distributors, charity fundraisers—becomes a significant element in higher education's regional role. Specific examples range from student-run pharmacies to legal aid centers to local sustainability efforts and even weight management—well beyond the traditional range of student philanthropy.[3]

Accelerating the interactions. Three outreach areas may warrant additional institutional attention going forward, without calling for huge policy adjustments and without occasioning major costs. A halting trend toward formal partnerships among universities and local entities, from museums to start-up facilities, may provide a framework for further efforts as well.

Use of public audiences. Some colleges and universities do a better job of attracting outside speakers and making their appearances available to the local as well as institutional public than they do with their own faculty. Highlighting faculty presentations—in addition to Speaker's Bureau services—may help draw the public to campus in mutually useful ways. A program of this sort will also provide some faculty a proving ground for exploring responses to particular research agendas beyond purely academic or disciplinary confines—thus contributing to the process of defining research significance and encouraging wider service as public intellectuals.

Many institutions, including liberal arts operations, have every reason now to expand their regional connections toward enhancing meaningful student internships. Some schools have an enviable track record in this area already—Drexel and Northeastern are classic examples of programs that build in wide practical training—and many places are waking up to the need to provide more opportunities for what we now call "experiential learning." There is an investment need here, usually in a central career services office that amplifies what particular degree programs can do on their own. Building wider community commitment to this aspect of a contemporary educational program obviously benefits institutions and students, but in improving labor force preparation, it serves regional interests as well.

Beyond individual volunteer efforts, colleges and universities have a deep self-interest in extending their intentional commitment to regional professional guidance. Nursing programs, for example, inevitably spill over into service on hospital boards and regional health agencies; they contribute expert advice, but they also help build opportunities for their graduates. Business schools may find similar mutual benefits in offering regional services; criminal justice programs have made major strides in connections with actual regional policing; and examples could easily be multiplied.

Priority number one in this category is education itself. Colleges and universities have a huge stake in contributing to local discussions about schooling, to interactions with teachers, even to appearances in school settings directly. This is particularly true, of course, where there are formal education programs—where outreach is at least as logical as for nursing or other professional fields—but the commitment should be wider: many programs have a responsibility to offer support and enrichment for practicing teachers, and the services should not be monopolized by the education folks alone. Good relations with local school leaders, in areas like science, writing or social studies and global affairs, should be a standard part of the institutional agenda.

Previous chapters have not belabored some of the obvious issues colleges and universities face in the educational preparation of the students they receive: it's important to play well the hands we are dealt. However, it is obvious that many local P–12 programs are not as strong as one would like. Further, any future project toward expanding higher education enrollments—given the lack of significant population growth—will almost certainly depend on improving preparation for college; school systems must be involved. Universities and their faculty need to be careful in offering assistance to regional school networks; they are not the major players in the eyes of state or federal education agencies, and it is really important not to seem arbitrary or patronizing. There are many opportunities to reach out to teachers as colleagues (particularly when, as is often the case, they were once our own students), as well as to contribute to curricular or policy debates. Building effective community educational interactions should be seen as a standard part of the institutional agenda.

The Arts Centers

Over the past decade or so, the proliferation of major community arts centers on college campuses has been a striking extension of regional service—with a few questions attached. Arranging performances from visiting artists as well as student and faculty groups is not a brand-new university function, but the interest in substantial new facilities reflects a wider commitment. At least 39 centers have opened in the past decade, 60 since 1996. And while 2009 was the peak year for the genre, with eight inaugurals, considerable momentum persists. In 2014, major projects included Oklahoma State, University of Alabama Tuscaloosa, Texas State—at an average construction cost of over $55 million. Overall, institutions at various levels, private but even more commonly public, in all parts of the country have participated in the trend. In several cases, facilities have emerged under university sponsorship but in active partnership with local governments.[4]

With few exceptions, the primary goal in this facilities surge has been regional service, though arts students (including the growing arts management segment) and faculty performers benefit as well. Scheduling reflects community tastes (not always at the high art end of the spectrum) and revenue prospects, with student interest and training taking a deliberate backseat in many cases. Western Illinois, with its $72 million commitment scheduled for completion in 2018, proudly and probably accurately notes the intent to serve "as a cultural and performing arts destination for the campus community, the city, and the entire region." Quite apart from facilities themselves, centers have been pouring significant money into the arts more generally, making colleges and universities major sponsors—as one observer put it, responsible for "unheralded contributions . . . to keeping culture alive and well in the United States." The function is not cultural alone: the regional economy benefits by services that help enliven and exemplify the community, touching base with what Richard Florida has noted about the importance of artistic amenities in attracting and retaining a creative business community.

Of course there are issues, not as substantial as those attached to intercollegiate athletics but of similar nature. While philanthropy backs many of the building projects, it does not always cover whole costs, not to mention ongoing operating expenses. Audience levels vary, again not always measuring up to expectations—among other things, arts patronage is very sensitive to economic downturns. In the breech, other university funds—including direct allocations from student fees—often must be pulled in to cover any gaps.

Bumps in the road. Two related problems complicate institutional outreach programs; while neither is entirely new, both do take on greater significance as they compete, however modestly, with the more basic higher education priorities.

Faculty reward is factor one, apart from whatever individuals decide to volunteer at a retirement learning community or a local program for high school teachers. Some of the regional commitments—like service on nursing panels or relationships with major hospitals—take serious time, without falling directly into either the teaching or research categories through which faculty are primarily rewarded. Figuring out how to credit this kind of service may need renewed attention. Even more obvious is the importance of allowing adequate time without, in current circumstances, routinely detracting from teaching obligations; a common faculty request for course reductions, as opposed to credit in a broadened research-service category, now needs a more thoughtful response.

This slides into factor two: the necessity of taking a slightly harder look at the institutional cost of some regional activities or expectations. It's not surprising that many communities have fallen into a pattern of seeking college or university freebies; without retreating into Scrooge-like calculations, some schools inevitably face a need to review. Measuring the cost/benefit ratio of athletic programs that are justified in part in terms of community service and interest is an obvious candidate already discussed (though hardly resolved). Cherished arts programs may need a more careful eye; they win regional praise and in fact often measurably build communities in ways that have economic as well as cultural impact, but the revenue/contribution combination they generate may well fall short of expenses. Clearer focus on student costs and benefits may prove essential in deciding on any further investments. Simple space demands by worthy community groups often carry costs, even when the relevant classroom is not technically in use. Community habits, in looking to one of the big institutions in the region; programs that earn revenue but short of costs; and the possibility of some undesirable distraction from basic goals—these are modest warning flags that probably need greater visibility in the outreach field. Without claiming a crisis where none exists, some institutions may need to sharpen and clarify the criteria they use to evaluate what they offer and do for the surrounding community.

The Global University

More than with regional outreach, different institutions face widely varied global challenges and opportunities. Elite liberal arts colleges, for example, have long taken a lead in study abroad (mainly with European targets at least until recently); the interests and resources of their study body differ greatly from the norms at public universities. Big research institutions by now have an essentially inevitable set of global linkages because of the progressive internationalization of scholarly teams and the reputational heft that at least the leading American universities maintain; the percentage involvement with international colleagues is rising rapidly. This section can only touch on some of the specific issues and opportunities the variety of global engagements generates.[5]

There is increasingly, however, a common global imperative that cuts across, or should cut across, institutional diversity. Admittedly, some American colleges may be tempted to bypass significant global involvement amid all the other issues they currently face—like the public university president in the New York State system who decided to save money by eliminating access to foreign language training except for Spanish. No formal imperative, in the United States, actually requires global education at present—in contrast to the clear interest that has developed abroad, where many countries use global measurements as part of their basic institutional evaluation. The Obama ratings scheme, for example, has no global components of any sort. As a result—foreign language facility is a prime example—many American students actually lag globally, which makes aspects of a global agenda all the more demanding, another possible goad to a preference for avoidance. Current changes in the student mix—the rise of first-generation entrants, for example, who historically have been less interested in study abroad opportunities than undergraduates—may complicate the global category still further. Public clamor for more global effort clearly takes a back seat to the frenzy for more STEM. So why, some readers may wonder, not include global category on the list, back in Chapter 2, of desirable but now secondary goals in favor of concentration on the clear priorities? In a book urging careful focus at this moment in higher education, why add another, and admittedly complex, dimension?

The response is simple: the world around us compels new levels of attention. In fact, a greater and more explicit commitment to global education and global opportunities has simply become part of fundamental quality at the college and university level, in the United States as in other countries. This does involve additional change, although it adds to the excitement as well as the challenge of contemporary higher education. Further, without downplaying the reorientation involved, key aspects of a global agenda mesh directly with other core priorities, complementing, even facilitating, more than contradicting.

Rationale. While the term globalization is relatively new—a couple of decades old, though the Japanese had an equivalent word earlier—the phenomenon has been accelerating for quite a while. Global connections, from trade processes to new efforts at international control of disease to the emergence of elements of a global youth culture, increasingly shape key aspects of society. Accelerating communication makes awareness of cultural differentiation, as well as the capacity for cultural adjustments, increasingly important. For Americans, to add to the intensification of globalization itself, the decentering of Europe, the rise of major powers in Asia and elsewhere, requires even further adaptations from committed internationalists.

Global education seeks to make students more fully aware of the basic features of the world in which they live, and in which they will live, so that they can function better as citizens and have a fuller basis for appreciating issues and opportunities by which they will define important elements of their futures. It reflects the need to adapt definitions of educational quality to new and fundamental features of the contemporary human condition—just as changes in technology have required inclusion of core features of Information Technology in any higher education agenda. Reshaping aspects of the humanities for a clearer focus on exploration of diverse (but not always totally dissimilar) cultural frameworks joins with new opportunities to reorient aspects of political science, economics and even public health toward creating a greater awareness of global processes and global issues. The need to include global topics in the definition of educational quality, even if it is not fully sanctified by prior tradition, is compelling.

There is also a practical component, though it should not be exaggerated. Many students will find an ability to function in global settings (including linguistically) a practical advantage in seeking first jobs and, even more, in exploring fulfilling careers. Business executives sometimes wax more enthusiastic about their need for globally minded employees than their personnel officers decide to implement, but a professional advantage will materialize for some of the students exposed to the global orientation in a variety of specific fields.

Global education advocates are often quite fervent, and they may overdo their aspirations to provide every student at a given institution a meaningful global experience: well-intentioned rhetoric can outpace reasonable expectations. But the basic arguments for global education, for its addition particularly to the quality priority in higher education, reflect the need to adjust universities and their students to key aspects of the changing world around them.

Tactical issues. Global education does not require a hopelessly large set of new commitments and, more particularly, new expenses. Universities have been figuring out how to organize decisions in this category without detracting unduly from other vital concerns. Often, some kind of global office proves useful—beyond the more conventional study abroad operation but embracing this—to provide overall coordination. Participation by many faculty, from many disciplinary perspectives, is also vital, as advancement of global education becomes a legitimate part of shared governance. Within this context, several specific areas warrant attention.

International students. Wider recruitment of international students has become a basic fiscal strategy over a wide range of American campuses as admissions officers seek to tap the currently richest pool for out-of-state students and their welcome tuitions. Many institutions are not just reaching out but are also developing better transition programs, in terms of language and relevant study skills, to make this expansion more successful for all concerned. How many campuses will really turn the corner into significant internationalization of their students remains unclear: there is great competition, varying degree of tactical sophistication, and ultimately some probable limits to the market overall. At the least, however, there's no need to convince most American institutions of the importance of this aspect of global education; it ties directly to the budget priority.[6]

It's worth noting that recruiting international graduates and undergraduates is not necessarily the only strategy possible in this area: a number of countries, such as Japan, Mexico and Turkey, are also interested in arrangements for summer or semester abroad programs, which can fit into a larger global education effort and also enhance overall revenues.

A variety of practical arrangements attach to any successful effort at international recruitment, but two issues predominate. First, any expansion program must be informed by serious thought about how international students—even visitors—can be responsibly connected to a variety of American students to contribute to mutual education both within and without the classroom. (Residence life arrangements can play a big role between the poles of ghettoization and disorientation.) Many faculty note that having international students in, say, a management class really improves the opportunity for the whole class to deal with important contemporary issues, but the connections must be made, the faculty themselves in some cases assisted in best service to a larger international cohort. International students, in other words, can form part of a larger global education program without damage to their own interests, but the result warrants careful planning; it does not just happen.

Second, if some significant revenue improvement results, it's worth giving some thought to using a part of it on other global education categories—and there can still be serious fiscal benefits left over. Oregon State, for example, has devoted part of its earnings from international students to supporting study abroad for additional American undergraduates. Additionally, some revenue might be applied to fellowships for international students themselves, particularly from regions that will otherwise be underrepresented.

Study abroad. Here, of course, is the classic American response to international education opportunities, dating back to the 1920s. There is no question that study abroad can be a transformational experience for many of those involved; there is also no question that expanding opportunities (and making sure that destinations other than Europe and Australia are involved) is a highly desirable goal for any global education program.[7]

Cautions as well as enthusiasms are unavoidable. Many study abroad programs may not contribute all that much to global awareness: the fastest growing categories, understandably, are two- or three-week tours, with materials exclusively in English; a cynic has noted that the best result, sometimes, is that students at least acquire a passport. Some programs are poorly prepared; we know that students benefit most when they have relevant training on the home campus before departure and follow-up study on return—but this increases the institutional effort involved. Most troubling, and not at all new, are the differentials among students who participate: too few scientists and engineers, notably more women than men and too few minorities or students from lower socioeconomic brackets. All of which adds up, first, to a realization that we need further work on study abroad to make it more widely possible and educationally useful; and second that we cannot put all of our global education eggs in the study abroad basket.

Successful study abroad efforts involve devising attractive programs, embedding them in a larger educational context and also—important point—carefully assessing results. The crucial challenge in this domain, however, centers on coming up with strategies that will make more students, and more student categories, find the experience desirable and feasible. Better curricular arrangements may help: engineering students, for example, might be relieved from the surfeit of requirements in favor of a wider experience that just might end up helping them as engineers. But the most obvious issues, unfortunately, take us back to budget. Many institutions clearly face the need to decide what, if any, subsidy can be offered to encourage study abroad, particularly in current circumstances. Many already support the administrative structure involved, though this is not always the case, leaving students to pay directly only for the educational experience and associated travel and subsistence costs. Seeking outside funding to provide some travel assistance and other scholarship inducements proves helpful in some cases, though despite the internationalist protestations of global corporations, actual solicitation can be tough going. A few programs benefit from lower educational and housing costs abroad, another inducement, but the question of whether need-based assistance in study abroad might justify some modest deployment of university funds—even student fee money—is worth discussion in this global age, adding this group to the athletes, honors students, musicians and student leaders who already get some extra support in return for measurable benefits to the campus educational climate.

Study abroad is not the only way to provide some meaningful, internationally relevant experience. In some parts of the United States, internships with international organizations can be fruitful and more feasible for some students than study abroad. Technology can also play a role. Organizing joint courses with partner universities abroad, mediated by the superb face-to-face interactions that the best technology now provides on subjects ranging from foreign policy or human rights to environmental issues, can expose students to serious international perspectives and even joint undergraduate research projects. Quite a bit of attention is now going to "stay at home" options that would really provide international experience. Obviously, some effort is required for these alternatives, and it will be important not to cheat and claim more than the actual activity generates, but the result broadens the range of options. Innovation most definitely applies to the global educational arena. Exploring in-country international experiences, but also making sure that they generate real contributions to global learning, is one of the current hot topics in the field.

Partnerships. The international standing of American higher education, and the push to globalize learning in many other countries, creates an array of opportunities to collaborate with many other institutions, creating wider global horizons for the individual campus. Student exchange remains one option; it can help a lot on the cost side for American students, while bringing additional international flavor to campus. Constraints, however, include the difficulty (often) of finding enough American students with the appropriate language facility to balance international enthusiasm for programs in the United States. Faculty exchanges can work as well, again depending on interest. Opportunities for short reciprocal visits, where faculty can work into existing courses for a couple of weeks, providing relevant international perspective, deserve attention alongside more classic semester- or yearlong arrangements. Many American institutions are trying to encourage faculty as well as students to take advantage of global opportunities—even subsidizing in some cases—and partnerships can facilitate this process. More ambitious collaborations, in addition to international research teams, will in the future increasingly help organize campus discussions of an array of problems but in a clear global setting—with American definitions and solutions juxtaposed with, and challenged by, views from other places.[8]

Of course, collaborations take time. Many projects seem worth exploring but fail to materialize. Maintaining even successful partnerships demands sustained effort—another reason for many American institutions to have some kind of global office. Any college or university needs to be able to make clear decisions about how many ventures can be contemplated. Always, however, some basic criteria are clear enough: ventures with international partners may provide a number of benefits, including enhancing the sometimes tarnished reputation of the United States. The arrangements must always be tested against basic priorities, including budget impacts but above all the capacity for international activities to provide additional learning opportunities for students themselves.

Curricula. The heart of any global education effort rests in the curriculum, which is where the deep relationship between global understanding and a contemporary definition of educational quality really strikes home. The process of rethinking conventional offerings in light of appropriate global standards is already well underway, in the gains, for example, of world history programs over more limited Western civilization approaches or the inclusion, in many general education platforms, of a definite global perspective—contemporary as well as historical.

Two basic categories are involved, with specifics varying according to institutional capacity. Some undergraduates, and graduate students, need opportunities to explore global issues in depth through an appropriate set of majors or segments of majors. Many new opportunities have shown rapid growth, as in the interdisciplinary approaches to global affairs, but more conventional disciplines contribute as well. Decisions about serious language training also fall into this category, where students need some definite opportunities and encouragements and where a purely European menu is increasingly inadequate. However, serving the often highly motivated internationalists in the student body cannot be the only focus. Decisions are essential about the global education segment that will apply to undergraduates more generally, whatever their special interest—and about how their learning can be measured.

Evaluating Global Programs

Somewhat ironically, given the twin popularity of assessment and global education, really successful measurements of overall global learning outcomes have yet to emerge widely. Assessment folks have had plenty of other pressing needs recently, and no one (in the United States) is yet demanding attention to outcomes in this category. In some cases as well, the American commitment to basic global goals falls short of urgency—as witnessed by the fact that American faculty are measurably less interested in global projects than their counterparts in many other countries—but there's a need here that ultimately must be met.[9]

Several challenges are obvious. The lack of a federal agency with sweeping higher education responsibilities, whatever the advantages in other respects, removes one obvious source of interest in global learning assessments where American results might be compared against other nations; states are simply not very interested. Further, many of the faculty and administrators most devoted to global goals are so convinced of their worthiness, or so eager to link them to other politically correct measurements like environmental impact, that they either see no reason for serious evaluation or complicate the effort by adding in other fashionable criteria.

We do, of course, have input measures. Many institutions would respond to a global query by pointing to numbers involved in study abroad programs. But as noted, study abroad projects, while usually better than nothing, are not necessarily very robust, given the popularity of the two- to three-week programs conducted in English. Another easily counted component involves the number of international students, another undeniably important field; but sheer numbers say nothing about how well students are integrated into the campus as a whole or what impact they have on the educational experiences, broadly construed, of the American-born students. Curriculum is another candidate for attention. There may be a tendency to look primarily at the numbers of students involved in clearly global majors—international relations or the increasingly popular, more interdisciplinary, global affairs approach; this is indeed important, and often rather encouraging, but it does not get at the global learning, or lack thereof, of the less-committed student majority. Foreign language exposure is another even more familiar component, but institutions are too often content simply with tallying students who take, or are required to take, an elementary course without accepting the more serious responsibility for figuring out how many students, in our linguistically parochial society, can and do actually gain the capacity and will to use a second language. As in other learning categories, the easiest tallies, though not to be forgotten, are clearly inadequate.

> Current international rankings efforts do not provide a lot of additional help in this area. They may count international students and study abroad; beyond this, they are usually bent on figuring out how many faculty publish in international outlets or what percentage of the faculty come from other countries—interesting data but not automatically applicable to students' global learning.
>
> In fact, we actually know what to look for. The better discussions of global curricula, including even relevant general education requirements, have pointed to two crucial educational goals: the need for student familiarity with cultural alternatives and reasonable comfort with understanding at least one or two frameworks in other region; and the importance of grasping some basic contemporary global processes and problems—particularly in the economic and political arena—and how they interact with more local or national factors. These two goals, of cultural awareness and local/global facility, may be furthered, of course, by language study or by study abroad or by institutionally encouraged interactions with foreign students. As with any learning area, different students will bring in different levels of capacity and experience even before their college careers. The goals are widely important, which is why, ultimately, American institutions will need to figure out how better to measure them over a college career. It's an achievable, if not easy, assessment challenge, and lead institutions should take on the task during the coming decade.

Global curricular discussions are not easy. They require some faculty to think outside familiar boxes; sometimes, over time, they depend on adjustments in personnel—as in adding the now-crucial kinds of non-Western language specialists. Advances will also be constrained by costs. Evolving appropriate courses and programs is part of core university business, however, which is why the global mandate fits directly into standard operating procedures. Other enhancements will help—as in expanded study abroad or imaginative partnerships—but they must be tested against budget realities. Student life efforts, often combining domestic and international students, can add cocurricular elements—even global badges, if this proves to help the motivation process. The work is already well underway, but it will develop additional facets in the future as it folds into the larger priority of educational quality.[10]

Conclusion

Regional and global activities must ultimately be evaluated in terms of the basic priorities of contemporary American higher education. In certain cases, this kind of review will call for some readjustments. Regionally, and in a smaller number of cases globally, some colleges and universities may have indulged in a version of "mission creep" that is just as damaging as the more familiar effort to expand research claims. The grim budget reaper requires solid business evaluations of operations beyond the campus—though this does not preclude explicit decisions to invest a bit.

An appropriate range of regional and global outreach is also, however, essential to the priorities themselves. Internships and volunteer operations that flow from a solid regional base feed student success directly. Global educational commitments now serve the basic educational mission. Both categories can also, on occasion, contribute to the bottom line, so even the budget filter is not consistently negative.

Prudence, in sum, must combine with commitment. More careful business plans may be required for some projects, as against understandable regional or global enthusiasms. But there is no reason to forget the wider mission of higher education in seeking the benefit of new research discoveries and in providing learning opportunities beyond the formal classroom. Ongoing research already contributes to regional and global benefit, and a variety of outreach efforts and collaborations will carry the mission further—as against a few naysayers who seek to restrict the contemporary American university to local labor force training and nothing beyond.

Regional and global horizons also provide part of the excitement of contemporary higher education. The current appraisal of higher education is more cautionary than one might wish: we need to reconsider some faculty policies, we need to rein in administrative costs and we need to be careful about unsupported commitments to enrollment growth or research expansion. Against this, the opportunities in teaching, including teaching innovation, and in exploring new knowledge are still going strong. Enhancing regional outreach or extending global awareness and probing global issues add further dynamism, for faculty and students alike. Transformative is an overused word, but it is really true that regional engagement or involvement in global programs contribute fundamentally to changing students' lives and providing a new sense of purpose. The momentum continues.

Further Reading

A good introduction to regional economic contributions is Jason Lane and D. Bruce Johnstone, eds., *Universities and Colleges and Economic Development* (Albany: State University of New York Press, 2012).

On student volunteering: M. S. Garver, R. L. Divine, and S. A. Spralls, "Segmentation Analysis of the Volunteering Preferences of University Students," *Journal of Nonprofit and Public Sector Marketing* 21 (2009); see also Scott Seider, *Shelter: Where Harvard Meets the Homeless* (New York: Continuum Press, 2010).

On the arts: Lawrence Biemiller, "Arts Patrons for the 21st Century," *Chronicle of Higher Education*, May 6, 2013.

On lifelong learning (in addition to materials from Osher Institutes): John Field, *Lifelong Learning and the New Educational Order* (London: Trentham Books, 2006); and Charles D. Hayes, *The Rapture of Maturity: A Legacy of Lifelong Learning* (Wasilla: Autodidactic Press, 2004).

On community partnerships: Karen Fischer, "Reimagining the 21st Century Land Grant University," *Chronicle of Higher Education*, 2009.
On the global side: J. K. Hudzik, "Comprehensive Internationalization: From Concept to Action," NAFSA publications, 2011; V. B. Mansilla and A. Jackson, *Educating for Global Competence: Preparing Our Youth to Engage the World,* (Washington: Council of State School Officers, 2011); Association of American Colleges and Universities, "Greater Expectations: A New Vision for Learning as a Nation Goes to College," Washington, DC, 2002; and Peter N. Stearns, *Educating Global Citizens in Colleges and Universities* (New York: Routledge, 2009).
On a key special topic: C. B. Matta, *Comprehensive U.S. Higher Education Internationalization: Exploring Study Abroad as an Indicator* (Chicago: Loyola University Press, 2010). See also American Council on Education, "International Higher Education Partnerships: A Global Review of Standards and Practices," Washington, DC, 2015.

Notes

1 S. M. Breznitz, *The Fountain of Knowledge: the role of universities in economic development* (Stanford, 2014).
2 C. L. Martin, *"Learning in Retirement Institutes: the impact on the lives of older adults," Journal of Continuing Higher Education* 51 (2003); see also Osher Lifelong Learning National Resource Center: www.nrc.northwestern.edu
3 Melody Brumble, "Fewer College Students Volunteer Their Time," *USA Today,* Jan. 22, 2012; "College Students' Volunteering: factors related to current volunteering, volunteer settings, and motives for volunteering," *College Student Journal* 48 (2014): 386–96. Ty Cruce and John Moore, "First-Year Students' Plans to Volunteer," *Journal of College Student Development* 48 (2007): 655–73.
4 "The Role of Performing Arts Centers: a case for the City University of New York," *International Journal of Learning* 17 (2009), http://www.bestvalueschools.com/25-most-amazing-university-performing-arts-centers; Lawrence Biemiller, "Arts Patrons for the 21st Century," *Chronicle of Higher Education,* May 6, 2013.
5 Stephen Pelletier, "Special Focus on Global Education: ACE Blue Ribbon Panel Report Envisions Global Future of Higher Education," American Council on Education (Washington, 2015).
6 Tamar Lewis, "Taking More Seats on Campus, Foreigners Also Pay the Freight," *New York Times* Education Section, Feb. 4, 2012.
7 Institute for International Education (IIE) Network, "American Students Studying Abroad at Record Levels," news release Nov. 13, 2007; Mell Bolen, ed., *A Guide to Outcomes Assessment in Study Abroad* (Austin, 2007); Peter N. Stearns, *Educating Global Citizens* (New York, 2009), ch. 5.
8 American Council on Education, "International Higher Education Partnerships: a global review of standards and practices," (Washington, 2015).
9 William D. Hunter, "Got Global Competency?" *International Educator* 13 (2010): 6–12; Stearns, *Educating,* ch. 9.
10 Stearns, *Educating.*

9

ADDING IT UP

"The University of the 21st Century"

Many, probably most, of the key problems contemporary American universities are facing come more from the external environment than from internal flaws. The public universities did not cause the funding crisis; government decisions and reprioritizations did that. Colleges did not generate growing social inequality and the income gaps that compound the challenge of affordability. Higher education did not sponsor changes in parenting that leave many students less capable of self-management than was once the case; it did not initiate new patterns of medication for many young Americans. To be sure, greater foresight could have eased adjustments; some issues, such as the downsides of tenure or the extremes of administrative bloat, could reasonably have been taken up when the overall climate was less dire. However, whatever the disparagers may claim, colleges and universities are not the villains of the piece so much as victims of larger trends in society.

This assessment risks distraction from the more important point: we—those of us responsible for higher education, whether through faculty or through administrative roles—need to take charge of the repair work. Knowing the larger forces in play remains essential, both to highlight the existing strengths that must be preserved and to devise constructive remedies. However, the overriding goal for universities is to regain greater control of their own futures, not so much against intervening boards or legislatures, but against the larger trends particularly in the budget arena, that have buffeted the system over the past decade.

Let's face it: we have been drifting a bit—not *Adrift* but not always facing up to reality. Faculty have urged attention to one set of issues, the bloat problem, but without forcing a really effective response—and sometimes without the necessary and complicated data at hand. Administrators have been dealing with teaching load issues but sidestepping confrontation, hence the recourse on adding more and more adjuncts without a formal assessment of the consequences. The results have not been horrible—many vital signs, including retention improvements and the growing percentage of first-gens, are mildly promising—but they have not been optimal, and they risk breakdown if we rely on extending the stopgaps further in the future. The situation is serious enough to require reevaluations in a number of areas.

There are no panaceas, whatever some of the disrupters may still try to claim. There is every reason to continue to expand the role of technology in aiding instruction, increasing flexibility and in some cases facilitating access, but it's not the magic bullet. It needs careful oversight. A new budgeting system may prove useful—though it can also be distracting—but unless it comes with a printing press, it will not solve the funding problem. We need to be cautious about the public relations impulse—so strong in some administrative circles—that seeks to dazzle without paying attention to the preservation of basic quality and the kinds of assessment that, we increasingly know, actually do allow us to gauge learning outcomes.

Indeed, beneath some of the innovative rhetoric, we need to be really careful that we do not exacerbate real inequalities in higher education, offering the well-to-do continued exposure to the benefits of liberal breadth and the links to research, while pretending that mere access to degrees, overseen by undervalued faculty, will suffice for the rest. Budget constraints may force us to reduce quality by exposing unprepared students to an excessive dose of online offerings or reduced writing opportunities—though I very much hope this will not prove necessary. If we have to move in this direction, however, let us at least be honest about it and continue to assess the results. Let's not allow the subject of quality to be moved off the agenda or to be clouded in misleading rhetoric.

Ultimately, unless we accept a movement away from existing strengths plus new essentials like the global component, there is no alternative to a complicated set of adjustments, requiring contributions from virtually all the components of the modern university. We need to cut back or, at least, constrain administrative staffs—but there is no easy target, no unit that can simply be expunged, no percentage figure that will not cause real challenge. We need several changes in faculty assignments, from a fuller evaluation of research contributions to modifications of the tenure system; these will be disputed and difficult and indeed can take shape only over time. Some essential reforms require a degree of collaboration among major institutions, lest any one university be saddled with a damaging competitive disadvantage. Adjustments, again, are essential, but they will be arduous. While some constructive shifts are underway, there is no automatic process.

It is not clear how many policy areas must, or indeed can, be addressed at once. Many institutions have already begun the process of evaluating research output, and therefore teaching loads, more carefully—this is a good first step if matched by carefully articulated administrative shifts. If combined with a modest infusion of new public investment, this might actually turn the trick in stabilizing costs and ending the spiral of tuitions outpacing inflation—all with probably modest implications for quality. However, more may be needed, and some of the other targets for discussion are fairly clear. Some reconsiderations in the tenure system have more to do with quality and effective public relations than with budget, so they might desirably merit an early agenda as well.

Better communication is vital, which is one reason to take a look at the tenor of many existing PR operations. The changes universities must work on require better, more open and frankly more time-consuming coordination between administrations and faculties; shared governance—improved shared governance—will be essential, and we need to explore some new mechanisms to support this process. Better communication with the external environment is essential as well. We must try to build wider agreement about the basic priorities around the complex combination of budgets, student outcomes and quality. We need to seek recognition of the changes that must be undertaken to convince a sometimes excessively skeptical public that the system is accepting responsibility and that it is capable of constructive adjustment.

In the process, we can hope that we can also encourage a greater sense of responsibility among some of the external critics as well. Too much of the existing chorus repeats inaccuracies—whether around trivial issues like climbing walls, overreliance on the results of low-stakes testing or wild claims about inefficiencies. Obviously, universities cannot control this element. Higher education does deserve careful scrutiny, including the good ideas and experiments that will continue to come from outside the campus walls, but there is, or should be, a recommitment to responsibility as well.

Might a new dialogue be possible as well with state officials, based in part on a clearer set of internal policies about administrative expenses and teaching loads as well as a mutual commitment to restraining tuition growth? The policy discussion about higher education funding has never really occurred amid real or imagined budget pressures and the self-serving assumptions about university wastefulness. The discussion may be elusive still—may even become more difficult—if higher education becomes a more directly partisan issue around the conservative fascination with cutting back to first-jobs training. The desirability of promoting a more responsible approach remains; the nation will be seriously hurt, in its research base and in the training of its career labor force, if public funding is not partially repaired. When universities can come to the table with their own adjustments more clearly established, it may not be impossible to aspire to a more constructive conversation.

Save perhaps for the really wealthy privates, there is a real need for prudence in contemporary higher education—a word that I accept reluctantly in thinking about universities' futures. We need to agree upon, and communicate, the basic priorities: doing a better job with budgets, continuing and accelerating our assurance of student success and preserving vital strengths. Other areas—whether athletics, philanthropy or global partnerships—must be assessed in their relationship to this core, and this is another litmus test that will sometimes be painful.

From this base, however, administrations and faculty can and should continue to think about areas beyond the core, though linked to it, should compatible opportunities arise—including changes in public support.

Research remains high on the agenda. It is a vital existing strength, and universities would surely welcome opportunities to expand their contributions, accepting more rigorous tests of affordability and significance in the process. More collaborative possibilities and the great promise of more problem-focused interdisciplinary work, including but extending beyond the STEM fields, offer intriguing prospects for the future.

Explorations beyond the essential innovations in global education may prove desirable as well, again assuming an appropriate financial base. Higher education, and not just in the United States, should serve not only to reflect but to further global connections, and it would be foolish to close off from additional collaborative possibilities.

Expanding student numbers and more forcefully addressing social inequality should not drop off the list. Prudence requires careful responses to political pleas that we substantially expand the percentage of the population served; any move in this direction must be accompanied by assurances of quality outcomes and fuller public funding. Failing these, public universities must at the least commit to maintenance of size and access and better graduation results—already a key gain in a changing social environment. Discussions of responsible inclusiveness should gain greater command over outdated exclusivity, but if funding changes do permit us to allow still more aggressive recruitment and support in combination with other educational sectors, we should not close our minds.

Pay attention to new possibilities in using technology, including capacities to reach new student audiences. As noted, one must urge realism, sound assessment, valid business plans and appropriate treatment of faculty—and this adds up to some real caution. However, further experiments are both inevitable and desirable, and some additional best practices will surely emerge.

An entrepreneurial component remains vital. Some American universities may brag too often about their qualities in this area, but the fact is that those institutions that do the best try to figure out how to undertake a new venture rather than devising all the reasons it would be impossible or stalling until the project goes away. The stimulus of new thinking and new proposals about research, collaborations or teaching methods is one of the joys of having a talented faculty. Prudence will dictate a bit more caution, if only because of constraints on resources, but the willingness to experiment (and sometimes to fail) must not be lost. The academic side of the apparatus particularly must work to retain this quality. Higher education does not need to close itself to new opportunities.

This is, in fact, the final challenge toward appropriate balance. We need clearer emphasis on the basic priorities of budget/tuition, student success and quality, and we need more consistent attention to sound business plans in addressing internal and external audiences. But American higher education also needs dynamism, the capacity to continue to develop in meeting social needs. This capacity must not be lost.

Working conditions in universities are changing, and they will change more in the future. It will be hard for many not to look back on a golden age when things were easier. Realism about what the field involves, including honest discussions with those planning to enter faculty or administrative life, is more important than ever.

The excitement has not vanished, however, and the opportunities to contribute to the social good are as great as ever. Exploration of new teaching approaches is at a lively height. Interdisciplinary research opportunities will be gaining more attention as we try harder to link research to leading issues and problems. Higher education's potentially growing role in the global environment is fascinating. The fundamental pleasure of seeing students learn and thrive remains very real—one of the reliable sources of good news stories on campus, even as the student body continues to change. Helping to lead higher education's adjustment process will offer its own interest. There's no lack of motivation, no shortage of ways to build knowledge and learning.

The past decade has been tough, and American higher education does need to regain some of the initiative that has been lost to the challenging external climate and inadequate initial response. Great strengths remain, and many promising changes are already launched. Further adjustments need urgent discussion, but they are within reach. The next decade, approached with eyes wide open, can be more constructive than its predecessor. The university's service to American society, and to the world, will continue to expand.

INDEX

Aberystwyth 127
Academically Adrift 22–6, 40, 46, 150, 192
academic freedom 88, 140
accreditation 26, 57, 59, 70–3, 99, 100
adjuncts 18, 132–4, 136, 145
administrative evaluations 103–5
admissions 78
adult students 32, 155, 158
Advanced Placement 153, 155
advising 157–8, 168, 170
American Association of State Colleges and Universities 80
American Association of University Professors 51, 107
American Council on Education 64, 90
American Institute for Research 101
Arizona State 53, 134, 144
articulation agreements 94, 157
arts centers 181
assessment 24–6, 37; administrative evaluations 103–4; advising 157–8; global programs 188–9; public relations 94; shared governance model 69–72; teaching evaluations 122–3
Association of American Colleges and Universities 155
Association of Governing Boards 58–9
athletics 30; categorization 77; coaches' salaries 106; cost/benefit 182; faculty involvement 69; student athletes 159–61
Autism Spectrum disorders 166, 171
auxiliary enterprises 97, 162

background checks 68, 99
badges, 168, 189
Ball State 141
bloat, administrative 21, 75, 100–3, 192
Bok, Derek 25
Bologna group 153
book costs 97, 151, 172
budget 12–21, 28; boards 58–9; budget cuts 102–3; consultancies 90–1; coordination 78–9; faculty 65, 66–7, 112–13, 131–8; global education 190; online expansion 35; process and models 83–4; student services 162; study abroad 186
budget forums 21, 67–9
business major 44, 48, 70, 180

calculus 28
California 15, 177
campus police 89
career services 165, 180
Chief Financial Officers *see* Senior Vice President
China 19, 33, 42
Christensen, Clay 11
citation rates 126–7
citizenship 41
class size 28, 144
climbing walls 16, 149, 162
cocurricular 46–7, 49, 164, 167–9, 173
college graduates, number 26
College Learning Assessment Test 22, 24–5
commodity courses 48, 122

community colleges 41, 43, 61, 94, 157
community service, student 179
commuters 49, 168–70, 171, 173, 178
comparative data 26–7, 36
competencies 32, 72, 92, 157
conflict analysis 129
consultancies 90-2, 109
consumerism 151
Council of Independent Colleges 80
Council on Undergraduate Research (CUR) 130
counseling 166, 171, 173
credit 18
criminology 128, 189
crisis mentality 86–9
critical thinking 36, 42; advertising 96; faculty goals 71; history programs 41; liberal education 44–5, 47
Crow, Michael 3
curriculum 60–1, 187
cybersecurity 61, 68, 88, 128

deans 60, 62, 79–80, 98, 106–7
debt, student 15, 16
degree completion *see* graduation rates
demography, students 17, 31
Denmark 36
department chairs 7, 77, 80, 84, 98, 123
depression (emotional) 166
Deresiewicz, William 24
development 19–20, 91
disabilities 163, 166
discounting 16, 17
diversity 7, 32, 157–9, 160
Doctor of Arts 116
dormitories *see* residence halls
Drexel University 180
dual enrollment 41, 72, 156

education (programs in) 180
engineers 171, 185–6
enrollments 12, 17, 31–2, 35, 88
equity office 78
executive education 18
experiential learning 165–6, 180

faculty 59–69
faculty exchange (international) 187
faculty senates 9, 62, 65–6, 145, 160
federal government 6, 100
financial aid 98, 161
first-generation (students) 26, 54, 155–6, 158, 169, 173

first jobs 36, 41, 43
flipped classrooms 53, 118, 119
Florida 139
Florida, Richard 181
food service 97
foreign language 183, 187, 188
for-profits 8, 11, 125
four-year graduation 31

Gallup survey 42, 165
general education 47–8; adjuncts 133–4; class size 144; curricula 187, 189; evaluation 49; faculty senates 65, 70–1; learning outcomes 119
George Mason University 7, 12, 16, 53, 101, 114
Ginsberg, Ben 75, 100
global education 53, 65, 68, 183–9, 195
globalization 183
global office 184, 187
governing boards 1, 5, 58–9, 105
grade inflation 22, 69–70, 121–2
graduate office 79
graduation rates 22, 26, 31, 53
grievances 62

health and fitness 164–5
helicopter parenting 152–3
high schools 151
history programs 41
honors 160–1, 170
Houston, University of 50–1, 97
humanities 128, 184
human resources 78, 99

inclusiveness 155–6, 158, 160, 163, 169–70
infrastructure 77–8, 96–7
institutional research 77, 100
interdisciplinarity 45; collaboration 83, 98; evaluation 60; global affairs 187; institutes 77; research 125, 130, 146; teaching 114
international students 18–19; evaluation 188; global education 168, 184–5; honors programs 161; rankings 33–4; recruitment 92
internships 41, 47, 165–6, 168, 180, 186
Iowa 20
Ireland 36
Ivy League 137–8

James Madison University 25
joint international courses 186

Kent State 160
Kentucky, University of 98
Kentucky State 106

Latino Americans 54
Latino students 155, 158
leadership training 49, 80–1, 161, 164
learning research 118
lectures 53, 119–20, 150
liberal-professional education 43–4
libraries 77, 172
lifelong learning 178–9
living/learning communities 168, 170
Lombardi, John 59
Lone Star system 12

Maryland, University of 160
Maryland-University College 136
Massachusetts 20
Master's degrees 34, 178–9
mental health 166
merit aid 161
midterm grades 99
Minnesota 102
minority faculty 115–16
minority students 158, 160, 163, 185
MOOCs (Massive Open Online Courses) 2, 35, 157
Moody's 18
music 161

National Clearinghouse Research Center 155
National Research Council 51
National Science Foundation 128
National Student Clearinghouse 27
National Survey of Student Engagement (NSSE) 26, 150
Nebraska, University of 101–2
neuroscience 127
New York University 107
Nielsen, Larry 75–6
North Carolina, University of 69, 177
Northeastern University 33. 180
Northern Virginia Community College 157
nurses 171, 180

Obama administration 36, 40, 183
older students *see* adult students
online education 17, 34–5; books 172–3; faculty 61, 98–9, 136; for-profit 92; hybrid education 119, 135–6;
productivity 144; quality 93; student body 158–9, 160
Oregon State 19, 157, 185
orientation 153, 163
Osher Lifelong Learning Institutes 178–9
outreach 176–82

P-12 outreach 180
partnerships 92–4
partnerships, international 186–7
Pell grants 36, 37
performance-based budgets 83–4
performance-based funding 126
Ph.D. training 116–17
philanthropy 19, 177
plagiarism 88, 120
Ponds 15, 16
post-tenure review 138–40
presidents (university) 59, 63, 82, 85–6, 105–8
President's Council 82–3
priorities 2, 28–9, 40, 87, 183
productivity 115, 126
productivity (faculty) 60
promotion and tenure 60, 114, 125–6, 136–7
provosts 62, 76, 77–84, 85–6, 106–7
public commitments 14–15
public intellectuals 129, 180
public relations 78, 91, 94–6, 109, 178, 184
Purdue University 42, 165

quality 21–5, 193–6; academic control 93; faculty criteria 112–14; faculty senates 66; global education 183–4; honors students 161; jobs 40–1; leadership 108, 110; research 51, 115; tenure 140

rankings 1, 33, 36–7, 42, 189
Rate-my-Professor 122
regional economic development 49, 128
regulations 68
remediation 28
research 29–30; budget 49–50; collaboration 195; compliance 99; educational quality 45–6; faculty 111–13; research quality 124–31; staffing 100–1
research compliance 99
residence halls 97, 152, 169, 185
responsibility-based budgets 8, 34–4
restructuring 102
retaliation 69

retention 22, 53; administrative assistance 99; advising 168, 173; community 164; general education 48; housing amenities 152; international standings 27; online learning 35; preparation 157–9; teaching 115
retirement 138, 141–2
revenue, new sources 18, 97
risk management 87
Rochester, University of 33
Russia 34

safety *see* security
salaries, administrative 105–8
salaries, faculty 18, 105
search firms 62, 91
security 18, 67
self-esteem 104, 151
Selingo, Jeff 11, 23
Selling Students Short 143
Senior Vice President 77, 107
sexual assault 89
Shanghai Jiao Tong 1, 34
shared governance 2, 57–72; consultancies 91; faculty participation 135–6, 145; global education 184; online 93
shooter exercises 87
social entrepreneurship 179
Society for College and University Planning (SCUP) 83
Socratic methods 53
South Korea 7, 27
Southern Association of Schools and Colleges 70
Southern New Hampshire, University of 136
Speakers' bureau 178–80
state funding 12, 20
state politics 14–15, 195
STEM (science, technology, engineering, mathematics) 44, 52–3, 128, 155
Straighterline 48
strategic implementation committees 63
strategic planning 62–3
student athletes 159–60
student exchange (international) 186–7

student fees 159–63, 171
student leadership 153–4
student life 46–7, 78, 100–1, 148–73, 189
student services *see* student life
students 148–73
study abroad 100, 161, 182, 183, 185–6
study time 150–3
suicides 88, 167
sustainability 129, 168
swirl (student) 27, 37, 156, 158, 169
syllabus 119

teaching 112–14, 117–24
teaching centers 118
teaching evaluations 121, 122–3
teaching loads 115, 134, 136–7, 142–4
technology transfer 97, 177
tenure 138–40
tenured faculty 132, 136, 143–5
term faculty 132, 134, 136
testing 120
Test of Leadership 22
Texas 139
time management 152–3
town-gown relations 177–8
transfer students 156, 158, 161, 169
t-shirts 163
tuition 15, 51, 171–2

undergraduate research 46, 51, 53, 129–30
United Kingdom 126, 127
US *News* 7, 33. 95, 157, 161

veterans 158
Virginia 31, 36, 51
volunteering 179

weather 88
well-being 165
Western Governors' University 125
Western Illinois University 181
Westmount College 141
Wisconsin 20, 97, 143
work-study balance 151
world history 187
writing 18, 41, 91, 120